NATIONALISM IN EUROPE, 1815 TO THE PRESENT

Nationalism has become so integral a part of life in Europe today that it is virtually impossible not to identify oneself with a nation state, and yet nationalism is historically a modern phenomenon. This reader helps the student to gain an understanding of this important subject by offering:

- a substantial and wide-ranging introduction
- key texts, including John Stuart Mill and Otto Bauer
- a selection of texts from the nineteenth and twentieth centuries which emphasize how the understanding of nationalism has changed over time
- a comparative European emphasis
- pieces previously not published in English
- a number of lengthy texts to offer students the possibility of studying in depth

As well as providing the central building blocks for informed theoretical discussion, Stuart Woolf also tackles controversial issues such as the difference between the development of nationalism in western and central-eastern Europe and the relationship between nation state and national identity.

Stuart Woolf is Research Professor of History at the University of Essex. His previous publications include *Napoleon's Integration of Europe* (1991) and his edited collection, *Fascism in Europe* (1981).

NATIONALISM IN EUROPE, 1815 TO THE PRESENT

A reader

Edited by Stuart Woolf

London and New York

First published 1996
by Routledge
11 New Fetter Lane, London EC4P 4EE

Simultaneously published in the USA and Canada
by Routledge
29 West 35th Street, New York, NY 10001

© 1996 Stuart Woolf, selection and editorial material
© 1996 Routledge, translated material

Phototypeset in Garamond by Intype, London
Printed and bound in Great Britain by
Clays Ltd, St Ives plc

British Library Cataloguing in Publication Data
A catalogue record for this book is available from the British Library

Library of Congress Cataloguing in Publication Data
A catalogue record for this book has been requested

ISBN 0–415–12563–4
0–415–12564–2 (pbk)

CONTENTS

CONTENTS

1

INTRODUCTION*

Stuart Woolf

Nations it may be have fashioned their Governments, but
the Governments have paid them back in the same coin.
                    Joseph Conrad, *Under Western Eyes* (1911)[1]

> I against my brother
> I and my brother against our cousin
> I, my brother and our cousin against the neighbours,
> All of us against the foreigner
>   Bruce Chatwin, *The Songlines* (1988)[2]

Nationalism has become so integral a part of life in Europe today
that it is virtually impossible not to identify oneself with a nation
state: we think of ourselves as Italians, French or English; we have
been prepared to fight wars to affirm the independence or rights
of our nation against what we regard as the threats of other states
or, tragically, other 'ethnically' different peoples, such as Serbs,
Croats and Bosnian Muslims, Armenians or Azers. To belong to
a nation state has become so natural that, on the one hand, almost
any people capable of articulating its identity as a nation and its
sense of persecution by the existing state demands the right to
independence and a territory, while on the other hand nation states
build political and legal barriers to exclude all but their own
citizens. The passport – in origin a *passe-partout* issued to protect
the traveller – has now become an obligatory document of legal
existence, symbol of this dependence of the individual on the
nation state, so inconceivable is the concept of 'statelessness'.

Three different elements have become inextricably superimposed
in our understanding of the nation state: the nation, as a collective
identity; the state as an expression of political independence; and

1

the territory as a geographical area with frontiers demarcating the necessary coincidence between nation and state.

Yet nationalism, in its identification of a people with the territorial nation state, is a historically modern phenomenon, generally accepted as dating from the French Revolution. 'Patriotism', in the sense of a readiness to sacrifice oneself for one's community (king, country ...), has a far older lineage, from the Roman *patria* to medieval kingdoms (Kantorowicz, 1984), but it was an expression of individual loyalty (or, at most, the self-identification of a group, such as the Polish *szlachta*, with the 'nation'), not the collective action of a people. 'National characteristics' (also used by nationalists in support of the continuity of the distinctive identity of peoples) form part of a well-established and distinguished literary rhetoric, dating back to the sixteenth century, when Shakespeare and Montaigne employed the expression as a commonplace means of categorizing the differences between the new-found strength and identity of the early modern dynastic states. Far more recent, and part of the nationalist self-image, is the claim that national patriotism is a primordial instinct, like the family, inherently superior to other loyalties, and that the 'nation' is a 'natural' unit that has always existed, albeit for long in a passive and dormant state.

THE HISTORIOGRAPHY OF NATIONALISM

From the earliest expressions of modern nationalism, historians, antiquarians and *savants* played a significant part in articulating a sense of national identity through their researches aimed at discovering (or inventing) the distant origins and ancient glories of their people. History, language, folklore, territory, culture or religion could all be used to demonstrate the past traditions of a nation, symbolic evidence of its historic continuity and hence its authenticity.

But far more important in the diffusion of the ideological affirmation of the 'naturalness' and inevitability of the nation state was the role of academic historians. Clearly by the 1840s, but almost uninterruptedly from the later nineteenth century until the second world war, such historians (for example, Heinrich von Treitschke) intepreted the history of their country in a teleological manner, as culminating inevitably in the nation state, whether monarchical or republican. The 'destiny' of the nation not only explained its past, but often justified the state's imperialist ambitions. For in reality, in these interpretations the state embodied and incorporated the nation. Hegel's dictum – 'nations may have had a long history before they finally reach their destination – that of forming themselves into states' (Gellner, 1983, p. 48) – became the interpretative canon not just of German historians, starting with Ranke (for whom the state had moral, almost theological connotations), but throughout Europe, culminating in the heyday of positivist historiography. It formed part of the process of deliberate 'nation-building', which spread through Europe in the later nineteenth and twentieth centuries as the political elites sought to strengthen the ties of their peoples to the old and newly formed nation states.

It would be erroneous and unjust to accuse these historians of deliberately distorting their national past (although there were those, like the Englishman John Seeley or the Italian Gioacchino Volpe, who were too easily attracted to the political power respectively of imperialism and fascism). Rather, the very triumph of the nation state confirmed and consolidated nationalist historiography in all countries. The assumption that a 'national spirit' could be followed like a red thread through the centuries, laid down with academic authority to a lay audience by Ernest Lavisse in France, J. R. Green in England, Pietro Silva in Italy, became, through endless simplification and repetition in school and family, uncritical dogma. Historians thus contributed, at the best, to the pride and collective ideals intrinsic to a sense of national sentiment; but also, at the worst, to the aggressive political projects of extremist right-wing regimes, such as those that dominated the 1930s (Kennedy, 1974; Lanaro, 1993).

The first world war, resulting in the disappearance of the multinational empires of eastern and central Europe and the affirmation of the principle of 'self-determination', strongly influenced historical interpretations. For self-determination, however imperfectly applied and whatever the problems of ethnic minorities that it brought to the forefront (P. Smith *et al.*, 1991), appeared to confirm the legitimacy of nationalist claims about the existence of the nation as a primordial factor, a demiurge outside history. Hans Kohn, the most productive historian of nationalism of the interwar period, could still write after the second world war, at the end of a long and distinguished career: 'What remains constant in nationalism through all its changes is the demand of the people for a government of the same ethnic complexion as the majority.

3

scientists and sociologists, in terms of modernization theory and economic development (Deutsch, 1962; Cameron, 1967).

Contemporaneously, the study of nationalism in Europe underwent unusually sharp historiographical revision. Although rarely stated explicitly, initially underlying such revisionism was a sense of the disastrous wars that aggressive nationalism had brought on Europe. The negative judgement on nationalism's international consequences reflected back on its claims that it expressed the legitimate, indeed the predestined aim of peoples – their political emancipation. Instead of being seen as positive and inevitable, nationalism was seen as a negative ideological creation: 'Nationalism is a doctrine invented in Europe at the beginning of the nineteenth century', wrote Elie Kedourie as early as 1960. 'It is nationalism which engenders nations, and not the other way round', elaborated Ernest Gellner (Kedourie, 1960, p. 1; Gellner, 1983, p. 55).

In central-eastern European historiography a more positive evaluation was given of the nationalist tradition, in that the struggles for independence embodied the forces of progress against the autocracy of the empires, whatever the subsequent ambiguities of nationalist movements (Hroch, 1989). A similar distinction between national movements – understood as the legitimate expression of popular sentiment – and nationalism, defined as a far narrower ideology or party, is characteristic of some Western, particularly French, historiography (Suratteau, 1972). But in English-language historiography in particular, where the debate has been most active, both national movements and later nineteenth-century nationalism are treated as essentially belonging to the same category. In such interpretations, nationalism has been reduced to an ideology of unusual efficacy, an instrument of political manipulation, increasingly (although certainly not inevitably) associated with the Right (Kedourie, 1960; Kamenka, 1976; Schieder and Dann, 1978; A. D. Smith, 1979; Breuilly, 1982; Gellner, 1983; Hobsbawm, 1990; Schieder, 1991).

An obligatory consequence of this radical revisionism has been to shift the focus of attention away from overtly political history. Since nations were not ahistorically predestined, the contexts and conditions that permitted the construction and diffusion of a sense of national identity and its transformation into a political force required analysis in terms of the social mechanisms through which the ideology of nationalism spread, the composition of its social bases, the functioning of its cultural symbols.

The detailed study of specific historical contexts has gained in analytical power from the conceptual approaches of other social sciences. From political science and sociology Gellner, Smith and Breuilly have adopted the concepts of modernization and industrialization, whose attributes they regard as necessary albeit insufficient preconditions for the emergence of modern nationalism. For whatever the constitutive elements of a national identity, some have failed to become national movements, in part at least for reasons of levels of social and economic development (Eley, 1981). The anthropologists' insistence that a social group defines itself in relation to the existence of the 'other' has become essential to any historical explanation of how the articulation of cultural differences, such as language or religion, can become the basis of a sense of national identity, of an 'imagined community' as Benedict Anderson defines it (Anderson, 1983). Why language has been so potent a unifying force for nationalism has gained from the contributions of socio-linguists, such as Fishman; while the theoretical contributions of students of symbolism, such as Bourdieu, have broadened the study of the unifying mechanisms of national symbols, such as the figures of Joan of Arc and Marianne in France or the ceremonies of nazism (Agulhon, 1979, 1992; Krumeich, 1989; Bourdieu, 1991; Mosse, 1975).

These new approaches have undoubtedly made the history of nationalism more intelligible by their concentration on the processes of construction of ideologies of nationalism, the conditions which facilitated (without necessarily ensuring) their diffusion, and the social mechanisms through which they operated. But in so doing, possibly because of the polemical force of their criticisms of the nationalist self-image, they have left unclear why national sentiment, the individual's pride in belonging to a nation – even when frustrated by or hostile to its state organization or, in the most extreme cases, such as in time of war or under a fascist regime, risking imprisonment or life to oppose its political policies – has become an unquestionable reality and an ideal source of attachment and commitment. Nor do they explain satisfactorily the transition from an individual sense of national pride to the sectarian exclusion of all others that has so frequently characterized nationalism in the twentieth century.

Today there are two approaches to the study of nationalism,

which are so fundamentally different that their proponents have difficulty in appreciating each other's arguments. On the one hand, *national movements* and *nationalism* are studied as manifestations of political power, in which social, economic and cultural aspects are considered as explanatory factors, but only in their relationship to the state. On the other hand, *national identity* is analysed as a cultural construction, not a fixed objective reality, but an ongoing and changeable process, dependent on and deriving from social relations, and hence not exclusive of other identities. The degree of reciprocal interdependence between national movements or nationalism and national identity makes it essential to understand and bring together the two approaches.

THE LIBERAL PHASE OF NATIONALISM (1789–1870)

Nationalism was born in western Europe, the region where sovereign states had developed most strongly since the middle ages. The implications of this obvious historical fact (too often ignored by students of nationalism) is that political nationalism, from its outset, turned to the state as its constant reference point. Between the fifteenth and eighteenth centuries, a national patriotism developed within the 'political nation' of the ruling elites as an important coagulating element in the construction of the early-modern dynastic state. It was a patriotism which was expressed most vocally against the threat of other states (for example, in Shakespeare's historical plays) and which was articulated through a panoply of 'national' institutions, such as a centralized government, a parliament, the Court, a national religion, each with its own ceremonies and symbols, but all insistent on the priority of national loyalty. Because most states were ruled by sovereigns, national and dynastic loyalty were most frequently equated; but the same national patriotism was expressed in non-dynastic *Ständestaaten*, such as the venerable republic of Venice, the newly established Dutch republic or Cromwell's England.

The state structuring of western Europe also meant that there were recognizable 'nationalities', perhaps most usually described in terms of the 'national characteristics' of the different peoples (French, English, Spanish, and so on). These descriptions both included different 'nations' within existing states and extended beyond the large dynastic states to a few other peoples – such as Italians or Germans – recognizable primarily through their lan-

8

guage. Presumably they were included in this panorama of plati-
tudinous knowledge because of their established presence in a
common cultural patrimony constructed in good part from literary
references, commercial contacts and the educational 'grand tour'.
The *Encyclopédie*, in the 1770s, provided an excellent summary of
what was understood by 'national characteristics': 'Each nation has
its own character: it's almost proverbial to describe a Frenchman as
light, an Italian as jealous, a Spaniard as solemn, an Englishman
as malicious, a Scotsman as vainglorious, a German as drunk, an
Irishman as lazy, a Greek as cunning, etc.' (*Encyclopédie*, 'Nation',
vol. 11, 1752). Such a listing of the peoples with 'national characteristics' is of interest because it includes most of the nationalities that
were to be regarded by the early-nineteenth-century nationalists as
historically important, either because they could claim a historical
state (like the French or Spanish) or because they were judged
significant in terms of cultural or historical evocations, population
or territory.

There was a hierarchy of nations which could claim the attention
of international public opinion, as Eric Hobsbawm has pointed
out, based on a crucial material and symbolic threshold size. For
Mazzini, the historic nations were the Italians, Germans and Poles,
to whom (after 1848) he added the Hungarians (Della Peruta, 1969,
pp. 222, 246). The 1848 revolutions in the Austrian empire cruelly
revealed the difficulties for the 'peoples without history' to assert
their right to existence, even in democratic circles such as those of
Mazzini.

Underlying this division of peoples into those with or without
the right to a political existence was no rational consideration
of the practical impossibility that all nations become states, but an
ideological conviction that the progress of civilization could be
traced through the history of specific nations. The Enlightenment
confidence in the passage from primitive tribes via feudalism to
contemporary civilization led to the cruder conclusion, common
to all nineteenth-century western intellectuals, from John Stuart
Mill to Friedrich Engels, that size was an indicator of human
progress and a pre-condition of the nation state. The more
advanced civilization of the greater nations was beneficial to the
smaller, more backward peoples, who would only gain from their
incorporation within the state frontiers of the former. As Mill
wrote in 1861:

Nobody can suppose that it is not more beneficial for a Breton or a Basque of French Navarre to be ... a member of the French nationality, admitted on equal terms to all the privileges of French citizenship ... than to sulk on his own rocks, the half-savage relic of past times, revolving in his own little mental orbit, without participation or interest in the general movement of the world. The same remark applies to the Welshman or the Scottish highlander as members of the British nation.

(Hobsbawm, 1990, p. 34)

Even as late as 1882, when ethnicity had become the core issue of dispute in the Austro-Hungarian and Russian empires, the great French scholar Ernest Renan could affirm that: 'The ethnic element, of fundamental importance in the origins of history, has always lost its importance in correspondence to the advance of civilization' (Lanaro, 1993, p. xxix).

Modern nationalism is conventionally dated to the French Revolution because of the revolutionaries' immediate and unequivocal equation of nation, state, territory and language. The nation not only embodied popular sovereignty, but was automatically identified with the unity of the French state and territory ('la France une et indivisible'). In this, it reflected, on the one hand, the long-established existence of the French state, and on the other the more recent Enlightenment conviction that it was through individual nations, and in particular the French nation, that civilization progressed (Woolf, 1989). The Revolutionary definition of the nation state, constantly reformulated according to the exigencies of the internal struggles and foreign wars, contained most of the elements of subsequent nationalism: it was voluntaristic during the phase of the 'nation in arms', when use of the French language was the basic criterion for citizenship; it was deterministic in its historical memories of ancient origins and insistence on natural frontiers, as in its exclusion of foreigners; above all, it proposed that individual citizens possessed a direct and unmediated relationship with the nation state, which increasingly expressed its 'national' individuality through its institutional procedures. The claim, in the 1795 Constitution, that a public vote of the people was enough for its independence and sovereignty to be recognized, confirmed the subversive nature of the Revolution, destructive of the established order of international relations, through its appeal to the peoples (however theoretical this soon became), backed up by the powerful militarism of the Revolutionary and Napoleonic armies.

If the constitutive elements of the ideology of modern nationalism can be located so precisely to Revolutionary France, it is doubtful – despite the assertions of national historiographies – whether the Napoleonic occupation led to an analogous raising of national consciousness in any other country, except among some (mainly Prussian) intellectuals. Even the mass popular risings in Spain and Russia offer ambiguous evidence, as they were primarily liberation movements against the foreign invader, in defence of local region, dynasty and religion rather than expressions of a nation state. But there can be no doubt about the rapid development of nationalism during the Restoration.

Characteristic of the earlier nineteenth century was a spirit of romanticism that expressed itself, beyond the tortured self-questioning of the private individual, in an altruistic willingness to sacrifice oneself for a greater, public cause. The rapid spread of nationalism owed much to the language of romanticism common to the educated classes. Without such a mentality, it would be impossible to explain the network of politically active phil-hellenic associations that sprang up across Europe in the 1820s, for whom independence from the oppression of the Muslim Turks of the Christian descendants of ancient Greece, the mother of western civilization, marked the march of progress. Political romanticism signified the cult of a folkloric (and hence distant and authentic) past, language as the Herderian expression of a *Volk*'s soul, the Staëlian intellectual as interpreter of the unspoken wishes of the people, the Giobertian reconciliation of religion and progress, the new 'organic' age of Saint-Simonian association and Mazzinian nationalism. Romanticism explains the disproportionate role of an intelligentsia – writers, students, lawyers, administrative officials, educated officers – in the early national movements. And although romanticism was compatible with all political shadings, until the revolutions of 1848 and even as late as Garibaldi's great *epos* of 1860, it confirmed the tie between liberalism and nationalism, precisely because the one and the other could be viewed as combining progress with the realization of the innate dreams of particular peoples.

This first phase of political nationalism (as distinct from cultural expressions of national consciousness, without a political programme) is thus intimately associated with liberalism, and is often contrasted, as if it were intrinsically different, with the more closed nationalisms of the late nineteenth and twentieth centuries. Hence it is important to understand the nature of this association.

In part the tie between nationalism and liberalism resulted from the unusual international situation. The breakdown of the Holy Alliance rapidly led to the emergence of two blocs of great powers, in which the hostility of the conservative, traditionalist states (Austria, Russia, Prussia) towards all manifestations of change encouraged an analogous convergence of reformist political positions and movements across frontiers, even if in practice they never liaised. Liberalism and nationalism were necessarily associated because the anti-liberal states were also anti-national. Liberal reforms, seen by Great Britain and France as the effective way to avoid revolution, appeared to the local exponents of progress increasingly impossible without political independence, whether from the foreigner (Italy) or from territorial fragmentation (Germany).

The very system of a 'Concert' of powers – a distinctive phase in the *longue durée* of the history of international relations, that regulated the European balance of power until 1870 and partially to 1914 (Hinsley, 1963) – created the conditions that permitted the development of some nationalist movements. Although normally working for the maintenance of the status quo and systematically rejecting any intrinsic right of a people to its political independence, the Concert allowed for and, at moments of crisis, could legitimate and even impose political change. The Concert of powers was responsible for the success of the first nationalist movement of the nineteenth century – that of the Greeks in 1828 – and English and French intervention was decisive in preventing the suppression of the Belgian and Italian movements of independence.

Nationalism, in this first phase, was associated with liberalism because both ideologies were identified with progress and middle-class values, the evidence of whose material benefits was evident in England and France. The values asserted by Belgian, Italian and German reformers were the same – individualism, economic progress, political representation, freedom of the press and an effective state bureaucracy. They combined what in retrospect were seen as the positive aspects of the Napoleonic experience with idealized models of England and France. According to national context and individual convictions, opinions could vary. Thus, Belgian liberals, with fresh memories of the advantages they had gained from the unified Napoleonic market, felt sacrificed within the kingdom of Holland; whereas Italians and Germans insisted on the economic benefits of unifying their territories. German liberals argued for secularization and education, themes ignored in Catholic Italy and Belgium or Orthodox Greece. Italian and German liberals held ambivalent attitudes towards the state, accepted by many as potentially the most powerful instrument of progress, but never regarded as politically neutral.

The revolutions of 1848 demonstrated that liberalism and nationalism were not two faces of the same coin, and led to painful self-questioning by both Italian and German liberals whether national independence might not be a necessary prerequisite for liberal reforms and the furtherance of progress. In Italy, the Cavourian National Society successfully affirmed the primacy of political unity over what it claimed were divisive discussions about the future organization of the state. In Germany in the 1850s–60s, the same debate underlay the differences between the conservative pro-Prussian proponents of a *Kleindeutschland* and the liberal supporters of a *Großdeutschland*, intended to prevent or at least dilute the predominance of Prussian militarism.

The practical consequences of this subordination of liberal reformism to political unity were to weigh heavily in both states. In Italy, the adoption of the centralized Piedmontese model of administration and a highly restrictive suffrage imposed a straitjacket on a country with markedly different state traditions and 'thicknesses' of social relations in civil society. In Germany, the southern German states, where liberalism was most advanced, had opposed a *Kleindeutschland* outcome; with Bismarck's triumph, the opponents of the Prussian-dominated federation – the Catholic world and then the social democrats – were soon branded as 'enemies of the Reich'. By the late nineteenth century, liberalism had lost its privileged relationship with nationalism, as indeed (contested by socialism) it had lost its monopolistic claim to embody progress.

Even though there is a general similarity in the constitutive elements, forms of associative sociability and symbolic functionality of the cultural references of the individual nationalisms, the specific contexts within which nationalist leaders constructed their movements explain many of the differences and particular emphases. For example, language was the most concrete indicator of cultural identity for Italians and Germans from Dante and Luther in terms of literary continuity and (though less widespread in Italy) of educated conversation; it was so fundamental to the authenticity of Greek national identity that ancient Greek formed the basis for the formalization of the new national language; but it played no role in the successful Belgian struggle for independence, precisely because of the fundamental linguistic divide between French and Flemish (even though this was only subsequently to become a bone of contention). Similarly, history – to which Greeks, Italians and Germans could appeal egregiously – was less potent in the Belgian case, because it referred to a less distant and subordinate past (the southern Netherlands provinces of the Spanish and Austrian empire, or the very recent departments of the Napoleonic empire). On the other hand, Greek, Belgian and Italian patriots could overcome their differences in the common struggle against a foreign enemy, which (despite points of anti-French xenophobia) was far more difficult for Germans in search of unity.

The distinction between voluntaristic and deterministic nationalism conventionally attributed to Italy and Germany on the basis of the ideas of specific writers also acquires more substance through a comparison of the particular contexts of the two countries. At the core of the distinction are the questions of ethnicity and territory, contentious and inseparable issues that soured the romantic ideal of nationalism in 1848 and have made nationalism so ambiguous a reality to the present day.

Historically, ethnicity has rarely been defined by dominant nationalities in strict terms of blood and kin, and then only in the most extreme cases (for instance, by the nazis, or Serb and Croat nationalists today); and it is biologically improper throughout Europe (except perhaps for Iceland), given the successive movements and settlements of tribes and populations over the centuries. The normal definition of an ethnic grouping is looser and broader, 'almost always connected in some unspecified way with common origin and descent, from which the common characteristics of the members of an ethnic grouping are allegedly derived' (Hobsbawm, 1990, p. 63).

Unlike Germany, territorial boundaries were never an ethnic issue during the struggles for independence or unity in Greece, Belgium or Risorgimento Italy. The resentment shared by the

14

inhabitants of the provinces of the future Belgium against their enforced incorporation in the kingdom of Holland was more immediate and urgent than any sense of ethnic identity among the Flemish (Zolberg, 1974). In Greece and Italy, on the other hand – in the eyes of the patriots – the frontiers of the newly independent states (in 1828 and 1861) fell far short of including all their nationality: the Greeks of Macedonia and Italians of Venetia were still under foreign domination. It was only subsequently, when politically determined frontiers were achieved, that ethnic minorities became apparent, and then – compared to central and eastern Europe – on a relatively marginal scale.

In Germany, on the other hand, the conflict between ethnicity and territory emerged precociously in the 1848 revolutions. In part this was the legacy of the processes of state expansion of the previous centuries, both of the Habsburg emperors towards the south-east, and of the Habsburgs and Prussian Hohenzollerns in the partitions of Poland. In part it derived from the very difficulty for Germans – because of the millenary tradition of the Holy Roman Empire – in defining what they understood as the German nation. In cultural terms of language and civilization, there were many German 'nations' living within the confines of the Empire, including for example Danes and Poles. The German *Volk* was an invention of German intellectuals of the late eighteenth century to describe a political expectation of the future, when Germans – including the various 'nations' (Prussians, Austrians, Bavarians, Danes, Poles, etc.) – would become a sovereign people. For Goethe in 1815, Germany's cultural richness derived from the diversity of its 'nations' and states, whatever unity it might possess in the eyes of other states.

The term *Nationalstaat* was only employed in 1848, when the insistence on the frontiers of the German Confederation (heir to the Holy Roman Empire) inevitably conflicted with those of ethnic nationality. Underlying the contemptuous dismissal of the claims of other nationalities was the conviction of the German revolutionaries at Frankfurt, like that of the Hungarian magnates at Budapest, of their national mission as defenders of western civilization against the rising tide of Slavs. The ethnic hostilities that emerged in the 1848 revolutions revealed the differences between nationalism in western and in central-eastern Europe.

NATIONALISM IN CENTRAL AND EASTERN EUROPE

Two preliminary but fundamental distinctions can be made between nationalism in central and eastern Europe and in the West. The first relates to the consequences of the long-term processes of historical evolution in the two regions, the second to changes in the character of international relations from the later nineteenth century. To avoid confusion, however, it is necessary to distinguish in central-eastern Europe between the 'historic' nations, which had once been independent states and whose 'political nation' possessed a strongly developed identity (Poland, Hungary, Bohemia), and – to use Engels' eloquent phrase – the far more numerous 'nations without history', whose claims to national identity only emerged in the 1848 revolutions or much later. When historians contrast western and central-eastern Europe, they are referring for the most part to the latter.

Central-eastern Europe, to employ the terminology of Armstrong, was a region characterized by 'nation states', in contrast to the 'state-nations' of western Europe (Armstrong, 1982). The play on words is a useful shorthand to describe how, in the former, national identities were forged within multi-national empires prior to and as the basis of a political programme to obtain an independent state, whereas states had long existed in the West. Structural reasons help explain such different developments.

Unlike western Europe, where sedentary agricultural settlements were established from the high middle ages, the frontier regions of eastern Europe, from south Russia to the Balkans, remained highly unstable until the eighteenth century, because of the prolonged struggle with the Muslim Ottoman empire. Across a broad swathe of territory – which cut across the Balkans and stretched north-east through Poland and south-western Russia – the repeated changes in the religious frontier from the fourteenth to the eighteenth century led to the periodic transplantation of peoples with different cultural and religious backgrounds. This led, on the one hand, to a precocious sense of ethnic consciousness, deriving from their sense of mission, among specific groups settled as an 'antemurale' along the military frontier, like the Orthodox Vlach in Transylvania or the Cossacks in south-east Russia; and, on the other hand, to a widespread overlap and confusion between different cultural, religious and linguistic groups inhabiting the same territories as the direct or indirect result of the displacement of populations.

The political processes by which the empires had expanded had led to the settlement in the conquered territories of a ruling class and landowners of the dominant ethnic nation – Germans in the Baltic, Russians and Prussians in Poland, Austrian Germans and Magyars in the Habsburg territories – to whom the great native magnate families, with vast estates, like the great urban Jewish financiers, had assimilated. By the nineteenth century this ruling class enjoyed a privileged position and a higher social status relative to the local elites in the administration and often as landowners or merchants. In such feudal societies, ethnic, linguistic and often religious differences accentuated the permanent antagonism between landowners and peasants.

Religious differences within the Christian world were not only far older than in the West (dating back to the fourth-century split between the western and eastern churches), but bore little relationship to state frontiers, such as were established in sixteenth to seventeenth-century western Europe. Over the centuries such differences had consolidated into a sense of separateness, and often of intolerence, above all in the Balkans, between the followers of the Orthodox, Catholic, Uniate and Protestant churches. Political frontiers could modify religious credos: Latvian and Estonian Protestant peasants converted to the Orthodox Church under pressure from the Russian hierarchy in the 1840s, Lithuanians in east Prussia were Protestants. But where religious differences coincided with political and social subordination, this created the terrain for an identification of religion with ethnic identity: the Catholic clergy played an important role in the diffusion of a sense of ethnic identity among the Slovak or Polish and Lithuanian peasantry under Russian rule, as did the Orthodox and Uniate churches among the Rumanian peasants of Transylvania.

If such processes of unstable settlement and religious divisions already provide long-term explanations of why ethnicity should constitute so distinctive a characteristic of nationalism in central and eastern Europe, the dominance of vast empires in the region helps explain the difficulties for their dynastic rulers in developing unifying 'national' institutions, as in the smaller and more centrally administered western states. A strongly dynastic loyalty only existed towards the tsar, who personified 'Holy Russia' in its religious and frontier mission against Muslims and Asian tribes.

For religious reasons, such loyalty was inconceivable for the Christian peoples under Ottoman rule (despite the latter's effective tolerance). In the Austrian empire, the religious and ethnic differences that accompanied the repeated resettlements accentuated divisions within the elites as well as between landowners and peasants.

Thus by the nineteenth century in central and eastern Europe, nationalist programmes were almost necessarily based on the construction of ethnic identity precisely because of the friction generated by the frequently close juxtaposition of different groups on the same territories within empires whose administrators were essentially incapable of developing dynastic loyalties or, where they existed (as in Russia), of institutionalizing them through centripetal state structures. The sovereign nation state, which by 1870 appeared as the norm in the West (even though in reality many of its states included more than one nation), became the ideal for nationalists throughout Europe.

The second distinction between western and central-eastern Europe relates to the change in the nature of international relations. The self-balancing Concert of great powers had always been reluctant to recognize the claims to statehood of national movements; at most it had permitted, at moments perhaps even encouraged, the successful political struggle of some 'historic' nations like the Italians and Germans. After 1870 the weakening of the Concert, which resulted from the tendency of all states to act independently, created an environment contemporaneously unfavourable towards minority nationalisms, but generative of increasing tensions. Once they had achieved their own nation states, Italy and Germany were hostile to the claims of national movements in either the Russian or Austrian empires because of their subversive consequences for the international system. As Bismarck stated: 'What could be put in that part of Europe now occupied by the Austrian state? New creations in this territory could only be such as bear a permanently revolutionary character?' (Hinsley, 1963, p. 252). Even if different standards were applied to the powerless Ottoman empire, the balance of power prevailed over any principles of nationality.

Nevertheless, the development of nationalist movements within the empires in central and eastern Europe also had a constantly disturbing effect on international relations. Nationalism in Poland, kept vigorously alive by the extremely numerous diaspora and insurrectionary *szlachta* and later through political parties, repeatedly threatened international stability. Wherever Germans, Slavs and Italians constituted ethnic minorities, they could appeal to their respective great powers, only too ready to use them as instruments of their own international rivalries. Nationalism was the immediate cause of the First World War in the form of the question of Serbian sovereignty. Since then, it has undermined the stability of international relations in Europe in all conjunctures of political and economic crisis, whether in the interwar years or since 1989.

International conditions are, however, inadequate as an explanation of why nationalism from the late nineteenth century appeared to become so general and central a political issue and, in its intolerance, so different from its earlier association with liberalism. This new phase of nationalism cannot be dissociated from a process of change in the relationship of state and society general to all Europe, but whose effects were particularly marked in the multinational empires of central and eastern Europe.

From the last two decades of the nineteenth century, states began to assume a more direct and continuous presence in the life of their citizens (Hobsbawm, 1990). The process of state-building, administrative modernization and the opening-up of the political system towards ever broader sectors of the population, which coincided with increasing urbanization and (in some countries) industrialization, led governments and bureaucracies to extend their responsibilities in many directions (for example, to social welfare schemes or obligatory universal education). The political presence of mass social movements in this new conjuncture reinforced the concern of governments to obtain a closer knowledge and more direct relationship with their populations. Practical and symbolic initiatives were encouraged or directly undertaken – from conscription to national anthems, ceremonies and monuments – in order to mobilize and influence citizens in the name of the nation state. The state appropriated the nation by its confiscation of patriotism.

This process, visible in all European countries, was accentuated by the greater diffidence and rivalry between states which accompanied the prolonged cycle of economic depression of the 1880–90s. The nation state needed to affirm its strength against other states and used such rivalry to impose its priorities of social imperialism within its own frontiers. Its accentuation of the need for the unity of the nation state could easily lead to intolerance or persecution of those regarded as enemies of the state. It is not accidental that pseudo-scientific theories of social Darwinism, racism and anti-semitism began to circulate from the 1880s, as they constituted, in their shrill extremism, attempts to legitimate such intolerance.

In multi-national states, whether of western or eastern Europe, majority nationalities have always been remarkably insensitive towards the protests of minorities. But in the West, with rare exceptions (of whom the Irish are the most prominent example), the traditional acceptance of a single official language and the consolidated practice of open recruitment to the service of the state for long inhibited the exponents of minority nationalisms from transforming a cultural identity into an effective political platform.

In central-eastern Europe, by contrast, dynastic loyalty was an inadequate substitute for strong state structures in the multi-national empires. Although we do not yet fully understand the processes of diffusion of models, it is evident that the consciousness of national identities within these empires had been heightened by the very example of successful Western nation states. Within the majority nationalities, there were those who saw minority national identities as a threat to the solidity of the state. The Austrian Habsburgs, following their military defeats in Italy and Germany, attempted to hold together their empire by a policy of concessions to the different nationalities, graded according to their capacity to make themselves heard; in practice, this meant the devolution of power to the nationalities regarded as most powerful or troublesome – the Hungarians and Poles. From the 1880s, in Austrian Poland and in the Hungarian part of the Dual Monarchy – as in Russia – a deliberate policy of 'national homogeneity' was imposed by the dominant ethnic nation in an attempt to repress the linguistic and cultural identity of the minorities. In the Russian empire, where the nationalists were urged on by the Orthodox church pressing for religious uniformity, such a policy had already been imposed by the minister Uvarov in the 1830s–40s at the expense of Lithuanian Poles and Ukrainians, in the name of 'the great idea of developing Russian nationality on its true principles, and thus making it the centre of the life of the state and of moral culture' (Seton Watson, 1967, p. 269).

The discriminatory measures of the Russian and Hungarian governments were directed in particular against the use of minority languages in schools and in the public administration: in the kingdom of Hungary, the number of elementary schools using Slovak as the primary language fell between 1874 and 1900 from 1,971 to 510; by 1914 there were only 345 native Slovak teachers and 129 German, compared to 4,257 Magyar (Macartney, 1934, p. 90). But so repressive a policy had a boomerang effect, for it crystallized and accelerated the political consciousness and hostility of ethnic minorities, even among populations like the Baltic peoples (as well as the German elites in the Baltic cities), hitherto without a broadly based political nationalism; indeed, it forged a single ethnic identity between the Finns and minority Swedes in common defence against the Russians (Hroch, 1989).

There is little agreement among students of nationalism as to why individuals, families and social groups should, at a certain moment, see themselves as forming part of a 'nation', and what they perceived as the elements that so defined them. The change from a generic sense of belonging to an ethnic or national group into political self-consciousness has never been automatic nor, where it occurs, has it proceeded at any standard rhythm. Some ethnic groups, like Jews and Ruthenes ('proto-nations', as Hobsbawm calls them) have long possessed a marked sense of the separateness of their nationality without any political claims to a territory or a state, until their sense of being discriminated against or persecuted – in an age when the nation state had become the dominant mode – made their elites more receptive to political arguments. The role of these elites has always been crucial, for it is they who articulate the ideals and possibilities of identity and thus set their parameters. The channels of social communication with their 'peoples' have varied according to the material, political and technological means available to them (such as associations, cercles and periodicals in the nineteenth century, political parties and television today), and have often proved inadequate, particularly in the short term.

The early nineteenth-century distinction between 'historic nations' and other ethno-cultural groups without political merits summarized a perception of the difference between 'nations' whose social and cultural sense of identity and interrelatedness was subsumed into a programme of political solidarity and statehood, and other groups, with shared characteristics (language, religion, traditions, etc.), who had not yet (and might never) articulate them in political terms as a defensive form of social affirmation. It is not coincidental that the 'historic' nations, whose political claims

21

were modelled on those of the realities of dominant nations in existing states (such as the English, French or Castilians), were normally associated with historically documentable state structures (such as the former states of Poland and Hungary, or the institutional structures of Croatia or the Holy Roman Empire); Italians alone had to invent a surrogate in the shape of the 'two Romes' whose glory justified Mazzini's 'third Rome'.

The 'peoples without history' – subordinate ethnic groups like the Slovaks, Romanians or Baltic peoples – initially lacked the two essential forces to discover or create their own history and identity: the solidarity of their upper classes and the practical means of constructing and communicating their own ethnic culture. Their elites had been assimilated into the dominant ones. It was necessary for members of these elites to rediscover their own culture – usually in reaction to the insensitivity of the ruling groups – for the process of construction of an ethnic or national identity to be initiated, following the same pattern of that of earlier 'historic' nations: the elaboration of a standard language, a selective history, folkloric traditions, territory or ethnicity, sometimes a common religion. The forging of such an ethno-cultural identity could be more or less rapid – or might be abortive. But once it existed, it could not be ignored and was more likely to be consolidated than repressed by policies of cultural uniformization. John Stuart Mill had noted its irrevocability as early as 1861: 'When nations, thus divided, are under a despotic government which is a stranger to all of them ... and chooses its instruments indifferently from all, in the course of a few generations identity of situation often produces harmony of feeling and the different races come to feel toward each other as fellow countrymen. But if the era of aspiration to free government arrives before this fusion has been effected, the opportunity has gone by for effecting it' (Fishman, 1972, p. 108).

In central and eastern Europe, ethnic nationalism was self-reproductive because the language of political power was ethnically articulated. On the one hand, the state produced (or excluded) ethnic identities by classifying them, whether for purposes of administration, education, political representation or statistics. On the other hand, the ethnicity of minorities was crystallized by the construction of a corpus of pre-existing practices, values and beliefs claimed by their members as proof of their authenticity and continuity. Religion and language were of particular importance because of their efficacy in creating and consolidating a sense of national identity across classes, while functioning as markers of difference from other national groups.

Miroslav Hroch has offered, on the basis of a comparative study of seven national movements in small countries, an analysis of nationalism in three phases: from the elaboration by intellectuals of the attributes of the nation, to the concerted political action of small groups of patriots through clubs, journals and associations, leading in the third phase to popular mass mobilization (Hroch, 1989). Such a comparative framework clarifies the significant differences in the social composition of nationalist movements in the two areas of Europe, which in turn influenced their political orientation.

As in the West, the social mechanisms by which nationalism gained support in central-eastern Europe, particularly among the 'nations without history', were predominantly urban. In the West, the urban intelligentsia and middle classes played a primary role, gaining substantial support among the urban working classes, but (except in Greece) to the virtual exclusion of the peasantry. This could not be so in central and eastern Europe, given its economic, social and religious structures. The political role of the towns (even if, relative to their populations, it remained disproportionate), was necessarily less exclusive because the towns (except in Bohemia) were more marginal in such overwhelmingly peasant economies. Nor could the urban bourgeoisie provide the backbone of patriotic movements, as in the West, because commercial activities were often dominated by Jews, in a region where they remained segregated and suspect (even though in the anti-Russian revolts of 1830 and 1863 Polish Jews had fought alongside Polish patriots).

Instead, by the late nineteenth century the petty bourgeoisie played an important part in the diffusion of nationalist movements, to the point that many historians conclude that their role was central. As the demands of administrative modernization and econmomic development disrupted earlier socio-cultural equilibria, many who felt their status and income threatened were led to search for security in an 'imagined community' of national ideals (Anderson, 1983; Hobsbawm, 1990). There is a need to be precise in the definition of petty bourgeoisie. For it is not clear that the artisans and shopkeepers of western Europe corresponded to the school teachers and petty bureaucrats in the multinational empires. Here the security of the new social strata emerging in

23

response to the process of modernization was put particularly at risk by the repressive policies of linguistic and cultural homogeneity. Low-grade officials and primary school teachers, in both town and countryside, became politically nationalist, like small urban businessmen and shopkeepers, in defence of their ethnic identity.

As nationalist movements sought to mobilize mass support, the urban intelligentsia played a less prominent role: village schoolteachers, parish priests, local officials, small traders and craftsmen elaborated the message of national identity through the countryside. Indeed, an exclusively peasant nationalism could develop, as in Lithuania under the leadership of the Catholic clergy, because of hostility towards the Jewish urban traders. Peasants were attracted to nationalist movements in central and eastern Europe primarily where religion or language reinforced the traditional class division from noble landowners. The deep class divisions of these feudal societies did not necessarily favour nationalists, as the ethnically foreign governments could outbid them for the loyalty of the peasantry by the concession of emancipation – as occurred successively in Prussian, Austrian and Russian Poland. It needed the hostile ethnic policies of Russians, Magyars and German agrarian elites and, following extensions of the suffrage, the inclusion by nationalists of agrarian reform within their programmes to turn the peasants' hatred of their foreign landlords into support for political nationalism.

By 1914 nationalism conditioned all domestic developments in central and eastern Europe. The only parallel in western Europe was the political success of Irish nationalism. Nationalism in the East was characterized by its virulent intolerance – in contrast to its earlier association with Western liberalism in such 'historic nations' as Poland or pre-1848 Hungary – because of the antagonistic process of construction of ethnic identities by both majority and minority nations. The shift towards national antagonisms that characterized international relations from the 1880s opened up new spaces for extremist nationalism, visible as fringe movements in the West, but so endemic in central-eastern Europe as to act as a permanent threat to international peace.

The principle of national self-determination was only finally accepted by the Allies in 1917, under President Woodrow Wilson's pressure and and through fear of the initial recognition of nationalities by the Bolsheviks in Russia. But it was not (nor could it be) applied consistently in the peace treaties of 1919–20. If plebiscites were held in some areas of ethnically mixed populations, 'historic rights' were sometimes accepted over ethnographic or economic characteristics (as in the inclusion of Slovakia and part of Silesia in Czechoslovakia), military or strategic reasons were preferred to ethnic consistency as in the inclusion of Albanian Kosovo in the new Yugoslavia), allies were given their due (Alto Adige and Trieste with its Slovene hinterland to Italy), military *faits accomplis* were accepted (the Romanian occupation of Bessarabia and Bukovina, or the Polish annexation of east Galicia) (Macartney, 1934).

The result was to create a legally new problem of 'national minorities', amounting to 25–30 million persons, or 20–25% of the total populations of the new states whose frontiers had been established by the peace treaties. 'Unredeemed' minorities (Hungarians in Romania, Slovenes in Austria, Germans in Czechoslovakia . . .) had been magnified on an unprecedented scale, and because their claims were now directed against the national states into which they had been incorporated (as distinct from the multinational empires before the war) and they could appeal to what they insisted were ethnically their national states, they constituted the prime element of tension both within their states and internationally until the Second World War. The spiral of ethnic hatred was irrepressible, as the newly-dominant nations applied the same uniformizing policies towards their minorities against which they had earlier protested so vocally. Nationalism which, before the war, had often extended its social base by its incorporation of social demands (in Poland, Finland, Georgia, the Jewish Bund), became authoritarian and virulently patriotic, easily associated with fascism as, a century before, it had been associated with liberalism. In the vacuum of power that has followed the collapse of communist regimes since 1989, both internationally and internally, we are witnessing a renewal of the same tragic phenomenon, with the presence of some 25 million Russians as minorities in the new states in what was formerly the USSR and the horrific policies of 'ethnic cleansing' of territories claimed by the newly dominant nations in former Yugoslavia.

NATIONAL IDENTITY, NATION-BUILDING AND NATIONALISM

National identity is an abstract concept that sums up the collective expression of a subjective individual sense of belonging to a socio-

25

political unit: the nation state. Nationalist rhetoric assumes not only that individuals form part of a nation (through language, blood, choice, residence, or some other criterion), but that they identify with the territorial unit of the nation state. Such an affirmation is ideological, in that it describes as a reality an ideal relationship that nationalists wish to exist. Historically, ruling elites were only too aware of the need to construct a bond of allegiance and loyalty between citizens and the nation state, expressed in Massimo d'Azeglio's famous aphorism, 'We have made Italy, now let us make Italians'. Today, few persons would deny their own sense of possessing a national identity, of belonging to a nation state, whatever their reservations about its policies or institutional forms. Hence it is a matter of more than historical importance to understand how and when national identity became a reality, what were the conditions that led inhabitants of different territories and allegiances to see themselves (and their ancestors and descendants) as sharing a common sentiment and affective bond as citizens of a nation.

Like the nation state itself, the construction of such a national sentiment can be dated to the French revolutionary ideology of democracy and participation. In *ancien régime* states, allegiance to the crown was of undoubted symbolic power, but its translation into social practices of loyalty was mediated through strong ties of solidarity and authority which bonded subjects to their lord, religion and locality. The initial voluntaristic basis of popular national loyalty in the Revolution, expressed most strongly in the mass armies defending the *patrie* against its enemies, proved inadequate – whether in France or other countries – in times of peace. Obedience to the state could be enforced by laws and police, legal citizenship defined by paternity or birthplace, but there was uncertainty until well into the nineteenth century, even in the old established states, about how widespread through society was willing, effective and primary identification with the nation state. By the late nineteenth century, ruling elites (and in particular those of a strongly nationalist bent) saw political, social, religious and class divisions as working against the solidarity of the nation, on which they believed the strength of the state depended.

Historians and social scientists have argued in terms of the construction of national identity through a process of 'nation-building'. Two main approaches are proposed, the first concentrating on the deliberate action of the state (Weber, 1977; Hobsbawm,

26

1990), the second stressing the almost inevitable consequences of modernization (Deutsch, 1962; Gellner, 1983; Smith, 1971).

According to proponents of deliberate state action, by the late nineteenth century the pressures that resulted from the processes of democratization of European societies, the restructuring of the world economy and the growing international rivalry increased the role of the state and accentuated its need to win support from and create a closer sense of identification with the 'nation'. Even in old established states like France, the need was felt, particularly after the defeat of 1870, to turn 'peasants into Frenchmen', to absorb the multitude of local identities and contain the deep divisions of French society within a national patriotism. By 1914, Weber argues, this had been achieved, in good part through deliberate actions by the state: the construction of roads and railways had brought all regions into contact with markets; conscription and compulsory education established the universal usage of the language of the dominant culture and allowed the elaboration of a common past, constantly evoked through national symbols and ceremonies. In short, for the political class and bureaucracy the French nation was a 'model of something at once to be built and to be treated for political reasons as already in existence' (Weber, 1977, p. 493). The First World War demonstrated their success.

If the political elite of an old state like France felt the need to actively boost or construct its citizens' sense of identification with their nation, it was obviously a matter of even greater urgency for the ruling class of the new nation states – particularly those which united territories that had formed part of different states – since disparate cultural traditions, administrative practices and economic circuits had to be forged into a new national identity. Administrative and political institutions, roads and railways, schools and conscription, all actively pursued in the new nation states, could create favourable conditions but certainly not ensure a common and enthusiastic sense of national sentiment among the great mass of the population. Alongside such material measures, symbolic forms of identification with the nation state were necessary in order to involve the people. There can be little doubt that the ruling elites were conscious of the importance, indeed the urgency, of such symbolic constructions, which they deliberately encouraged through the invention and public repetition of past traditions and history through flags and anthems, monuments and school textbooks, religious ceremonies and sports associations, exaltation of

27

king and empire. National symbols, like the figures of Marianne in France or Britannia in Britain, or the monument to Vittorio Emanuele II in Italy, offered visual representations of the unity of the nation. In Germany, the multiplicity of earlier state traditions inhibited the affirmation of a single dominant national symbol: alongside the multiple forms of commemorating the founding fathers Bismarck and Wilhelm I, different monuments, each resonant with its own symbolic meaning – from the cathedral of Cologne to the monument to Hermann, ancestral hero of the German *Volk* – placed regional pride firmly within the new Reich (Hobsbawm and Ranger, 1977; Agulhon, 1979, 1992; Nora, 1984–92; Tobia, 1991; Tacke, 1993).

The second approach to nation-building shifts the analysis away from the role of the state in raising the national consciousness of the people to the impersonal effects of modernization. Market forces and the modern state, for the American political scientist K. W. Deutsch, had the effect of breaking down the familial and local ties and value systems characteristic of traditional societies; mobility and literacy encouraged new forms of social communication, secular ideologies of mobilization and participation steadily thickened relations within the parameters of the nation state. For Gellner, building on these concepts of mobility and communication, the division of labour of industrial 'high culture', requiring individuals to acquire the skills to move from one occupational position to another, obliged the state to develop an educational system through which to socialize its citizens into this culture; through its monopoly of education, the state replaced earlier value systems with a new sense of identification with the nation state and patriotism. Implicit in Gellner's thesis is an explanation of why a sense of national identity only developed with such difficulty and unevenly in imperfectly modernized states, such as Italy, where levels of illiteracy were high and substantial areas of the national territory remained marginal to market forces three quarters of a century after political unification.

Few would deny the analytical utility of these approaches to an understanding of how national identities have emerged: they replace the nationalists' ahistorical assumption of an innate patriotism with an historical explanation of processes of social change and political decisions. But many difficulties remain, of which the most fundamental is the attribution to an outside actor (the state, capitalism) of the responsibility for the emergence of a national identity, of which an undifferentiated people are purely passive recipients. Yet the very subjectivity of identity makes it a highly individual matter; and social groups may attribute significantly different interpretations to their relationship with their nation.

Identity is neither a fixed nor an exclusive attribute. It is shaped within networks of social relations that constitute its environment and is expressed in a diversity of forms according to the particular context. There is a multiple quality to identity that corresponds both to the particular social environment and to the diverse social situations within which every individual lives and acts. When referred to the environment, it explains the relatively easily observable contrasts in comportment and beliefs that contemporaries have always associated with class, status and gender: as, for example, in nineteenth-century (or present-day) descriptions of a factory worker in an industrial city, a peasant in a remote village, a provincial landowner or an urban businessman. Contemporaneously, within these categories, each individual also displays different facets of his multiple sense of identity according to his role in the particular social situation within which he finds himself – for instance, as child, parent or dependent relative within the family; as parishioner or patron at religious functions; as man or woman among peers on festive occasions; in the use of dialect or formal language according to occasion and respondent; in his sense of identification with his parish, village, region or nation.

Individual identities change through the course of life with the accumulation of experiences. Youth has always been a characteristic of nationalist activists. But collective identities are also continuously modified through the intensity of contacts (which can be interpreted as liberating or constrictive) with other, often larger environments: the identity of a village can be transformed by the demands of conscription or by new market opportunities, a town suburb by an influx of immigrants. Collective identities, because they derive from social relations with others, in particular can often be the result of an external imposition as much as of an internal evolution: Jews and emigrants provide excellent, albeit contrasting examples. The intensity of Jewish identity cannot be dissociated from the millenary religious and racial persecution of Jews. The vast majority of peasants who emigrated massively from southern and eastern Europe across the oceans from the 1880s carried with them a cultural baggage which related primarily to family, village and region, local dialect and religion, rather than to nation or state; they became Italians, Greeks, Poles or Russians less because of the solidarity they initially sought in their new alien environment (a solidarity which related predominantly to kin and village of origin rather than to co-nationals), but far more because they were described and treated as such by the local inhabitants and officialdom.

The success of nationalism in grafting or constructing national identity onto multiple pre-existing individual and collective identities owed much to its capacity to relate its image of the nation to elements locally recognizable by individuals and groups, whether historically or linguistically. 'National' history has always been a capacious portmanteau, able to accommodate and revive memories of a distant and mythicized past, from Scottish kilts to Germanic Walhallas or Italian communal pageants (Hobsbawm and Ranger, 1977). Language possesses a unique capacity of communication between a writer or speaker and an anonymous audience which can be assumed to be culturally at one with him. The creation and diffusion of a vernacular language and literacy, through its structural closeness to many popular dialects, through its symbolism as proof of the authenticity and continuity of the past, through its oral and written imagery, has always proved particularly effective as an emotional link between individuals and the 'imagined community' of the nation (Fishman, 1972; Anderson, 1983). As a peasant nationalist recalled of prewar Poland: 'As for national consciousness, I have mentioned that the older peasants called themselves Masurians, their speech Masurian. They lived their own life, forming a wholly separate group, and caring nothing for the nation. I myself did not know that I was a Pole till I began to read books and papers, and I fancy that other villagers came to be aware of their national attachment in much the same way' (Kedourie, 1961, p. 120). It is not accidental that nationalist movements as different as the Catalan and the Lombard League in its early phase, the former wholly open to the 'southern' migrants of Andalusia, the latter closed to 'terroni', should both regard linguistic identity as fundamental (Ucelay da Cal, 1982; Diamanti, 1993, p. 56).

National identity can undoubtedly incorporate smaller, lower level identities and primordial ties of affection and obligation, such as those towards family and locality. But (contrary to the insistence of extreme nationalists), it did not (and does not) do so to the exclusion of such ties. For, in normal circumstances, for a majority of the population there has never been any contradiction between identification with family, region, class or religion and contemporaneously with the nation state. Indeed, the very language of nationalism draws heavily on the metaphor of family; and the retention of regional names for units of national armies – the Alpini, Royal Scots, etc. – is indicative of the recognition accorded by the ruling elites to the cohesive force of such regional symbols. Conflict between different identities only arises in extreme circumstances through the insistence of nationalists on the absolute value of national patriotism. It is the extremism of the inclusion–exclusion mentality of nationalists that has always been responsible for tensions within the social body of the nation state. The best known historical example is the outbreak of war in 1914, but the imposition of national loyalties and values in newly annexed territories such as Alsace or Alto Adige, or on any ethnic or cultural minority regarded (and regarding itself) as 'different', has inevitably, and usually deliberately, been generative of conflict.

These examples point to the complexity of what was (and is) understood by national identity. The nationalist appropriation of the concept – propagated universally as official doctrine – has accustomed us to equate it with identification with the state, to the point that, in a world of nation states, the 'nation' has only regained its autonomy in the face of the failure of the state. But the historical process of formation of national identity was never experienced in uniform manner by its actors. Nationalist movements have never been monolithic, but were always internally divided and competitive. It is only the historiography of nationalism that always attempts to impose an interpretative patina of concord, once success has been achieved. The historiography of Italian nationalism, for example, has regularly described the profound political divisions between leaders and movements during the struggle for independence, as if they were resolved by the achievement of a state and henceforth reduced to parliamentary differences. The monuments in the urban landscape of every European country remain as testimonies to the victors' unilateral consensual reinterpretation of the past.

But if there was agreement among the elites about the need to forge a national sentiment, its prolonged gestation was interpreted and mediated in multiple ways through class, regional or other identities, whose continued presence led to different and potentially conflictual experiences of national identity. Indeed, where nationalist leaders and movements had ultimately been forced to subordinate their competing aims to the common struggle for independence, once the creation of a new state had removed this supreme constraint it could not but lead to the renewed outbreak of rivalries and antagonistic definitions of the nation state.

In some nation states regional identity has been far more important than in others – in Germany, Spain, Italy or Yugoslavia, for example, compared to France, Portugal, Holland or Poland – because of the historical antecedents of diverse regions, whose elites could claim an earlier state or ethnic identity. Nationalist historiography has tended to ignore, or dismiss as traditional or reactionary, the strength of the social relations and networks within such regions, if they clashed with the new 'modern' ideology of the nation state. But the relationship between important, sometimes dominant segments of their elites and, in particular, the new nation states was often highly conflictual, precisely because of the new normative framework imposed by the state. Where regional attachment constituted an important element of the historical configuration of the national territory, national identity was interpreted even by those regional elites who were convinced supporters of the new nation state, particularly the urban bourgeoisie, as a sometimes polemical affirmation of their own role and power: monuments were erected to patriotic figures of local origin or regional identity stressed on national occasions, such as the pilgrimage to Vittorio Emanuele II's tomb in 1883 or the 1909 centenary of the revolt of Andreas Hofer in the Austrian Tyrol (Tobia, 1991; Tacke, 1993).

National identity depends on exclusion as much as on inclusion: the 'foreigner' whose expulsion is a precondition of national independence, or the ethnic minority whose pretentions threaten national unity, are the functional counterpart to the symbolic and material mechanisms of forging national cohesion, present in most historical processes of nation-building. But the definitions of who should be included and who excluded are fundamentally arbitrary, dependent on the very myths that underpin nationalist ideology (history, language, race, religion, territory . . .), expressed and sometimes imposed ruthlessly by elites in control of the state. The political manifestation of ethnic and regional identities may be seen as a product of the insistence on national identity and even more on nationalism, precisely because of the sense of exclusion or marginalization within the nation state. It is not a historical accident that regional nationalisms – from the Catalan and Basque to the Breton, Valdostan, Welsh and Scottish – only acquired political substance in the later nineteenth century, when nation-building throughout Europe pressed on civil society with a new intensity. And it was probably inevitable that regional elites should have always constructed their own nationalism with the same panoply of cultural attributes as the majority nations against whom they were (and are) asserting themselves, because of the symbiotic relationship between the two.

A clear distinction needs to be made between such national movements within regions and the formal institutionalization of regions by the nation state for its own purposes, whether administrative, economic, statistical or other. State-created regions may well have reinforced regional nationalisms where they already existed, as in Catalonia, Scotland or the Valle d'Aosta. Indeed, in recent decades, the adoption of regional structures of administration in states such as Italy or Spain may well be generating new regional identities where previously they existed barely or not at all, as in Campania or Extremadura.

Even when the existence of a national sentiment had undoubtedly become general, as in the western European nation states by 1914, class differences led to a very different understanding of its meaning. In Britain, the Welsh miners, who displayed their solidarity with the nationalist appeal to patriotism by volunteering at the outbreak of war, demonstrated their opposition to the war becoming an occasion for capitalist profit by striking in 1915. By 1917 the war was seen as an occasion for radical social transformation by soldiers in all the armies, whether in their existing states (England, France, Germany, Italy) or in the new nation states they hoped would emerge (the Austro-Hungarian and Russian empires) (Hobsbawm, 1990; Procacci, 1992).

It is evident that the creation of a national territory, clearly demonstrated by political frontiers, in the medium term normally worked in favour of the construction of a national identity, as national bureacracies, developing the Napoleonic model, applied uniformizing practices and regulations across the territory, building roads and railways for a national market and schools for a national language and culture. We can see *a posteriori* that in most nation states, both old and new, as the practice of political participation extended, civil society slowly conformed to the area of the national territory, in both public and private spheres: political and social organizations – professional groups, political parties, trade unions, etc. – structured themselves on a national scale; the comportment and way of life of individuals and families, even their demographic behaviour, gradually converged towards a national norm (Cotts Watkins, 1991). Group self-interest provided an increasingly strong basis for such national identity, certainly more constant than the highly charged but always exceptional expression of national patriotism aroused by war (Potter, 1963).

Political and economic stability ensures allegiance to the nation state; a willing, essentially passive but emotive form of national identity is consolidated by the passage of generations. It is a sense of identification with the nation state – rendered most explicitly in the American ideology of the 'melting pot' – which immigrants acquire and which their children share with long-standing residents, unless they are deliberately discriminated against. Immigrants or other ethnically distinctive groups will not necessarily lose their 'other' identity over some generations, not least because of the facile and habitual association between ethnic origin and socio-economic status made by the dominant elites of the 'national' society. At moments of particular tension, whether domestic or international, when sentiments of inclusion and exclusion are heightened, this sense of forming part of a nation could (and can) be incited, under extreme nationalist pressure, into more active manifestations of patriotism. But ultimately the daily practices of the nation state have fostered the sense of national identity.

Such a reassuring interpretation of the consensual consolidation of national identity has underlaid all attempts at nation-building and is implicit today in liberal democratic theory. As we have seen, in Russia and Hungary (and many other examples exist, such as Francoist Spain, fascist Italy or, now, ex-communist Yugoslavia), the insensitivity and rapidity of the drive for homogeneity within the state could have disastrously contrary effects, facilitating the transformation of the cultural identity of ethnic minorities into a political programme. But it is not just heavy-handed political authoritarian rule that is responsible for the emergence of a politically ethnic (or regional) identity. Majority nations within a nation state, however liberal or democratic, are structurally insensitive towards the susceptibilities of minorities not only because of their dominant role in the running of the state, but because the cultural and symbolic identifying signs of the nation state – its historical, linguistic, geographical or ethnic past – are primarily (and probably necessarily) couched in the language of this majority. In Belgium, Flemish nationalism was constructed against francophone Walloon cultural as well as economic hegemony; in England and elsewhere, ethnic groups remain necessarily ambivalent towards a white-dominated cultural representation of national identity. A subjective sense of discrimination is intrinsic to the construction of a separate identity, and ethnic ties would appear to be more binding and potentially antagonistic through their exclusiveness.

If stability may normally have ensured at least passive allegiance, by contrast, because of the appropriation of the nation by the state, whenever the state has experienced prolonged political or economic crisis, the demand voiced by minority elites for recognition of their national distinctiveness has constantly resurfaced, whatever the criterion employed for identification (language, culture, ethnicity, territory or history). In this sense, there is a similarity between the nineteenth-century ethnic nationalist movements of the central and eastern European empires, such 'historic' western European nationalisms as the Catalan, Basque and Flemish, the postwar regional nationalist movements (from the Valle d'Aosta and Sardinia to Scotland and Wales, and now the Lombard League), and the most recent recrudescence of nationalism in the former USSR and Yugoslavia. As the conditions for allegiance diminished, through economic weakness and/or political decline, the demands of a centralizing state lost their compensations (employment, rise in the standard of living, international reputation, empire . . .) and appeared increasingly as impositions that benefited a particular nationality or, quite simply, the state bureaucracy or party.

If the conditions for the repeated resurgence of national movements are similar, their social composition has changed, in tune with the impact on all societies of economic and technological change and universal literacy: an intelligentsia of the new technology has replaced the *literati* of the early nationalist movements, the social base involves countryside as much as town, the working class and small businessmen alongside middle-class professionals and shopkeepers (A. D. Smith, 1979; Nairn, 1977; Diamanti, 1993).

Precisely because the common aim of all such movements is recognition of their identity and autonomy on the basis of their internal cohesion as a national group, there is no theoretical limit to the self-reproduction of such 'nations', once the scale of identificatory criteria is reduced: the Cornish in England can claim as particular an identity in England as the Bretons in France, the Friulani in Italy as much as the Abkhazians in Georgia. Only the practical demands of the viability of a state can set a limit; and even then – as in the case of many of the states created after the first world war or recognized by the United Nations since decolonization – political or economic viability has often been subordinated to the credo of self-determination.

In a world of nation states (to employ Breuilly's distinction), it was (and is) inevitable that the demands of these movements should structure themselves on the model of the nation state. Their internal divisions over aims and policy – autonomy or independence, negotiation or direct confrontation, political or social priorities – continue to repeat the power struggles and ideals that have always divided nationalist movements. The capacity of their individual leaders to mobilize support for their respective positions continues to correspond to the ability or failure of the elites of the existing state (and of the international system) to renegotiate the institutional structures of the state: the Habsburg dynasty failed to win sufficient support to ensure that its empire survived the disruptions of the war; in Spain, the post-Francoist ruling class has utilized the transition to democracy to accept an unprecedented level of decentralization; in the former Soviet Union and the former Yugoslavia, the incapacity or rigidity of the state has facilitated the classic and simplistic demand of extreme nationalists for political independence as a priority.

The strength of nationalism, to the present day, lies in its capacity to identify with, incorporate and mobilize support for a wide spectrum of ideological positions. Its weakness lies in what at moments seems to be its almost innate tendency to allow the power of the state to impose a unilateral definition of patriotism that brooks no criticism. As nationalists multiply their demands for statehood and territory today, a historical understanding of nationalism in Europe is essential if we are to rise above the irresponsibility and mystification of emotive response.

The texts that follow have been selected to illustrate how the affirmation and diffusion of nationalism in Europe over the past two centuries have influenced both contemporary and historical analyses. Nationalism has penetrated and often permeated the mentality and conventional wisdom of every European state; but because intellectual traditions are so national and differ in their manner of representing themself and the Other, the texts have been chosen from various European countries. A historiographical approach has been adopted, as it reveals the growing awareness of the ambiguities and complexities of nationalism.

* I wish to thank Gerhardt Haupt, Michael Müller and the participants in seminars at the University of Essex and the European Forum of the European University Institute for their perceptive comments on earlier versions of this text.

NOTES

1 Penguin Classics, 1975, p. 72.
2 B. Chatwin, *The Songlines*, London, 1988, p. 224.

REFERENCES

Agulhon, M. (1979), *Marianne au Combat*, Paris.
—— (1992), *Marianne: Les Visages de la République*, Paris.
Anderson, B. (1983), *Imagined Communities. Reflections on the Origin and Spread of Nationalism*, London (2nd edn, 1991).
Armstrong, J. A. (1982), *Nations before Nationalism*, Chapel Hill, NC.
Bauer, O. (1907), *Die Nationalitätenfrage und die Sozialdemokratie*, Vienna.
Bottomore, T. and Goode, P. (eds) (1978), *Austro-Marxism*, Oxford.
Bourdieu, P. (1991), *Language and Symbolic Power*, Cambridge.
Breuilly, J. (1982), *Nationalism and the State*, Manchester.
Cameron, R. (1967), 'Some lessons of history for developing nations', *American Economic Review*, 57.
Chabod, F. (1961), *L'Idea di Nazione*, Bari.
Cobban, A. (1969), *The Nation-State and National Self-Determination*, London (1st edn, 1945).
Cotts Watkins, S. (1991), *From Provinces into Nations. Demographic Integration in Western Europe 1870–1960*, Princeton, NJ.
Della Peruta, F. (ed.) (1969), *Giuseppe Mazzini e i Democratici*, Naples.
Deutsch, K. W. (1962), *Nationalism and Social Communication*, Cambridge, Mass.
—— and Fultz, W. J. (eds) (1966), *Nation Building*, New York.
Diamanti, I. (1993), *La Lega. Geografia, storia e sociologia di un nuovo soggetto politico*, Rome.
Eley, G. (1981), 'Nationalism and social history', *Social History*, 6.
Fishman, J. A. (1972), *Language and Nationalism*, Rowley, Mass.
Gellner, E. (1983), *Nations and Nationalism*, Oxford.

Hayes, C. J. (1968), *The Historical Evolution of Modern Nationalism*, New York.

Hinsley, F. H. (1963), *Power and the Pursuit of Peace*, Cambridge.

—— (1973), *Nationalism and the International System*, London.

Hobsbawm, E. J. (1990), *Nations and Nationalism since 1780*, Cambridge.

—— and Ranger, T. E. (eds) (1977), *The Invention of Tradition*, Cambridge.

Hroch, M. (1989), *Social Preconditions of National Revival in Europe*, Cambridge.

Hughes, M. (1988), *Nationalism and Society. Germany 1800–1945*, London.

Hutchinson, J. (1994), *Modern Nationalism*, London.

—— and Smith, A. D. (eds) (1994), *Nationalism*, Oxford.

Kamenka, E. (ed.) (1976), *Nationalism. The Nature and Evolution of an Idea*, London.

Kantorowicz, E. L. (1984), *Mourir pour la patrie et autres textes*, Paris.

Kedourie, E. (1961), *Nationalism*, London (1st edn, 1960).

Kennedy, P. M. (1974), 'The decline of nationalistic history in the West, 1900–1970', in Laqueur, W. and Mosse, G. L. (eds), *Historians in Politics*, London.

Kohn, H. (1955), *Nationalism, its Meaning and History*, Princeton, NJ.

—— (1968), 'Nationalism', in *International Encyclopedia of the Social Sciences*, vol. 11, New York.

Koselleck. R., Geschnitzer, F., Schönemann, B. and Werner, K. F. (1992), 'Volk, Nation, Nationalismus, Masse', in Brunner, O., Conze, W. and Koselleck, R. (eds), *Geschichtliche Grundbegriffe: Historiker Lexikon zur politischen-sozialen Sprache in Deutschland*, vol. 7, Stuttgart.

Koshar, R. (1993), 'Building pasts: historic preservation and identity in twentieth century Germany', in Gillis, J. (ed.), *Commemorations. The Politics of Modern Identity*, Princeton, NJ.

Krumeich, G. (1989), *Jeanne d'Arc in der Geschichte*, Sigmaringen.

Lanaro, S. (1993), 'Introduction' to Renan, E., *Che cos'è una nazione?*, Rome.

Langewiesche, D. (1988), *Liberalismus in Deutschland*, Frankfurt.

Macartney, C. A. (1968), *National States and National Minorities*, New York (1st edn 1934).

Mill, J. S. (1861), *Considerations on Representative Government*, London.

Minogue, K. R. (1970), *Nationalism*, London.

Mosse, G. (1975), *The Nationalization of the Masses. Political Symbolism and Mass Movements in Italy (1812–1933)*, New York.

Nairn, T. (1977), *The Break-up of Britain. Crisis and Neo-nationalism*, London.

Nora, P. (ed.) (1984–92), *Lieux de Mémoire*, 3 vols, Paris.

Potter, D. M. (1963), 'The historian's use of nationalism and vice-versa', in Riasanovsky, A. V. and Riznik, B. (eds), *Generalisations in Historical Writing*, Philadelphia.

Procacci, G. (1992), *Soldati e Prigionieri Italiani nella Guerra 15–18*, Rome.

Renan, E. (1947), 'Qu'est-ce-qu' une Nation?', in *Oeuvres complètes de Ernest Renan*, vol. 1, Paris.

Schieder, T. (1991), *Nationalismus und Nationalstaat: Studien zum nationalen Problem in modernen Europa*, Goettingen.

—— and Dann, O. (eds) (1978), *Nationale Bewegung und Soziale Organisation*, Munich.

Seton Watson, H. (1967), *The Russian Empire 1801–1917*, Oxford.

—— (1977), *Nations and States*, London.

Smith, A. D. (1971), *Theories of Nationalism*, London.

—— (1979), *Nationalism in the Twentieth Century*, Oxford.

—— (1986), *The Ethnic Origins of Nations*, Oxford.

—— (1991), *National Identity*, London.

Smith, P., Koufa, K. and Suppan, A. (eds) (1991), *Ethnic Groups in International Relations*, New York.

Suratteau, J. R. (1972), *L'Idée Nationale de la Révolution à nos Jours*, Paris.

Symmons-Symonelewicz, K. (1970), *Nationalist Movements. A Comparative View*, Meadville.

Tacke, C. (1993), *Denkmal im Sozialen Raum. Eine vergleichende Regionalstudie nationaler Symbole in Deutschland und Frankreich im 19. Jahrhundert*, PhD. thesis, European University Institute.

Teich, M. and Porter, R. (eds) (1993), *The National Question in Europe in Historical Perspective*, Cambridge.

Tobia, B. (1991), *Una Patria per gli Italiani*, Bari.

Ucelay da Cal (1982), *La Catalunya Populista. Imatge, Cultura i Politica en l'etapa republicana (1931–1939)*, Barcelona.

Weber, E. (1977), *Peasants into Frenchmen. The Modernization of Rural France*, London.

Woolf, S. (1989), 'French civilization and ethnicity in the Napoleonic empire', *Past and Present*, 124.

—— (1991), *Napoleon's Integration of Europe*, London.

—— (1991), *Europe and the Nation-State*, San Domenico di Fiesole.

—— (1992), 'The construction of a European world-view in the Revolutionary-Napoleonic years', *Past and Present*, 137.

Zolberg, A. (1974), 'The making of Flemings and Walloons: Belgium 1830–1914', *Journal of Interdisciplinary History*, 5.

2

NATIONALITY*

J. S. Mill

John Stuart Mill (1806–73), the political philosopher, was less interested in nationalism than in liberalism and the political economy. But he was drawn to reflect on the power of this new force by the dramatic political events he witnessed, in particular the unification of Italy, which aroused widespread public interest in England. Like the historian Lord Acton, who published an almost contemporaneous essay on the same theme ('Nationality', *Home and Foreign Review*, 1862), Mill was concerned with the problematic relationship between liberalism and nationalism.

OF NATIONALITY, AS CONNECTED WITH REPRESENTATIVE GOVERNMENT

A portion of mankind may be said to constitute a Nationality if they are united among themselves by common sympathies which do not exist between them and any others – which make them co-operate with each other more willingly than with other people, desire to be under the same government, and desire that it should be government by themselves or a portion of themselves exclusively. This feeling of nationality may have been generated by various causes. Sometimes it is the effect of identity of race and descent. Community of language, and community of religion, greatly contribute to it. Geographical limits are one of its causes. But the strongest of all is identity of political antecedents; the possession of a national history, and consequent community of recollections; collective pride and humiliation, pleasure and regret, connected with the same incidents in the past. None of these circumstances, however, are either indispensable, or necessarily sufficient by themselves. Switzerland has a strong sentiment of nationality, though the cantons are of different races, different languages, and different religions. Sicily has, throughout history, felt itself quite distinct in nationality from Naples, notwithstanding identity of religion, almost identity of language, and a considerable amount of common historical antecedents. The Flemish and the Walloon provinces of Belgium, notwithstanding diversity of race and language, have a much greater feeling of common nationality than the former have with Holland, or the latter with France. Yet in general the national feeling is proportionally weakened by the failure of any of the causes which contribute to it. Identity of language, literature, and, to some extent, of race and recollections, have maintained the feeling of nationality in considerable strength among the different portions of the German name, though they have at no time been really united under the same government; but the feeling has never reached to making the separate states desire to get rid of their autonomy. Among Italians an identity far from complete, of language and literature, combined with a geographical position which separates them by a distinct line from other countries, and, perhaps more than everything else, the possession of a common name, which makes them all glory in the past achievements in arts, arms, politics, religious primacy, science, and literature, of any who share the same designation, give rise to an amount of national feeling in the population which, though still imperfect, has been sufficient to produce the great events now passing before us,[1] notwithstanding a great mixture of races, and although they have never, in either ancient or modern history, been under the same government, except while that government extended or was extending itself over the greater part of the known world.

Where the sentiment of nationality exists in any force, there is a *prima facie* case for uniting all the members of the nationality under the same government, and a government to themselves apart. This is merely saying that the question of government ought to be decided by the governed. One hardly knows what any division of the human race should be free to do if not to determine with which of the various collective bodies of human beings they choose to associate themselves. But, when a people are ripe for free institutions, there is a still more vital consideration. Free institutions are next to impossible in a country made up of different nationalities. Among a people without fellow-feeling, especially if they read and speak different languages, the united public opinion, necessary

41

to the working of representative government, cannot exist. The influences which form opinions and decide political acts are different in the different sections of the country. An altogether different set of leaders have the confidence of one part of the country and of another. The same books, newspapers, pamphlets, speeches, do not reach them. One section does not know what opinions, or what instigations, are circulating in another. The same incidents, the same acts, the same system of government, affect them in different ways; and each fears more injury to itself from the other nationalities than from the common arbiter, the State. Their mutual antipathies are generally much stronger than jealousy of the government. That any of them feels aggrieved by the policy of the common ruler is sufficient to determine another to support that policy. Even if all are aggrieved, none feel that they can rely on the others for fidelity in a joint resistance; the strength of none is sufficient to resist alone, and each may reasonably think that it consults its own advantage most by bidding for the favour of the government against the rest. Above all, the grand and only effectual security in the last resort against the despotism of the government is in that case wanting: the sympathy of the army with the people. The military are the part of every community in whom, from the nature of the case, the distinction between their fellow-countrymen and foreigners is the deepest and strongest. To the rest of the people foreigners are merely strangers; to the soldier, they are men against whom he may be called, at a week's notice, to fight for life or death. The difference to him is that between friends and foes – we may almost say between fellow-men and another kind of animal: for as respects the enemy, the only law is that of force, and the only mitigation the same as in the case of other animals – that of simple humanity. Soldiers to whose feelings half or three-fourths of the subjects of the same government are foreigners will have no more scruple in mowing them down, and no more desire to ask the reason why, than they would have in doing the same thing against declared enemies. An army composed of various nationalities has no other patriotism than devotion to the flag. Such armies have been the executioners of liberty through the whole duration of modern history. The sole bond which holds them together is their officers and the government which they serve; and their only idea, if they have any, of public duty is obedience to orders. A government thus supported, by keeping its Hungarian regiments in Italy and its Italian in Hungary, can long continue to rule in both places with the iron rod of foreign conquerors.

If it be said that so broadly marked a distinction between what is due to a fellow-countryman and what is due merely to a human creature is more worthy of savages than of civilised beings, and ought, with the utmost energy, to be contended against, no one holds that opinion more strongly than myself. But this object, one of the worthiest to which human endeavour can be directed, can never, in the present state of civilisation, be promoted by keeping different nationalities of anything like equivalent strength under the same government. In a barbarous state of society the case is sometimes different. The government may then be interested in softening the antipathies of the races that peace may be preserved and the country more easily governed. But when there are either free institutions, or a desire for them, in any of the peoples artificially tied together, the interest of the government lies in an exactly opposite direction. It is then interested in keeping up and envenoming their antipathies that they may be prevented from coalescing, and it may be enabled to use some of them as tools for the enslavement of others. The Austrian Court has now for a whole generation made these tactics its principal means of government; with what fatal success, at the time of the Vienna insurrection and the Hungarian contest,[2] the world knows too well. Happily there are now signs that improvement is too far advanced to permit this policy to be any longer successful.

For the preceding reasons, it is in general a necessary condition of free institutions that the boundaries of governments should coincide in the main with those of nationalities. But several considerations are liable to conflict in practice with this general principle. In the first place, its application is often precluded by geographical hindrances. There are parts even of Europe in which different nationalities are so locally intermingled that it is not practicable for them to be under separate governments. The population of Hungary is composed of Magyars, Slovaks, Croats, Serbs, Roumans, and in some districts Germans, so mixed up as to be incapable of local separation; and there is no course open to them but to make a virtue of necessity, and reconcile themselves to living together under equal rights and laws. Their community of servitude, which dates only from the destruction of Hungarian independence in 1849, seems to be ripening and disposing them for such an equal union. The German colony of East Prussia is cut off from Germany by part of the ancient Poland, and being too weak to maintain separate independence, must, if geographical continuity is to be maintained, be either under a non-German government, or the intervening Polish territory must be under a German one. Another considerable region in which the dominant element of the population is German, the provinces of Courland, Esthonia, and Livonia, is condemned by its local situation to form part of a Slavonian State. In Eastern Germany itself there is a large Slavonic population: Bohemia is principally Slavonic, Silesia and other districts partially so.[3] The most united country in Europe, France, is far from being homogeneous: independently of the fragments of foreign nationalities at its remote extremities, it consists, as language and history prove, of two portions; one occupied almost exclusively by a Gallo-Roman population, while in the other the Frankish, Burgundian, and other Teutonic races form a considerable ingredient.

When proper allowance has been made for geographical exigencies, another more purely moral and social consideration offers itself. Experience proves that it is possible for one nationality to merge and be absorbed in another: and when it was originally an inferior and more backward portion of the human race the absorption is greatly to its advantage. Nobody can suppose that it is not more beneficial to a Breton, or a Basque of French Navarre, to be brought into the current of the ideas and feelings of a highly civilised and cultivated people – to be a member of the French nationality, admitted on equal terms to all the privileges of French citizenship, sharing the advantages of French protection, and the dignity of French power – than to sulk on his own rocks, the half-savage relic of past times, revolving in his own little mental orbit, without participation or interest in the general movement of the world. The same remark applies to the Welshman or the Scottish Highlander as members of the British nation.

Whatever really tends to the admixture of nationalities, and the blending of their attributes and peculiarities in a common union, is a benefit to the human race. Not by extinguishing types, of which, in these cases, sufficient examples are sure to remain, but by softening their extreme forms, and filling up the intervals between them. The united people, like a crossed breed of animals (but in a still greater degree, because the influences in operation are moral as well as physical), inherits the special aptitudes and excellences of all its progenitors, protected by the admixture from being exaggerated into the neighbouring vices. But to render this admixture possible, there must be peculiar conditions. The combinations of circumstances which occur, and which effect the result, are various.

The nationalities brought together under the same government may be about equal in numbers and strength, or they may be very unequal. If unequal, the least numerous of the two may either be the superior in civilisation, or the inferior. Supposing it to be superior it may either, through that superiority, be able to acquire ascendancy over the other, or it may be overcome by brute strength and reduced to subjection. This last is a sheer mischief to the human race, and one which civilised humanity with one accord should rise in arms to prevent. The absorption of Greece by Macedonia was one of the greatest misfortunes which ever happened to the world: that of any of the principal countries of Europe by Russia would be a similar one.

If the smaller nationality, supposed to be the more advanced in improvement, is able to overcome the greater, as the Macedonians, reinforced by the Greeks, did Asia, and the English India, there is often a gain to civilisation: but the conquerors and the conquered cannot in this case live together under the same free institutions. The absorption of the conquerors in the less advanced people would be an evil: these must be governed as subjects, and the state of things is either a benefit or a misfortune, according as the subjugated people have or have not reached the state in which it is an injury not to be under a free government, and according as the conquerors do or do not use their superiority in a manner calculated to fit the conquered for a higher stage of improvement.

When the nationality which succeeds in overpowering the other is both the most numerous and the most improved; and especially if the subdued nationality is small, and has no hope of reasserting its independence; then, if it is governed with any tolerable justice, and if the members of the more powerful nationality are not made odious by being invested with exclusive privileges, the smaller nationality is gradually reconciled to its position, and becomes amalgamated with the larger. No Bas-Breton, nor even any Alsatian, has the smallest wish at the present day to be separated from France. If all Irishmen have not yet arrived at the same disposition towards England, it is partly because they are sufficiently numerous to be capable of constituting a respectable nationality by themselves; but principally because, until of later years, they had been so atrociously governed, that all these best feelings combined with their bad ones in rousing bitter resentment against the Saxon rule. This disgrace to England, and calamity to the whole empire, has, it may be truly said, completely ceased for nearly a generation. No Irishman is now less free than an Anglo-Saxon, nor has a less share of every benefit either to his country or to his individual fortunes than if he were sprung from any other portion of the British dominions. The only remaining real grievance of Ireland, that of the State Church, is one which half, or nearly half, the people of the larger island have in common with them. There is now next to nothing, except the memory of the past, and the difference in the predominant religion, to keep apart two races, perhaps the most fitted of any two in the world to be the completing counterpart of one another. The consciousness of being at last treated not only with equal justice but with equal consideration is making such rapid way in the Irish nation as to be wearing off all feelings that could make them insensible to the benefits which the less numerous and less wealthy people must necessarily derive from being fellow-citizens instead of foreigners to those who are not only their nearest neighbours, but the wealthiest, and one of the freest, as well as most civilised and powerful, nations of the earth.

The cases in which the greatest practical obstacles exist to the blending of nationalities are when the nationalities which have been bound together are nearly equal in numbers and in the other elements of power. In such cases, each, confiding in its strength, and feeling itself capable of maintaining an equal struggle with any of the others, is unwilling to be merged in it: each cultivates with party obstinacy its distinctive peculiarities; obsolete customs, and even declining languages, are revived to deepen the separation; each deems itself tyrannised over if any authority is exercised within itself by functionaries of a rival race; and whatever is given to one of the conflicting nationalities is considered to be taken from all the rest. When nations, thus divided, are under a despotic government which is a stranger to all of them, or which, though sprung from one, yet feeling greater interest in its own power than in any sympathies of nationality, assigns no privilege to either nation, and chooses its instruments indifferently from all; in the course of a few generations, identity of situation often produces harmony of feeling, and the different races come to feel towards each other as fellow-countrymen; particularly if they are dispersed over the same tract of country. But if the era of aspiration to free government arrives before this fusion has been effected, the opportunity has gone by for effecting it. From that time, if the unreconciled nationalities are geographically separate, and especially if their local position is such that there is no natural fitness or convenience in their being under the same government (as in the case of an Italian province under a French or German yoke), there is not only an obvious propriety, but, if either freedom or concord is cared for, a necessity, for breaking the connection altogether. There may be cases in which the provinces, after separation, might usefully remain united by a federal tie: but it generally happens that if they are willing to forego complete independence, and become members of a federation, each of them has other neighbours with whom it would prefer to connect itself, having more sympathies in common, if not also greater community of interest.

* From J. S. Mill, *Considerations on Representative Government* (1861), ed. with an introduction by R. B. McCallum, Oxford, Blackwell, 1948, pp. 291–7.

NOTES

1 The unification of Italy [Editor's note].
2 1848 revolutions [Editor's note].
3 Today's term for 'Slavonic' is Slav [Editor's note].

3

WHAT IS A NATION?*

Ernest Renan

Ernest Renan (1823–92) was a rationalist scholar of the history of languages and religions, famed for his *Life of Jesus* (1863). Professor at the Sorbonne, his lecture on what is a nation was a vindication of the voluntaristic definition that originated with the French Revolution. He argued polemically against the insistence on blood and soil that was being affirmed ever more widely in Germany.

Since the end of the Roman Empire, or rather, since the break-up of the empire of Charlemagne, western Europe gives the appearance of being divided into nations, some of which, in certain periods, have sought to exercise hegemony over the others, without ever meeting with lasting success. What Charles V of Spain, Louis XIV and Napoleon I were unable to do, probably no one will be able to do in the future. The establishment of a new Roman Empire, or a new empire of Charlemagne, has become an impossibility. Europe is too greatly divided for an attempt at universal domination not to provoke a coalition that would quickly bring the ambitious nation back within its natural borders. For a long time, a kind of equilibrium was established. For hundreds of years to come, France, England, Germany, and Russia will be still, despite the risks they will have taken, historical individuals, the essential pieces on a draughtsboard whose squares vary continually in size and importance, but never merge absolutely.

Understood this way, nations are something quite new in history. They were unknown in antiquity; neither Egypt, nor China, nor ancient Chaldaea were nations to any extent. They were flocks lead by a son of the Sun, or a son of Heaven: no more were there Egyptian citizens than there were Chinese citizens. Classical

48

antiquity had republics and city monarchies, confederations of local republics and empires; in no way were there nations as we understand the term. Athens, Sparta, Sidon, Tyre are small centres of admirable patriotism; but these cities have relatively limited territories. Before their absorption into the Roman Empire, Gaul, Spain and Italy were collections of tribes, often united amongst themselves, but without central institutions and without dynasties. Nor were the Assyrian Empire, the Persian Empire and the empire of Alexander *patries*. There never were any Assyrian patriots; the Persian Empire was a vast feudal system. Not one nation connects its origins with Alexander's colossal adventure, which has however been so rich in consequences for the general history of civilization.

[. . .]

What actually became of the Germanic peoples after their great invasions in the fifth century until the last Norman conquests in the tenth? They made no great difference to the composition of the races; but they imposed dynasties and a military aristocracy on more or less extensive areas of the ancient empire of the West, which then took the name of their invaders. Hence a France, a Burgundy and a Lombardy; and later, a Normandy. The rapid ascendancy of the Frankish Empire momentarily recreates the unity of the West; but this empire irremediably breaks down towards the middle of the ninth century; the treaty of Verdun [843] traces divisions that are immutable in principle, and thereafter France, Germany, England, Italy and Spain, by frequent detours and through a thousand adventures, move towards a fully national existence such as we see flourishing today.

What is it that really characterizes these different states? It is the fusion of the populations of which they are composed. In the countries we have just listed, there is nothing analogous to what we find in Turkey, where the Turk, the Slav, the Greek, the Armenian, the Arab, the Syrian and the Kurd are as distinct today as they were in the days of the conquest. Two essential circumstances contributed to this result. First the fact that the Germanic peoples adopted Christianity as soon as they were in tenuous contact with the Greek and Latin peoples. When the conqueror and the conquered share the same religion, or rather, when the conqueror adopts the religion of the conquered, the Turkish system, the absolute distinction of men in accordance with their religions, can no longer take place. The second circumstance was the forgetting, on the part of the conquerors, of their own language. The grandsons of Clovis, Alaricus, Gondebaud, Albinus, and Rollon already spoke a Roman tongue. This fact was itself the consequence of another important feature, which is that the Franks, the Burgundians, the Goths, the Lombards and the Normans had very few women of their own race with them. For several generations, the chiefs married only German women; but their concubines and their wet-nurses were Latin. The whole tribe married Latin women, which meant that after the Franks and the Goths settled on Roman territory, the *lingua franca*, the *lingua gothica*, had only a very short-lived fate. It was not like this in England, since the Anglo-Saxon invaders undoubtedly brought women with them; the Breton population fled, and besides, Latin was no longer, indeed never was dominant in Brittany.[1]

[...]

Forgetting, and, I would even say, historical error are an essential factor in the creation of a nation, and thus the advances of historical study are often threatening to a nationality. Historical investigation, in fact, brings to light the acts of violence that have taken place at the origin of every political formation, even those whose consequences have been the most beneficial. Unity is always created through brutality; the unification of northern and southern France was the result of continual exterminations and terror lasting for almost a century. The king of France, who, dare I say it, is the ideal type of the secular unifier, created the most perfect unity of nationality there has ever been. Viewed too closely, however, the king of France has lost his prestige; the nation he formed has cursed him, and today only cultivated minds know his worth and what he did.

It is by contrast that the great laws of the history of western Europe become palpable. Many countries failed in the endeavours that the king of France, partly through his tyranny and partly through his justice, so admirably brought to completion. Under the crown of St Stephen, the Magyars and the Slavs have remained as separate as they were 800 years ago. Far from combining the different elements of its dominion, the Habsburg dynasty has kept them apart and frequently at odds with each other. In Bohemia, the Czech and the German elements are superposed like oil and water in a glass. The Turkish policy of separating nationalities in accordance with religion has had the most serious consequences: it has caused the ruin of the Orient. Take a town like Salonika or Smyrna, and you will find there five or six communities, each with their own memories and with almost nothing in common between them. Now the essence of a nation is that individuals have many things in common, but also have forgotten many other things. No French citizen knows if he is Burgundian, Alani, Taifali or Visigoth; every French citizen must have forgotten Saint Bartholemew's Day,[2] the thirteenth-century massacres in the Midi. There are not ten families in France that could furnish proof of Frankish origins, and such proof would still be essentially defective in consequence of thousands of unknown instances of crossbreeding that may disturb all the genealogists' propositions.

The modern nation is therefore an historical result brought about by a series of phenomena converging in the same direction. Sometimes unity has been brought about by a dynasty, as is the case with France; sometimes by the direct will of the provinces, as is the case with Holland, Switzerland and Belgium; sometimes by a general sensibility, belatedly conquering the caprices of feudalism, as is the case with Italy and Germany. A profound *raison d'être* has governed these formations. The principles in such cases come to light by the most unexpected surprises. In our own day, we have seen Italy united by its defeats, and Turkey demolished by its victories. Each defeat advanced Italian affairs, while each victory ruined Turkey; for Italy is a nation, and Turkey, outside Asia Minor, is not. It is France's glory to have proclaimed, through the French Revolution, that a nation exists by itself. We should not take it badly that others imitate us. The principle of nationhood is ours. What then is a nation? Why is Holland a nation, whereas Hanover or the Grand Duchy of Parma is not? How does France persist as a nation, when the principle that created it has disappeared? How is it that Switzerland, which has three languages, two religions and three or four races, is a nation, whereas Tuscany, for example, which is so homogeneous, is not? Why is Austria a state and not a nation? How does the principle of nationality differ from the principle of race?

[. . .]

To listen to certain political theorists, a nation is above all else a dynasty, representing an ancient conquest that was initially accepted and then later forgotten by the mass of the people. According to the political theorists of whom I am speaking, the grouping of the provinces effected by a dynasty, through its wars, its marriages and its treaties, ends with the dynasty that formed it. It is quite true that the majority of modern nations were created

by a family of feudal origins who had contracted a marriage with
the land and had been, in some way, a nucleus of centralization.
The frontiers of France in 1789 were neither natural nor necessary. The large area added by the Capetian dynasty to the narrow
strip of the treaty of Verdun was indeed the personal acquisition
of this dynasty. In an era of frequent annexations, there were
neither natural limits nor was there an idea of them; neither the
rights of nations, nor the will of provinces. The union of England,
Scotland and Ireland was by the same token a dynastic act. Italy
only held back so long from being a nation because, amongst its
numerous ruling houses, none, before this century, became the
centre of unity. Strange thing that it was on the obscure island of
Sardinia, only just Italian soil, that it took on a royal title.[3] Holland, which created itself through an heroic act of resolve, nevertheless contracted an intimate marriage with the House of Orange,
and would run real risks, were this union one day to be
compromised.

Is such a law absolute, however? Doubtless not. Switzerland
and the United States, which were formed by conglomerations of
successive additions, had no dynastic basis. I will not discuss this
question as far as France is concerned. We would have to have
access to the secrets of the future. Let us just say that had the
great French royalty been so much a national concern, then how,
the day after its fall, was the nation able to continue without it?
Then the eighteenth century changed everything. After centuries of
degradation, man went back to the spirit of antiquity, to respecting
himself, and to the idea of his rights. The words *patrie* and 'citizen'
had reclaimed their meaning. Thus the most daring operation
that had been exercised in history could be performed, an operation that could be compared to what would be, in physiological
terms, the attempt to give life, as it originally was, to a body from
which the brain and heart had been removed.

It must therefore be admitted that a nation can exist without a
dynastic principle, and even that those nations that were formed
by dynasties can separate themselves from this dynasty without
thereby ceasing to exist. The old principle that takes account solely
of the rights of princes can no longer be maintained; besides
dynastic right, there is national right. On what criterion is this
national right to be based? By what sign can it be recognized?
From what tangible fact can it be derived?

I. By its race, many confidently say. The artificial divisions resulting from feudalism, princely marriages and diplomatic congresses are obsolete. What remains firm and permanent is the race of the population. This is what constitutes a right, a legitimacy. For example, the Germanic family, according to the theory I am expounding, has the right to recapture the scattered members of germanism, even when these members are not asking to be reunited. The right of germanism over a given province is stronger than the rights of the inhabitants themselves of this province. In this way we create a kind of primordial right analogous to the divine right of kings; an ethnic principle is substituted for that of the nation. This is a very great error, which, if it came to predominate, would ruin European civilization. The principle of the nation is as just and legitimate as the principle of the primordial right of the race is narrow and full of danger for genuine progress.

[...]

Ethnographic considerations have had nothing to do with the constitution of modern nations. France is Celtic, Iberian, and Germanic. Germany is Germanic, Celtic, and Slavic. Italy is the country that most embarrasses ethnography: Gallic, Etruscan, Pelasgic, Greek, not to mention the many other elements, have interbred here, forming an indecipherable blend. The British Isles, taken together, present a mixture of Celtic and German blood whose proportions are particularly difficult to define.

The truth is that there are no pure races and to base politics on ethnographic analysis is to rest it on a chimera. The noblest countries – England, France, Italy – are those whose blood is most mixed. Is Germany an exception in this regard? Is it a purely Germanic country? What an illusion! The entire south was Gallic. The east, after the Elbe, is entirely Slavic. Are those parts that they claim really pure, pure in fact? Here we touch on one of the problems concerning which it is of the greatest importance to get one's ideas clear and to prevent misunderstandings.

Discussions on race are interminable, because philological historians and physiological anthropologists have given the term two utterly different meanings.

[...]

For the anthropologists, the zoological origins of humanity are thoroughly prior to the origins of culture, civilization and language. The primitive Aryan, Semitic and Turanian groups were not of a piece physiologically. These groupings are historical events that took place in a particular era, let's say fifteen or twenty thousand years ago, whereas the zoological origins of humanity are lost in impenetrable gloom. What philologically and historically we call the Germanic race is certainly a quite distinct family of the human species. Is it, however, a family in the anthropological sense? Assuredly not. The appearance of Germanic individuality in history came about only a very few centuries before Jesus Christ. Apparently the Germans did not stand out on the earth in this period. Before this, blended with the Slavs into the indistinct mass of the Scythians, they had no separate individuality. An Englishman is indeed a type within the whole of humanity. Now the type that we quite improperly call the Anglo-Saxon race,[4] is neither the Breton in Caesar's time, nor the Anglo-Saxon in Hengist's; neither the Danish in Knut's time nor the Norman's in William the Conqueror's, but rather the result of all of them. The Frenchman is neither a Gallic, nor a Frank, nor a Burgundian. He is what has emerged from the great melting-pot in which, under the presidency of the king of France, the most diverse elements were fermented together. The origins of an inhabitant of Jersey or Guernsey in no way differ from the Norman population on the neighbouring coast. In the eleventh century, the most penetrating eye would not have grasped the slightest difference between the two sides of the Channel. Trivial circumstances meant that Philippe-August did not take these islands along with the rest of Normandy. Separated from one another for almost 700 years, the two populations not only became foreign, but also utterly dissimilar to one another. Race, as we historians understand it, is something that is made and unmade. The study of race is of the utmost importance for the scholar concerning himself with the history of humanity. It has no application in politics. The instinctive conscience that presided over the preparation of the map of Europe took no account of race, and Europe's first nations are nations of essentially mixed blood.

The fact of race, of the utmost importance originally, is therefore losing its importance ever more.

[...]

II. What we have just said concerning race must also be said about language. Language asks for reunification; it does not force it. The United States and England, the Spanish-speaking Americas and Spain speak the same language but do not form a single nation. By contrast, Switzerland, so well made since it was made with the assent of its different parts, includes three or four languages. There is in man something superior to language: his will. The will of the Swiss to be united, in spite of their various idioms, is a fact of far greater importance than linguistic similarity, often attained through persecution.

One worthy fact about France is that it has never sought to obtain linguistic unity by coercive means. Can we not have the same feelings, the same thoughts, and love the same things in different languages? A moment ago we were speaking of what the drawbacks were in making international politics depend on ethnography: there would be no fewer in making it depend on comparative philology. Let's allow these interesting studies full freedom in their discussions; don't involve them in what may spoil their dispassion. The political importance we attach to languages stems from our regarding them as signs of race. Nothing is more false. Prussia, where German is only spoken now, spoke Slavic some centuries ago; Wales speaks English; Gaul and Spain speak the primitive idiom of Alba Longa; Egypt speaks Arabic; there are innumerable examples. Even at their origins, linguistic similarity did not entail racial similarity. Let's take the proto-Aryan or the proto-Semite tribes; there were slaves there who spoke the same language as their masters; but the slave was very often of a different race from his master. To repeat: the divisions of the Indo-European, Semitic and other languages, created with such exemplary wisdom by comparative philology, with such exemplary wisdom, are not coincident with the divisions of anthropology. Languages are historical formations that tell us very little about the blood of those who speak them, and that could not, in any case, fetter human freedom when it comes to questions of determining the family with which one is united in life and in death.

Like the excessive attention paid to race, considering language in isolation has its dangers, its drawbacks. When we take this to extremes, we lock ourselves into a determinate culture that is held to be national; we limit ourselves, shut ourselves away. We leave the open air that we breath in the vast field of humanity to shut ourselves into the conventicles of patriotism. Nothing could be worse for the mind, and nothing is more regrettable for civilization.

[. . .]

III. Religion, too, is unable to offer a sufficient basis on which to establish a modern nationality. Originally, religion stems from the very existence of the social group. The social group was an extension of the family. Religion and rites were the rites of the family. Athenian religion was the cult of Athens itself, of its mythical founders, its laws and its customs. It did not involve any dogmatic theology. This religion was, in the strongest sense of the word, a State religion. One was not an Athenian if one refused to practise it. It was, at bottom, the cult of the Acropolis embodied. To swear on the altar of Aglauros[5] was to swear an oath to die for one's country. This religion was the equivalent of what for us is the act of being drawn by lot for military service, or the cult of the flag. To refuse to participate in such a cult was as it would be in our modern societies to refuse military service. It was to declare that one was not an Athenian. On the other hand, it is clear that such a cult had no meaning for those who did not come from Athens; nor was any proselytism exercised in order to force foreigners to accept it; nor was it practised by Athenian slaves. It was the same in some small republics in the Middle Ages. One was not a good Venetian if one never swore by St Mark; one was not a good Amalfian if one did not place St Andrew above all the other saints in paradise. In these small societies, what later was persecution and tyranny was legitimate, and was of as little consequence as, for us, the act of wishing the father of the family a happy saint's day and sending him greetings on New Year's Day.

What was true in Sparta and Athens was already not true in the kingdoms arising from Alexander's conquests, and especially not in the Roman Empire. The persecutions of Antiochus Epiphanes in order to induce the Orient to the Olympian cult of Jupiter, and those of the Roman Empire to maintain a so-called state religion were a fault, a crime and a genuine absurdity. This situation is perfectly clear in our day. No longer is faith invariant amongst the masses. Everyone believes and practises as he pleases, what he can and what he wishes. No longer is there a state religion; one may be French, English or German while being Catholic, Protestant or Jewish or not practise any cult. Religion has become an individual concern, a matter for each man's conscience. The division of nations into Catholic and Protestant no longer exists. Religion, which fifty-two years ago [1831] was such an important element in the formation of Belgium, retains all its importance deep within each individual; but it has become almost entirely extrinsic to the reasons that mark the boundaries of peoples.

IV. Community of interests is assuredly a powerful bond between men. Are these interests, meanwhile, enough to create a nation? I do not believe they are. Community of interests makes commercial treaties. Within nationality there is an aspect of feeling; it is at the same time body and soul. A *Zollverein* is not a *patrie*.

V. Geography, what are called natural frontiers, certainly plays a considerable part in the division of nations. Geography is one of the essential factors of history. Rivers have steered races; mountains have halted them. The first were favourable to historical movements, while the second limited them. Can we say however, as certain parties believe, that a nation's frontiers are inscribed on the map, and that this nation has the right to take for itself what is necessary in order to round out certain contours, to reach a particular mountain or river, to which we attribute a sort of *a priori* faculty of delimitation? I know of no more arbitrary nor more fatal doctrine. With this, we justify all violence. And anyway, is it the mountains or rather the rivers that form these allegedly natural frontiers? It is indisputable that mountains separate, whereas rivers unite instead; but then not even all mountains divide states. Which are those that separate and which are these that do not separate? From Biarritz to Tornea there is not one river mouth that has more of a demarcating nature than any other. If history had wished it, the Loire, the Seine, the Meuse, the Elbe or the Oder might have had the same status as a natural frontier as does the Rhine, which has led to so many offences being committed against that basic right, that is the will of men. There is talk of strategic reasons. Nothing is absolute: it is clear that concessions must indeed be made to necessity. But it is not necessary that these concessions go too far. Otherwise, the whole world will demand their military proprieties, which will mean war without end. No, soil no more makes the nation than does race. Soil provides the *substratum*, the field of conflict and labour; man provides the soul. Man is everything in the formation of that sacred thing we call a people. Nothing material is sufficient. A nation is a spiritual principle resulting from the profound complications of history, a spiritual family and not a group determined by the configuration of the land.

We have just seen what is insufficient to create such a spiritual principle: race, language, interests, religious affinity, geography and military exigencies. What else then is required? In the light of what has already been said, I shall not need to retain your attention for long.

A nation is a soul, a spiritual principle. Two things, which strictly speaking are just one, constitute this soul, this spiritual principle. One is in the past, the other in the present. One is the common possession of a rich legacy of memories; the other is actual consent, the desire to live together, the will to continue to value the heritage that has been received in common. Man is not improvised. The nation, like the individual, is the outcome of a long and strenuous past of sacrifice and devotion. Of all cults, the cult of ancestors is the most legitimate, since our ancestors have made us what we are. An heroic past of great men, of glory (I mean genuine glory): this is the social capital on which a national idea is established. To have common glories in the past and common will in the present; to have done great things together and to will that we do them again: these are the conditions essential to being a people. We love in proportion to the sacrifices to which we have consented and the evils we have suffered. We love the house we have built and leave in inheritance. The Spartan song: 'We are what you were; we will be what you are' is, in its simplicity, the epitome of a hymn for every *patrie*.

A heritage of glory and regrets to share in the past; one and the same programme to be realized in the future. To have suffered, enjoyed and hoped together is worth more than customs agreements and frontiers that conform to strategic ideas; and this is what we understand in spite of racial and linguistic diversity. A moment ago I said 'to have suffered together': indeed, suffering in common unites more than does joy. In matters of national memory, mourning has more validity than triumph, since it imposes duties which demand a common effort.

A nation is therefore the expression of a great solidarity, constituted by a feeling for the common sacrifices that have been made and for those one is prepared to make again. It presupposes a past; however, it is epitomized in the present by a tangible fact: consent, the clearly expressed desire that the common life should continue. The existence of a nation is (excuse the metaphor) a plebiscite of every day, just as the existence of the individual is a perpetual affirmation of life. Oh, I know that this is less metaphysical than divine right, less brutal than so-called historical right. In the order of ideas I am placing before you, a nation has no more right than a king to say to a province: 'You belong to me, therefore, I am taking you.' A province, for us, is its inhabitants, and if anyone has the right to be consulted in this matter, it is the inhabitant. A nation never has a genuine interest in annexing or retaining a country against its will. The nation's wish is, in the final account, the only legitimate criterion, the criterion to which one must necessarily return.

We have driven the metaphysical and theological abstractions from politics. After this, what remains? Man remains, his desires, his needs. Secession, you will say, and in the long run, the breaking up of nations, are the consequence of a system that places these old organisms at the mercy of often scantly clarified wills. It is clear that in such matters no one principle must be excessively advanced. Truths of this order are applicable only as a whole and in a highly general manner. Human wills change; but what does not change in this life? Nations are not something eternal. They began, so they will come to an end. A European confederation will probably replace them. Such, however, is not the law of the century we are living in. At the present time, the existence of nations is good, even necessary. Their existence is a guarantee of freedom, which would be lost if the world had only one law and one master.

By means of their various and sometimes conflicting vocations, nations serve in the common work of civilization; each brings one note to the great concert of humanity which, in short, is the highest ideal reality to which we have attained. Isolated, they have their weak links. I often say to myself that an individual who had the failings that nations hold to be skills, who lived on empty praise, who to that extent was jealous, egotistical and fractious and who could endure nothing without drawing his sword, would be the most insufferable of men. All these discordant details, however, vanish within the whole. Poor humanity! How you have suffered! What trials still await you! May the spirit of wisdom guide you and keep you from the innumerable dangers that plague your way!

To summarize, gentlemen. Man is the slave neither of his race, his language, nor his religion; neither of the courses of the rivers, nor the mountain ranges. One great aggregate of men, of sound spirit and warm heart, creates a moral conscience that is called a nation. Insofar as this moral conscience proves its strength through the sacrifices demanded by the renunciation of the individual for the good of the community, it is legitimate and has the right to exist. If doubts arise concerning its frontiers, consult the populations in dispute. They certainly have the right to an opinion in the matter. This will make the political professionals smile, those infallible men who spend their lives in self-deception and who, from the heights of their superior principles, take pity on our down-to-earth views.

'Consult the populations, indeed! What naivety! These then are the feeble French ideas that claim to replace diplomacy and warfare by means of an infantile simplicity.'

Let's pause for a moment, gentlemen; let the reign of the professionals pass away; let us know how to withstand the disdain of the powerful. Perhaps, after many fruitless experiments, they will come back to our modest empirical solutions. The way to be right in the future is, at certain times, to know how to resign oneself to being out of date.

Translated by Iain Hamilton Grant

* From E. Renan, 'Qu'est-ce qu'une nation?' (1882), in *Discours et conférences, Oeuvres complètes*, vol. 1, Paris, 1947.

NOTES

1 Renan was referring to the autochthonous British in England, regarded as of the same race as the Bretons of Brittany [Editor's note].
2 Massacre of Huguenots in 1572 [Editor's note].
3 The Savoy dynasty owes its royal title only to its possession of Sardinia (1720).
4 The Germanic elements are not much more important in the United Kingdom than they were in France in the period when she possessed Alsace and Metz. The Germanic language was dominant within the British Isles solely because Latin had not entirely replaced Celtic idioms, as had taken place amongst the Gauls.
5 Aglauros is the Acropolis itself, dedicated to saving the country.

4

THE NATION*

Otto Bauer

Otto Bauer (1882–1938) was a leader of the Austrian social democratic party and one of the major marxist intellectuals before the
first world war. Confronted by the realities of the deep national
divisions among the working classes in the Austro-Hungarian
empire, he argued against the mainstream of marxist thought,
expressed most forcefully by Karl Kautsky, which dismissed the
appeal of nationalism in terms of internationalism. Strongly influenced by positivist writings about the progress of humanity, Bauer
attempted to reconcile marxism with a remarkably modern vindication of the legitimacy of cultural nationalism in a multi-national
state.

A nation's inherited qualities are nothing other than the sedimen-
tation of its past, its *history frozen*, so to speak. Ancestors' ways
of life affect their children necessarily as by the process of natural
selection they determine which qualities will be passed on and
which gradually lost. The effect of natural selection is perhaps
strengthened by the fact that the qualities the ancestors acquired
due to their specific living conditions are also passed on to their
descendants. Whatever the case may be, inherited character is
determined by nothing other than history, the ancestral past. This
means that the members of a nation are physically and mentally
similar, for they are descendants of the same ancestors and have
therefore inherited all those qualities developed by their ancestors
through natural and sexual selective breeding in the struggle for
survival, and perhaps also those acquired by their ancestors' efforts
to support themselves. This is how we understand the nation as a
product of history. If one wants to study the nation as a natural
community, it will not suffice to see a certain substance – such as

a germ plasm passed on from parents to children – as the substratum of the nation. Instead one needs to study the history of ancestral conditions of production and exchange and seek to understand the qualities passed on to descendants from their ancestors' struggle for survival.

[. . .]

THE CONCEPT OF NATION

The character of the individual is never simply the sum of inherited qualities; it is always also determined by the culture passed down to and influencing him, by the way he is educated, the laws to which he is subject, the customs according to which he lives, the views of God and the world handed down to him, of what is moral and immoral, beautiful and ugly, by the religion, philosophy, science, art and politics affecting him, but above all by that which determines all these phenomena: the way in which he conducts his struggle for survival and supports himself among his compatriots. This brings us to the second major way in which the individual is determined by the struggle for survival, namely the oral transmission of cultural assets. The nation is never simply a natural community but also a cultural one. Here too it is largely the destiny of past generations which determines the individual: the child is subject to the effective influences of the existing society into whose economic life, law and intellectual culture he is born. Here too, though, only the continuous community of relations can provide a community of character. The great instrument of such relations is language. It is the instrument of education, the instrument of all economic and all intellectual relations. The effect of culture reaches as far as the boundaries of common language extend. The community of relations only extends as far as the community of language.

[. . .]

On the other hand, though, common language alone is no guarantee for national unity: Danes and Norwegians, Catholic Croats and Orthodox Serbs are subject to different cultural influences despite sharing a common language. But when the culturally divisive effect of religion disappears, Serbs and Croats will correspondingly become one nation, through the community of relations conveyed by a common language and of the similar cultural influences to which they are exposed. This also explains the national significance of the victory of a uniform language over dialects. The necessity of closer relations created uniform language, and the existence of uniform language subjects all its speakers to an identical cultural influence. Mutual effect on one another unites them into a cultural community. The Dutch provide a clear example of the relationship of cultural differentiation and common language: despite originating from three offshoots of Germanic tribes, they are no longer part of the German people. The fortunes of the Dutch economy, so different to those of the German one, have created a different form of culture in Holland: economically and culturally divorced from the Germans, the Dutch have broken off the community of relations they shared with the German tribes. The bond that joined them to each other was too tight, the bond tying them to the other Germanic tribes too loose. Consequently they created their own language as the instrument of their culture and had no further part in the process of cultural unification of the German nation by one German language.

[. . .]

Our investigation has shown that the effectiveness of common culture in constituting a nation is quite different under differing social situations. We have so far encountered essentially three types of national cultural communities.

The first type, which in our historical presentation is represented by the Teutons in the age of kin communism,[1] shows us a nation in which all its members are as much tied by common blood as they are joined by a common culture inherited from their ancestors. As we have noted several times, this national unity disintegrates with the transition to a settled form of existence. Differences appear between the inherited qualities when intermarriage ceases between the geographically divorced tribes subject to different conditions in their struggle for survival; the common inherited culture will evolve differently within each tribe. The nation thus carries within itself the seed of its own decay.

The second type is represented by the nation based on the differences between social classes. The mass of the people is further exposed to the process of differentiation with which we are familiar. Without sexual interrelations, even physically they grow steadily more unalike. Linked by no bond of communication, they develop different dialects from the original common language. Exposed to different conditions in the struggle for survival, they develop different cultures, which in turn lead to differences of character. In this way, as the original common inherited qualities are lost over the centuries and as the original common culture is concealed and undermined by later different cultural elements, national unity is progressively lost to the mass of the people. The nation is no longer held together by the masses' unity of blood and culture, but by the cultural unity of the ruling classes who place themselves above these masses and live off their work. They and their followers are bound together by racial and cultural relations of all kinds. Thus the knights in the Middle Ages, and the educated in modern times, constitute the nation, while the broad masses – the farmers, artisans and labourers – whose labour upholds the nation, are no more than the nation's lessees.

A third and final type is represented by the socialist society of the future, which reunites all members of a nation in an autonomous national whole. In this case, however, the nation is no longer fused together by common descent but rather by common education, work and enjoyment of culture. For this reason the nation is no longer threatened by disintegration, for it is given a secure guarantee of national unity by common education, participation in the enjoyment of culture, close links within the polity and in working for society.

The nation, then, no longer seems something rigid to us, but rather is a process of becoming, whose nature is determined by the conditions under which its people struggle for their subsistence and to preserve the species. A nation does not come into being at the early stage at which men merely seek their food without having to work for it and support themselves by simply appropriating or occupying ownerless property they find, but instead at the stage where man extracts the goods he requires from nature by labour. The emergence of a nation and the special characteristic of each nation is thus determined by people's modes of labour, by the means of labour they deploy, by the productive forces they control and the relationships of production they enter into. It is Karl Marx's historical method which has enabled us to solve the great task of understanding the emergence of the nation, of every single nation, as part of mankind's battle with nature.

[...]

The diversity in national character is an empirical fact that can only be denied by a doctrinaire who sees only what he wants to see and not what is obvious to all. Despite this, differences in national character have been repeatedly denied, maintaining that language is the only thing that distinguishes one nation from another. Such an opinion is held by many theorists whose concepts are based on Catholic theology. It was repeated by the humanist philosophy of the bourgeois Enlightenment. And it has become the inheritance of many socialists, who hoped to use it in support of proletarian cosmopolitanism which, as we shall see, represents the first and most primitive response of the working class towards the national struggles of the bourgeois world. This supposed insight into the insubstantiality of the nation lives on in Austria today in the linguistic usage of the social-democratic press, which loves to refer to comrades 'of the German or Czech tongue' instead of calling them German or Czech comrades. The view that national differences are simply linguistic is founded on the atomistic–individualistic view in which society appears merely as the sum of externally connected individuals, and the nation appears simply as the sum of individuals related externally, namely by language. To profess this view is to repeat the error made by Stammler,[2] who believed that the constitutive characteristic of social phenomena was to be found in external regulation, in legal statutes and conventions. For us, however, the nation is not simply the sum of individuals, but rather every individual is a product of society. Thus we do not see the nation as the sum of individuals relating to each other by means of a common language: on the contrary, the individual himself is a product of the nation; his individual character has been formed solely by constant interaction with other individuals and their character in turn by interaction with his. Such relations have determined the character of each of these individuals, thereby amalgamating them in a community of character. The nation appears in the *nationality* of each individual compatriot, which means that the character of each individual is determined by the destiny experienced by all compatriots as a whole, a destiny lived in common and in constant interaction. Language, however, is no more than a means to this interaction, albeit in all cases an indispensable and omnipresent one, just as any external regulation is basically a form of cooperation between individuals united in a community. Those who cannot believe what they see, even when the differences in national character are visible in everyday life, must at least accept the theoretical consideration which causally demonstrates that different communities of character must of necessity result from the differing destinies experienced in constant community of relations.

Our understanding of the nation's essence not only renders the individualistic denial of the reality of national character impossible, it also rules out the much more dangerous misuse of this concept. National character, in fact, is nothing other than the certainty of the direction of will of each compatriot through the community of destiny[3] he shares with all his compatriots. Once it has come into being, national character appears as an independent historical force. Difference of national character means difference in direction of will; given the same conditions, each nation will therefore act differently. The development of capitalism in England, France and Germany, for example, gave rise to movements that were admittedly similar but on closer inspection in fact different. National character, then, appears as historically potent. Theory may see national character as an historical product, but everyday experience views it much more as a creative force determining history. While theory teaches us to understand it as the outcome of relationships between men, direct experience sees it much more as determining and regulating these relationships. Such is the fetishism of national character. Our theory exorcizes this ghost at one stroke. If we recognize that every member of a nation is a product of his nation and that national character is nothing more than that direction of will produced by the community of destiny in each member of a nation as his individual peculiarity, then it no longer seems mysterious that national character ostensibly determines the intentions and actions of each member of a nation. National character too no longer appears as an independent force once we see it as the outcome of the history of the nation. We now understand that the apparently autonomous historical action of national character conceals nothing other than the fact that the history of our ancestors and the conditions of their struggle for survival, the productive forces at their disposal and the productive relationships they entered upon also determine the behaviour of their natural and cultural descendants. If, earlier on, we came to see natural heredity and the inheritance of cultural assets simply as means by which the fate of past generations determines their descendants' character, national character itself now seems to us to be the mere means by which ancestral history still affects their descendants' life, their thoughts, feelings, desires and actions. The very act of recognizing the reality of national character removes its apparent autonomy and presents it simply as a means for the activity of other forces. But this also robs national character of its apparently substantial character, namely its appearance as the lasting, continuing element in the passage of events. As it is no more than the outcome of history, it changes from hour to hour, with every new event experienced by the nation; it is as mutable as the very event it reflects. Positioned in the midst of universal events, it is no longer a continuing Being but constant Becoming and wasting away.

Finally, we propose to consolidate our attempt to determine the essence of the nation by comparing it to existing theories on the subject.[4] Metaphysical theories of the nation – national spiritualism and national materialism – have already been touched on. Psychological theories of the nation which seek its essence in the consciousness of belonging together or in the desire to do so will be dealt with in a later context. Here, then, it is only necessary to contrast our theory of the nation with the attempts of those who have constructed a series of elements which, when they occur together, are taken to constitute the nation. Italian sociologists present the following as such elements:

1 common territory of residence
2 common origin
3 common language
4 common morals and customs
5 common experiences, common historical past
6 common laws and common religion.[5]

It is clear that this theory combines a number of characteristics which cannot really be juxtaposed, but can only be understood in a relationship of interdependence. Apart from the supposed first element of the nation, common territory of residence, the fifth element, common history, stands out among the others. It is this which determines and gives rise to the others. Only common history gives common origin its certainty of content by deciding which qualities will be inherited and which will die out. Common history gives rise to common morals and customs, common laws and religion, and therefore – to keep to our linguistic usage – to a community of cultural tradition. Both common origin and common culture are merely the instruments common history makes use of to achieve its end of constructing national character. The third element, common language, cannot be equated with the others either: rather it should be seen as a secondary level instrument. For if common culture is one of the means by which common history is effective in forming national character, common language is in turn a means of the effectiveness of common culture, the instrument by which the community of culture is created and maintained as an external regulator, as the form of social cooperation of individuals acting together, forming and repeatedly recreating a community.[6]

Let us first replace the mere listing of a nation's elements with a system: common history as the effective cause, common culture and common origin as the means to its effectiveness, common language in turn as the mediator of common culture, simultaneously its product and producer. This enables us to understand the reciprocal relationship between these elements. For what has so far proved so problematic for the theorists of the nation – namely the fact that these elements can appear in greatly differing constellations and with one or another element missing – now becomes understandable. If common origin and common culture are means of the same causal factor, it is obviously without significance for the concept of nation whether both means take effect or not. This means that a nation can be based on community of origin but is not necessarily so, whereas mere community of origin can only form a race and never a nation. This then explains the interrelationship of the various elements of a community of culture: common laws are without doubt an important means in the formation of a community of character, but a community of character can also exist and come into being without them, so long as the effectiveness of the other elements is strong enough to bring individuals into a community of culture. Differences of confession can divide peoples speaking the same language into two nations: religious differences prevent a community of culture, while a common religion is the basis of a common culture, as has so far been the case with Serbs and Croats; whereas the Germans have remained one nation despite their religious disunity because the confessional rifts were not strong enough to prevent a general German cultural community from coming into being and continuing. This also finally enables us to understand the relationship of language to the other elements of the nation: without a community of language, there is no community of culture and therefore no nation either.[7] But a community of language is not enough in itself to give rise to a nation when differences in other respects prevent the community of language from becoming a community of culture: for example, religious diversity in the case of the Croats and

Serbs, or differences of descent, social and political conditions, as between the Spanish and the Spanish-speaking South Americans.

It now only remains for us to consider the first of these listed 'elements' of the nation, common territory of residence. We have noted several times that territorial separation splits the unity of a nation. The nation as a natural community is gradually destroyed by national separation because the different conditions of the struggle for survival graft onto the geographically separated parts of the nation different characteristics, which cannot be evened out by mingling blood.

The nation as a community of culture is likewise destroyed by territorial separation, because each geographical part, leading its own struggle for survival, also modifies the originally homogenous culture. Owing to the absence of relations between them, the originally homogenous national culture disintegrates into a number of differing cultures, as is quite plainly seen in the shift from a single homogenous language into a variety of tongues following the excessive loosening of relations between the various geographical parts of the originally homogenous nation. If, then, geographical difference divides nations, common territory of residence will indeed be one of the nation's conditions of existence, but only in so far as it is the condition for a community of destiny. In so far as a community of culture, and conceivably even a community of nature, can be maintained despite geographical separation, this latter is no obstacle to a national community of character. The German in America who remains influenced by German culture – be this only by German books and newspapers – and who gives his children a German education remains, despite all geographical separation, a German. Community of land is only a condition of a nation's being in so far as it is a condition of a community of culture. In the age of print, post, telegraph, railway and steamship, however, this is the case to a far lesser extent than it used to be. If community of residence, then, is understood not as one element of a nation among others, but rather as a condition of the effectiveness of the others, the limits of the oft-repeated statement that a common territory of residence is the condition of a nation's existence will be clear. This is a matter of no small importance, for we base our understanding of the relationship between nation and the state, the most important territorial unit, on our concept of the relationship between nation and land. This is why we shall have to return to this question and illustrate our answer with precise examples. Here, however, we have only been concerned to demonstrate how our theory of the nation is able to understand those factors juxtaposed as 'elements' of the nation by the older theory as the effective forces of a system, in their interdependence and collective action.

Yet our theory must still prove itself by a task which has proved the downfall of all previous attempts at determining the essence of a nation, namely to delimit the concept of a nation in relation to the narrower geographical and tribal groups within the nation. It is certainly true that community of destiny has united Germans in a community of character. But could this not also be said of the Saxons or Bavarians, the Tyrolese, Styrians or indeed of the inhabitants of every single Alpine valley? Have not our ancestors' various destinies, the diversity of settlement and land division, of the fertility of their soils and climate made the inhabitants of Zillertal, Passiertal, Vintschgau and Pustertal into quite distinctive communities of character? Where are the boundaries between communities of character that can be regarded as independent nations and those we consider as narrower groups within the nation?

At this point it should be remembered that we have already encountered these narrower communities of character as the products of the disintegration of the nation that was based on the community of origin. The descendants of the original Germanic tribe have grown ever more dissimilar since they began to live apart and isolated, geographically separated, chained to the soil by agriculture, without relations or intermarriage with one another. Even though they began in a single community of nature and culture, they are on the path to forming numerous communities of nature and culture which are autonomous and quite distinct from one another. There is a tendency for these narrow groups originating from just one nation each to develop into a particular nation. The difficulty in delimiting these narrower communities of character from the concept of a nation thus lies in the fact that they themselves represent evolutionary stages towards the nation.

As we already know, a counterforce to this tendency to national disintegration is at work, seeking to bind the nation closer together. But this countertendency initially only affects the ruling classes. It binds together the members of medieval courtly society and the educated classes of the early capitalist period in a narrow nation clearly distinct from all other communities of culture; it establishes close economic, political and social relations among its members, creates a uniform language for them, allows the same intellectual culture, the same civilities to permeate them. This close bond of a community of culture initially binds the ruling classes in a nation. There can be no doubt as to whether any educated person is German, Dutch, Slovenian or Croatian: national education and a uniform national language differentiate between even the most closely related nations. On the other hand, whether the peasants of some village or other should be counted still as low German or already as Dutch, still as Slovenians or already as Croatians, can only be decided arbitrarily. Only the boundaries of a nation's members are clearly delimited, not those of the lessees of every nation.

Modern capitalism gradually demarcates more clearly the boundaries of the lower classes of the nation, as they too begin to gain access to national education, the nation's cultural life, to the uniform national language. The tendency towards unification also affects the working masses, but it will only triumph in a socialist society. Then all peoples will be as clearly distinguished from each other by differences in national education and usages as at present is only the case with the educated of each nation. There will surely be narrower communities of character within a socialist nation too; but in their midst autonomous communities of culture will be impossible, since even every local community will be under the influence of the whole nation's culture and engaged in cultural contact and exchange of ideas with the whole nation.

Only now do we come to the complete definition of the concept of nation. The nation is the totality of people bound by the community of destiny in a community of character. 'By the community of destiny': this is the trait that differentiates them from international communities of character such as profession, class or membership of a state, which are based on similarity of destiny, not on community of destiny. 'The totality of those with the same character': this differentiates them from the narrower communities of character within the nation, which never formed a self-determining community of nature and culture through their own identity of destiny, but are in close relations with the whole nation, and therefore are also determined by its destiny. The nation was clearly delimited in this way in the age of tribal communism: the nation was then formed by the totality of all those descended from the original tribe on the Baltic coast, whose spiritual being was determined by the destiny of this tribe in virtue of its natural heredity and cultural tradition. The nation will be clearly delimited once again in socialist society: it will be constituted of the totality of all those benefiting from national education and the nation's cultural assets and whose character is thus formed by the destiny of the nation which determines the content of these cultural assets. When society is based on the private property of the means of production, the ruling classes – formerly courtly society, today the educated – constitute the nation as the sum of those in whom the same formation, modelled on the nation's history and transmitted by the uniform language and national education, gives rise to an affinity of character. The vast popular classes, however, do not constitute the nation – they no longer constitute it because their age-old community of origin no longer binds them closely enough together, and do not yet constitute it because the developing community of education does not yet encompass them. The difficulty in finding a satisfactory definition of the concept of nation, which has proved the downfall of all previous attempts, is thus historically determined. The search to discover the nation has been directed towards our class society, in which the old, clearly defined community of origin has collapsed into a host of local and tribal groups and in which the new community of education in the process of formation cannot yet unite these small groups in a national whole.

Our search for the essence of the nation thus reveals a magnificent historical picture. In the beginning – in the age of tribal communism and nomadic agriculture – was the unified nation as a community of origin. Then, after the transition to settled agriculture and the development of private property, came the division of the old nation into the cultural community of the ruling classes on the one hand and the lessees of the nation on the other – the latter enclosed in confined local areas, the products of the decomposition of the old nation. Later, with the development of social production in capitalist form, came the widening of the national cultural community: the working and exploited classes remained the nation's lessees, but the tendency towards national unity based on national education gradually became stronger than the particularistic tendency of the decomposition of the old nation based on common descent into ever more starkly differing local groups. Finally, once society has divested the social production of its capitalist shell, the unified nation rises as a community of education, work and culture. The development of the nation reflects the history of the mode of production and of property. Just as private ownership of the means of production and individual production arose out of the social structure of tribal communism, and in turn gave rise to cooperative production on the basis of collective property, so the unified nation split into a national society and lessees, then divided into small local districts, which grew closer together again with the development of collective production, finally to merge into the unified socialist nation of the future. The nation of the age of private property and individual production, divided into a national society and lessees and split into many close-knit localized groups, is the product of the decomposition of the communist nation of the past and the material of the socialist nation of the future.

Thus the nation itself proves to be an historical phenomenon in two respects. It is an historical phenomenon according to its material certainty, since the national character which exists in every people is the outcome of an historical evolution, since the nationality of every people reflects the history of the society of which the individual is the product. It is an historical phenomenon in its formal sense, since at the various stages of historical evolution districts of varying size are linked by various means in various ways to form a nation. The history of society not only decides which concrete characteristics of a nation's members constitute its national character; it is also the case that the form in which the historically effective forces produce a community of character is historically determined.

The national conception of history, which sees conflicts between nations as the driving force behind events, is striving after a mechanism of nations. It sees nations as elements which cannot be further dissolved, as fixed bodies bumping into each other in space, working on one another by pressures and shocks. We, however, dissolve the nation itself into a process. We no longer see history as reflecting the battles of nations: for us it is rather the nation itself which is a reflection of these historical conflicts. For the nation only becomes apparent as national character, in the nationality of the individual, and the individual's nationality is nothing other than one side of his existence being determined by society's history, by the evolution of methods and conditions.

NATIONAL CONSCIOUSNESS AND NATIONAL SENTIMENT

As long as man is only familiar with members of his own nation he will only be aware of how they differ from him, not of how they resemble each other. If my dealings are always with Germans, if I only ever hear of Germans, I have no chance of becoming aware of the fact that the people I know have one thing in common with me, namely their Germanness. Instead, I only ever see the differences between us: he is Swabian, I am Bavarian; he is bourgeois, I am a worker; he is blond, my hair is black; he is grumpy, I am cheerful. Not until I get to know foreign peoples do I become aware that these people are foreign to me, whereas I am linked to all those with whom I have previously had dealings and to millions of others by the bond of belonging to one nation. Knowledge of foreign people is the precondition for all national consciousness.

[...]

National consciousness does not in any way mean love of one's own nation or desire for the political unity of that nation. To understand social phenomena one must insist on a clear division of greatly differing psychological patterns and on maintaining such a distinction by the use of appropriate terminology. Thus no other meaning should be attached to national consciousness than the simple recognition of belonging to a nation, the uniqueness of the nation and its difference from other nations.

The nation as a community of character determines the actions of its individual members even when they are not conscious of their nationality. For the nationality of the individual is one of the means by which historical–social forces determine the individual's resolutions. Yet the individual only becomes conscious of being determined by his nationality when he has recognized himself as belonging to a nation. It is national consciousness, therefore, which makes nationality a conscious motive power of human, especially political, action.

That is surely the reason why such great importance has been attributed to national consciousness for the existence and essence of the nation. There are some who have even wished to make national consciousness the constitutive characteristic of the nation: the nation would thus be the entirety of men who are aware of belonging to it and of being different from other nations.

[...]

Today, however, it can safely be said that anyone belonging to the cultural community of a nation is also conscious of this fact. But this dissemination of national consciousness is to a large extent a product of our capitalist age which, with its unprecedented wealth of relations, has brought nations into such close contact with each other that no one taking part in his own nation's culture can remain wholly foreign to other nations. Even someone who has never come face to face with anybody from a foreign nation learns about such foreign nations through literature and newspapers, albeit in caricature. Even such a person develops a consciousness of his own nationality by his knowledge of foreign nations. Only in such an age could the false view develop that national consciousness is responsible for uniting men into nations.

National consciousness only becomes the determining reason for human actions when it is linked to a singular sentiment, national sentiment.

[...]

This singular sentiment, which always accompanies national consciousness – through recognition of the uniqueness of one's own and its dissimilarity from other nations – we call national sentiment.

When I first get to know a foreign nation, what I see seems to me something new and unusual.

[...]

Human consciousness is ruled by the law of inertia. In the process of our intellectual development we have acquired a system of representations. If new perceptions threaten to upturn this construction, this lethargy of our consciousness will put up resistance.

[...]

In precisely this way the observation of the singularities of a foreign nation is often accompanied by a feeling of aversion. The beautiful women of Italy with their unaccustomed appeal may attract me at first, but soon I will long for the blond beauties of my home land. Italy's culture may delight me at first, but in time I find it hard to accustom myself to this foreign people with their foreign views and customs; the singularity of a foreign way of doing things may at first be amusing or pleasing, but aversion soon comes to the fore when I see the same external stimulus having a different effect on foreigners than I could have expected observing my compatriots in my homeland a hundred times.

[...]

Recognition of a foreign nation's way of life is thus often accompanied by a feeling of aversion. In such instances, the image of one's own national ways is accompanied by a feeling of pleasure. Knowledge of foreign nations thus often awakens love of one's own nation. National sentiment wells from that dangerously fearful power of the old and familiar, the displeasure with which the human intellect in its lethargy faces all that is new and therefore all that is foreign.

[...]

But that is not all: my national consciousness does not mean recognition of a foreign nationality, but that of my own, of my own way of being. If I become aware of belonging to a nation, I recognize that a close-knit community of character binds me to it, that its fate has shaped me, its culture has determined me, that it is an effective force even in my character. The nation is not foreign to me but is part of me that recurs in the way of being of others. The concept of the nation is thus tied to the concept of my ego. Whoever reviles the nation reviles me too; if the nation is praised, I have my part in that praise, because the nation does not exist outside me and my kind. Linked to the concept of nation is thus the strongest feeling of pleasure: it is not, as has sometimes been thought, true or supposed community of interests with my compatriots but rather the recognition of the bond of community of character, the recognition that nationality is nothing other than my own way of being which causes the concept of nation to be accompanied by a feeling of pleasure and awakens in me the love of my nation. I love myself because I am ruled by the animal instinct for self-preservation: the nation seems to me simply part of myself and national singularities part of my character – which is why I love my nation. Love of one's nation is therefore no moral achievement, not the outcome of a moral struggle for which I could praise myself; it is no more than the product of my instinct for self-preservation, love of myself as I am, a love which extends to all who are like to me and are linked to me by community.

There is a further motive power to national sentiment alongside all these. It springs from the enthusiasm which, as Goethe said, history arouses. For those with a knowledge of history the concept of nation is tied to the concept of its destiny, to the memory of heroic battles, unceasing struggle for knowledge and art, to triumphs and defeats. All the sympathy one can show for the struggles of men in the past is now translated into love for the vehicle of this fate rich in diversity, the nation. What is being introduced here is not in fact a new element but an extension of the last two points. Just as the concept of nation owes a substantial part of its wealth of sentiment to its close connection with the concept of my own youth, so its connection to the ideas of those who teach us to love and admire history kindles new love for it. And in learning to love the nation and recognizing my own essence in its individuality, its history becomes dear to me. In its destiny stretching back into the grey mists of time, I believe I can recognize the forces which have engraved the traits of character of the descendants of those distant generations and my own character. All that romantic desire for what is long past thus becomes a source of love for the nation. A national work of art, such as Wagner's *Meistersinger*, has a national influence, because it is a part of the nation's history and so teaches us to love the nation itself.

Knowledge of the nation's history produces a lively national sentiment above all among intellectuals. But the greater the extent to which this knowledge is spread by primary schools, newspapers, lectures and books, the more the national sentiment of the broad masses is kindled by the history of the nation.

National sentiment originating in this way gives rise to a curious national way of attributing a value to things. For as the concept of the German people is connected to a feeling of pleasure, I almost feel justified in calling anything German which for me is connected to a feeling of pleasure. If I speak of a man as a true German man, I do not simply intend to convey his nationality but to praise and laud him. Good German becomes a term of praise, un-German a reproach. The name of the people assumes a value: I believe I am praising a deed by calling it good German, criticizing it by calling it un-German. This is what is meant by the remarkably romantic overtone which resonates, according to Bismarck, when we speak of the German people.

THE PRINCIPLE OF NATIONALITY

The revolution in the traditional state system was consummated in the nineteenth century under the banner of the principle of nationality. Every nation was to form a state, every state to include just one nation. The struggles for the unity of Germany and freedom of Italy, the liberation of Greece, Rumania, Serbia and Bulgaria from Turkish rule, the Irish struggle for home rule, that of the Poles for the restoration of the Polish state, the break-away of the South American states from Spain are all manifestations of the great struggle to realize the principle of nationality.

This phenomenon is so striking that many theorists take the will to live together in an independent polity as the nation's constitutive character. Renan[8] and Kirchhoff,[9] for example, see the nation as the sum of all those living together in an independent polity who defend this polity and are willing to make sacrifices for it. Here we are dealing with a psychological theory of the nation. But whereas the theory with which we are familiar (which seeks to make national consciousness, the recognition of belonging together, the characteristic feature of the nation) is an intellectualist theory, the doctrine that finds the essence of the nation in the will to political unity and freedom is voluntarist.[10]

Our objections to this doctrine are the same as those with which we countered the psychological–intellectual trend. This theory too is unsatisfactory because it evades the question of why we should want to be united with one set of people in a polity and not with others. It is also incorrect because it is in no way true to state that all people belonging to a polity form a nation by dint of this – some Czechs see the existence of Austria as necessary for their nation and agree with Palacky in thinking that Austria would have to be invented if it did not exist already; but this does not mean that the Czechs belong to an Austrian nation. Further, it is just as incorrect to claim that all those belonging to one nation want to see their nation politically united: the Swiss Germans and many Germans in Austria have no desire whatever to see the dream of German unity realized.

The fact that the nation state is considered the rule and the multi-national state as a mere exception, a remnant of times past, has led to a disturbing confusion of the terminology used in political science. The word 'nation' is often used to mean no more than all the citizens or all the inhabitants of an economic region. In Germany policies intended to supply the existing class state with the necessary instruments of power – soldiers, artillery and battleships – are called national, like revanchist and colonial expansionist policies in France. When the national economy is named, it is not the economy of the nation – for example that of Germans in all countries – but the economy of the German economic area, which by no means includes all Germans, but French, Danes, Poles and Jews instead, as well as smaller numbers of members of the most diverse nations. Those who speak of the protection of national labour do not mean the protection of German labour in Austria or in the USA, but the protection of the labour force in the German economic area, and so on. We are not concerned with the 'nation' in this sense here. This linguistic usage is based on a confusion of the nation with the population of the state and economic area.[11]

Whenever the relationship between nation and state is discussed, the theory is usually content to maintain that it is natural for every nation to want to become a state. This does not solve the issue facing scientific theory, but presents it. We have to ask why people find it natural and sensible that each nation and always only one nation should form a political polity. The principle of nationality, then, clearly contains two demands: first, the will to national freedom, the rejection of foreign rule, the demand that every nation be a state! Second, the will to national unity, the rejection of particularism, the demand that the whole nation forms one state. It now has to be explained how these demands arose in the nineteenth century and how they could become powerful enough to cause the downfall of the traditional state system.

The impetus for the nation state movement came unquestionably from the demand to end foreign rule. In instances where rule by a foreign power also meant oppression and exploitation of the whole nation, there is no need to explain such a demand. This was, for example, the case in the Serb revolution. The Serbs, radically separate from the dominant Turks in terms of nationality and religion, severely exploited and oppressed, laboured under the yoke of Turkish military feudal rule. The Turkish rulers appropriated a considerable part of the product of the labour of this nation of peasants; the inhabitants had to buy their right to exist from their rulers through a poll tax. Hated measures, such as the ban on carrying arms or mounting a saddled horse, made the despised *Rajah* (herd) feel the weight of their oppression daily. This oppressed people had to rise against their foreign rulers as soon as they had a chance of success. When the internal breakdown of the Turkish empire and Russia's policy in the Balkans appeared to present such an opportunity, the enthralled people rose to fight for their freedom, their nation state. It was no different where – as in Greece – the mass of the people lived in serfdom alongside an aristocracy of civil servants and a rich bourgeoisie who contributed substantially to exploitation by the ruling state. In this case national revolution became a revolution of the enthralled masses, in which, however, the bourgeoisie also played its part. A rich bourgeoisie finds the contempt of the ruling nation particularly hard to accept. The sons of the Greek financial and office-holding aristocracy studied at western universities, from which they brought home the longing for freedom kindled by 1789; indeed, had not Schiller himself challenged the Greeks among the students at his lectures to act for the liberation of their people? A craving for independence can thus be awakened among the bourgeoisie of the enslaved nation. This class becomes the leader of the national struggle because the power in the nation state for which they are fighting inevitably falls to it.

It is different when foreign rule means no worsening of the economic situation for the masses, but perhaps even an improvement. The Polish uprisings were mainly a rebellion of the nobility, the *Szlachta*. They failed because of the indifference and partly even the opposition of the peasants who feared the renewal of boundless exploitation by their lords from the restoration of the Polish state. In this case, the nation state revolution meant above all a rebellion of the oppressed nation's ruling class for whom the loss of the nation state also meant the loss of their hegemony; it was not a movement of the broad working masses, whose condition in the nation state would have been no better and perhaps even worse than under foreign rule. And yet, even in such cases the idea of the nation state spread among the masses. The same phenomenon can be seen in Germany under Napoleon I. When the greater part of Germany fell under French rule, this obviously led to the dethroning of the narrow ruling strata of the nation, while for the broad masses foreign rule brought advantages rather than disadvantages: participation in the great achievements of the French revolution, removal of feudal fetters, the introduction of the new bourgeois legal system. Despite this, the war of liberation was far from being simply a movement of the courts and bureaucracies dethroned by French domination, but was a movement of broad social strata. How can we explain this phenomenon? Where did it come from, this remarkable phenomenon of the broad masses of the people rising up against domination by a foreign nation even when they had lost nothing by such foreign rule, when at most they had exchanged the oppression of one lord for that of another, indeed when foreign rule had even improved the lot of the lower social strata?

In every state, even in the nation state, the petty bourgeoisie, peasants and workers are exploited and oppressed by foreign domination – by landlords, capitalists and bureaucrats. But such foreign rule is veiled, as it were; it is not clearly visible, but has to be perceived. Foreign rule by another nation, on the other hand, is clearly and immediately visible. When a worker goes to an authority, when he appears before a court, he does not understand that it is a foreign power dominating him through the civil servant or the judge, for the civil servant and the judge present themselves as the mouthpiece of his nation. But if the civil servant or the judge is a member of another nation, if he speaks a foreign language, then the fact of the subjection of the mass of the people to a foreign power becomes undisguisedly visible and hence intolerable. The peasant's son also serves as an instrument of a foreign power in the army of the nation state. But this foreign power, the ruling classes whose purposes are served by this army, knows perfectly well how to conceal this fact: it knows how to convince people that the army is an instrument of power of the whole nation. But if the officers belong to a foreign nation and give their commands in a foreign language, even the peasant's son feels immediately that he is subjugated to a foreign power when he has to obey the command. In a unified national society the capitalist, the feudal lord, appears as the spokesman, the intermediary agent of the nation which has entrusted him with the task of directing production and distribution. But if he belongs to a foreign nation, the peasant subjected to *corvées* and the waged labourer feel at once that they are serving a foreigner, working to the advantage of a foreigner. This is the great significance of foreign rule: it makes exploitation and oppression, which should be perceived differently, clearly and immediately visible and therefore unbearable.

There is another reason for the masses' hatred of rule by a foreign power, especially when this is a new, previously inexistent situation. In the eyes of a child, the harbinger of evil is always its cause. In the childlike legal perception of less developed peoples, whoever does damage is guilty of damage and the judge does not need to trouble himself with intention, incitement or accessories to the crime. The German peasant in the war of liberation did not concern himself with the fact that the disaster of the French wars had been brought on him by German princes who had conspired against the French Revolution because of their hatred of the political and economic freedom of citizens and peasants. He only saw the French soldier bringing war to the country, the French armies killing his sons and destroying his wealth, which awakened his hatred of the French. How, then, was he supposed to bear French domination of his country? And all the fury, all the desire for revenge was directed not against the rulers of his own nation who instigated the war, but against the foreigners, the obvious and visible culprits who killed the sons of the people, took their daughters and laid waste their fields. The hatred unleashed by war thus becomes the motivating force behind the desire for national freedom.

One can demonstrate that the desire to repulse foreign rule was the motivating force behind all the nineteenth-century movements for a nation state. The conspiracy of Europe's absolute princes against the French Revolution threatened the French people with the danger of having to submit to a foreign will, sacrificing the freedom they had conquered to a foreign power; the revolutionary struggle of the French people thus became a national cause. And when the armies of Napoleon I subjugated Germany, the demand for national freedom exploded here too and Arndt, the enemy of the French, preceded Schenkendorf, the Kaiser's herald.[12] The struggles for freedom of the Italians, Irish, Poles, Greeks and the Slavs of the Balkan peninsula were also struggles against foreign rule. Young Europe's longing for national freedom grew out of hatred of foreign rule.[13]

The desire for a nation's political unity also stemmed from this hatred. Only a strong polity uniting the whole nation seemed able to prevent the continuance or reestablishment of foreign rule. To cite Treitschke, since rule by many had come to mean bondage for all, the Germans demanded a strong, unified German empire.

However, the effect of these forces unleashed by the development of modern capitalism was similar. Capitalism requires a large, densely populated economic area; the needs of capitalist development thus work against the political fragmentation of the nation. If capitalist states were linked to each other by the free exchange of goods, fused into one economic area, capitalism could well bear the fragmentation of the nation into a number of independent states. In reality, however, the state in the capitalist world almost always becomes a more or less independent economic area; the exchange of goods between states is limited by protective tariffs, taxation policy, the level of railway charges and the differences in legal systems. The vast majority of goods produced in a state also serves the needs of consumers living within that state. Capitalism's demand for a large economic area thus becomes a demand for a large state. Let us now try to outline the reasons which necessitated the development of large states in the nineteenth century.

[...]

The smaller state is of course weaker not just in terms of economic policy, but also politically. Capitalism, though, constantly requires the strong arm of the state in order to realize its goals of expansion. How could German capital seek profitable investment abroad? How could German businessmen travel in foreign markets without knowing themselves to be protected by the military power of their state? This is why capitalists see the small state as incapable of guaranteeing its citizens adequate protection abroad, as an inadequate, incomplete instrument of their power – all the more so because the small state is generally also a very expensive instrument. For, given the same conditions in other respects, the administration of a large state is comparatively cheaper than that of a small state, with a correspondingly lesser pressure of taxation.

Nations in the nineteenth century were directly faced with all these advantages of the large state. It was widely known how France had flourished after the abolition of the internal tolls that had separated its provinces. Hence it was hardly surprising that the desire of the Germans and Italians to make their countries into large unified economic areas should have grown stronger.

Translated by Amanda Chisnell

* From O. Bauer, *Die Frage der Nationalitäten und die Sozialdemokratie*, in *Otto Bauer Werkansgabe*, vol. 1, Vienna, Europaverlag, 1975, pp. 87–8, 174–6, 179–81, 186–203, 229–35, 238–43.

NOTES

1 Characteristic of nomadic tribes [Editor's note].
2 R. Stammler, *Wirtschaft und Recht* (Economy and Law), Veit, Leipzig, 1896 [Editor's note].
3 Identity of character in a community, produced by the same causal agents [Editor's note].
4 A collection of various definitions of the nation is given by F. J. Neumann, *Volk und Nation* (People and Nation), Leipzig, 1888.
5 Ibid., p. 54.
6 Language is, admittedly, not just a means of handing down cultural assets, but is also a cultural asset in its own right. A Frenchman is not

only different from a German because his language hands down different cultural assets, but also because his language is a cultural asset handed down to him, the particular qualities of which determine his speech, his thought and his character. If French rhetoric differs from the German art of speech, then the difference in language undoubtedly plays a part in this.

7 To speak of a Swiss nation is based either on a confusion of the people of a state with a nation – when one is simply referring to the fact that the Swiss belong to a state – or, when the community of character between the German, French, Italian and Rhaetian Swiss is pointed out, on the mistaken view that every community of character already constitutes a nation.

8 *Qu'est qu'une nation?* (What is a nation?) Paris, 1882. [See above, ch. 2. Editor's note.]

9 *Zur Verständigung über die Begriffe 'Nation' und 'Nationalität'* (On the understanding of the concepts 'Nation' and 'Nationality') Halle, 1905.

10 We can now group the theories of the nation discussed so far as follows: 1. Metaphysical theories of the nation: national spiritualism and national materialism; 2. Psychological theories of the nation: pychological–intellectualist and psychological–voluntarist; 3. The empirical theory of the nation, which simply lists the elements essential to the nation. Against these theories we set our theory of the nation which is based on the materialist concept of history, in which the nation is a community of character originating in the community of destiny.

11 On the distinction between people and nation see Neumann, *Volk und Nation.*

12 E. M. Arndt (1769–1860), a poet famous for his appeals to the German people to rise against Napoleon [Editor's note].

13 *Young Europe* (1834–7), a revolutionary organization created by Giuseppe Mazzini [Editor's note].

5

NATION, NATIONALITY, INTERNATIONALISM*

Marcel Mauss

The first world war radically transformed the academic approach to nationalism, as well as the realities of the latter, but in contradictory ways. **Marcel Mauss** (1872–1950) was a sociologist and ethnologist of immensely wide intellectual interests and knowledge. His unfinished essay on nationality, which was written shortly after the war but never published in his lifetime, is an elegant deconstruction of nationalist claims. Without denying the realities of national identity, Mauss shared the hopes of many western intellectuals, like Gilbert Murray and Norman Angell, of a new international order, which he argued must emerge from the unprecedented interdependence between states.

We now have the idea, utterly foreign to the *ancien régime*, that an individual can serve only his Country [*la patrie*]. Even in a country as uncertain as Russia, public morality has become extremely sensitive on matters of relations between public figures and foreign countries, even allied ones. Everything in a modern nation standardizes and individualizes its members. Like a primitive clan, it is homogeneous, and is composed of allegedly equal citizens. It is symbolized by its flag, as the clan is by its totem; it has its cult of *la patrie*, just as the clan has its cult of ancestral animal-gods. Like a primitive tribe, its dialect is raised to the level of a language, and it has domestic laws that conflict with international law. Like the clan, it pursues demands for compensation, such as France made for the murder of Sgt Mannheim, in the manner of a vendetta. From the foreigner appearing before its tribunals, it seeks bail until judgement is delivered. It has its currency, its exchange rates and its credit; it has its customs, its frontiers and its colonies, which it generally lays exclusive claim to exploit, and of which it is always the only governor. Individuation is so far-reaching as to have an impact upon two orders of phenomena with which it may have been thought incompatible: in mind and in the race, in the highest forms of intellectual life and in the most fundamental forms of biological life. The thought of a single language rich in tradition, allusion and sophistication, with a complex syntax, an abundant, ongoing and manifold literature, centuries of reading, writing, education and, especially in the last fifty years, a daily press; this thought has been universalized to a degree unknown in the highest civilizations, ancient and modern. All this means that the mentality of a Frenchman is even less similar to that of an Englishman, than the mentality of an Algonquian is to that of a Californian Indian. It also means that there is an infinitely greater separation between how an Italian and a Spaniard think and feel, although both come from a single civilization, than there is in popular morals and imagination, for the extraordinary uniformity across the world of the latter expresses the unity of the primitive human mind.

In fact, this individuation in the formation of nations is a significant sociological phenomenon, while its novelty is not usually properly appreciated. You could even say that sociology in its entirety continues to suffer from the defect in this flawed perspective. By a mistaken dialectic of contradictions, such as equally exists in the history of the sciences, it has alternately viewed every society, even the most primitve, from the perspective of modern nations and, under this rubric, has considered them to be more individuated than they are; or, on the other hand, by considering the history of societies to be unitary, thus basically reduced to the history of civilization *per se*, it has overlooked national individualities, especially in modern times.

Up until modern times, none of the majority groups was characteristic of a given society. Their frontiers, even those of language and law, were not necessarily those of the tribes and the states that used them. They were only exceptionally the object of those beliefs that bring a people to associate themselves with their institutions. Neither Greek nor Latin became a people's cult-object such as French has been since the seventeenth century and the French Academy; as German has been since Lessing and Fichte, and Italian since Dante. In the modern nations by contrast, all, or a certain number, of the signs that we have recognized as being insufficient to define the limits of a society in space and time, can be, especially in the unified nations, the object of that superstitious attraction which, in the most primitive formations, was inspired only by the law and the juridical elements of religion.

A modern nation believes in its race. This is a greatly mistaken belief however, especially in Europe, where every known population, excepting perhaps the Norse populations and a few Slavs, were of course the product of recent and profuse interbreeding. This does not, however, hinder the Germans, especially since the romantics, from imagining that there exists a German race; Fichte, with swathes of linguistic and philosophical fantasy, took great pains to prove that, in Europe, the Germans alone are an *Urstamm* [a primal tribe: the Teutons]. The Scots believed in their purity, and [Henry Thomas] Buckle[1] would convince us of it, if that were possible. The Irish were persuaded of it. Hence the extremely questionable deployment of so-called 'ethnographic' notions in history, still more dubious in diplomacy. Numerous Slavs were denationalized; they lay claim to Slavic descent, and we see in our own day certain Bohemian groups laying claim to the Wends and the Lusatian people, who have become authentic Germans nevertheless, pan-germanism having wanted to see if not the German flag, then at least rights for Germans everywhere a colony of Germans exists, even in foreign countries. Race creates nationality in a good number of minds, as in the case of the Zionist Jews when they claim shared nationality with the great numbers of Jews who are, however, perfectly adapted to their countries. But all these paradoxes, paralogisms and sophisms of political interest are created by one basic fact that they show up: new races are formed at the core of modern nations. The trends of migration and displacement; the existence of large urban centres where people of all origins meet; new ways of living such as the barracks in the last years of the peace,[2] or the civil servant whose career leads him across an entire country, have begun to carry out the fusion of ancient stocks of the population, of which a large number still remained here and there. At the very least a physiological, muscular, if not an osteological type has developed. In other nations new races are actually created, produced by recent migrations where all sorts of ethnic elements begin to merge: such as the Australians with whom we had the honour of living, and who are a mixture of the physical and moral qualities of the English, the Scots and the Irish who came together there as they did not in the old countries. This process is so important that it has given rise to an

overstated theory; it even led Mr Boas,[3] one of our most distinguished ethnologists, to believe he could demonstrate, reacting
against the givens of anthropo-sociology, that lifestyles and diet
could transform the race even without any interbreeding having
taken place. By means of plentiful statistics he believed he had
proved that within one generation, pure-race Italians or Jews, who
had resettled in New York, acquired the basic characteristics of
the American race. Critically analysed, the figures actually show
only the improving conditions of these offspring of poor parents.
This, however, is certainly a fact. It is also certain that a great deal
of interbreeding, in conjunction with enormous advances due to
the spread of wealth through ever broader sectors, created new,
more vigorous and more beautiful examples of humanity in the
pre-war period, which latter is now considered in a more favourable light. In short, because the nation created the race, it was
believed that the race created the nation. This was simply to extend
certain beliefs to the entire populace, that until then had been
restricted to the divine race of the kings, to the blessed stock of
the nobility, and to the castes who had to maintain their pure
blood, who had gone so far as consanguineous marriage to ensure
it. It is because every last Frenchman or German takes pride in
his nation that he has ended up taking pride in his race.

Next, the nation believes in its language. It puts a great deal
more effort into preserving it than into keeping it alive; much more
effort goes into making it more widespread, even by artificial
means, than goes into enriching it with new words and new speakers; and more goes into fixing it than into improving it. Linguistic
conservatism, proselytism, and fanaticism are the very latest
phenomena to express this fundamental individuation, both of
modern national languages, and, by the same token, of the nations
that speak them. The French Academy is France's recent imitation
of the British Academy: the intervention of the state itself in
questions of orthography, with such pedantry and prudence! A
French Alliance, copied exactly from the Germanic or Pan-Slavic
model, and so many other completely novel facts in the history
of languages: vernacular languages, of course, since purism was
contemporaneous with writing; archaisms contemporaneous with
the earliest traditions, and superstitions surrounding words and
formulae date from the very origins of language. This superior,
strange, archaic or purified language, however, used to be an object
revered only by an elite; by contrast, the people were indifferent

to it and, with the exception of Greece, where education was comprehensive, were only involved in reflecting civilization, articulating its enormously rich technical vocabulary, its astonishingly poor moral vocabulary and its utterly simple images through their own dialects. It was here that language came alive. It lived a natural life, however, without deformations or circumlocutions, without refinements; strong and free, with no political ambitions and without believing in its superiority. With the formation of nations, the language of culture becomes popular language, and the emotions of which it used to be the object extend to the people as a whole. Fine talk, linguistic excellence, the distinction between those who speak the language and those who do not; all this has all become conventional wisdom. For the average German, every German must speak the high Saxon German that became successively the language of the courts, the language of literature, the language of religion with Luther, that of the military with Frederick and, following the *Aufklärung* [Enlightenment], the language of the university. The history of the French language is the same, but older and richer in events because the *langues d'oc*, the languages of southern France, had a more outstanding history than did the Germanic dialects. Printing, that is, making written language available to a mass audience, as we know, gave primacy to the language of culture and extended the beliefs that used to attach to them to the masses, who began to put them into practice, and who believed in them as had the elite who abandoned Latin, but carried over into French, Italian, Spanish, English and German, all the pedantry and the superstitions with which they surrounded the dead languages. This phenomenon has intensified and spread throughout modern Europe. It has not yet come to an end. It is even gradually spreading to the majority of the world's languages, and currently the Arabs, Chinese and Japanese are experiencing the most serious difficulties due to their shift from the languages written and spoken by the elites towards the languages of European culture and concurrently, towards the national languages that the people want to, and believe they must, speak correctly.

But rather than going into any further detail concerning these fundamental linguistic facts, let's move on to the dominant fact. The last century has seen the creation of national languages by peoples who used not to have one. Those peoples who had never written – or rather who had never continuously and intensely written a 'civilized language' – set to the task of constructing one.

Others went back to ancient, long-forgotten languages: Greek, Irish, Slovak, Slovene, Flemish, Finnish (whose self-styled epic, the *Kalevala*, is nothing but a handbook of folklore). Nationalities have often even been preceded by the language. Thus Ruthenian has none but a political existence, a Little-Russian dialect from Galicia having been arbitrarily selected, whether by the Russians to oppose the Cisleithanian Austrians,[4] whether by the latter to oppose both the Russian Little-Russians and the Russians, or whether by the Ruthenians themselves to oppose their Polish oppressors in Galicia. In this we can see the will of a people to intervene in the processes that until then had been left to unconscious variations and developments. It would be a mistake, however, to think of this as an exceptional piece of artifice. A father's will to see his children receive a complete education in their mother tongue gives natural expression to this linguistic effort. It conveys the need of generations tied together by a single language not to undo it, either through bilingualism such as we have with the Bretons, the Basques and the Alsatians, or through forgetting some dialects, as we are seeing in provincial France. The Flemish campaign for a University of Ghent, the Ruthenians' for a University of Lemberg, the Croats' for a University of Agram: these are only the final episodes in the linguistic nationalism of peoples who want to add the colour of their languages to European culture, and who, in order to do this, build up, maintain and perfect a language at the cost of notable stresses and effort.

If, however, the various nationalities do create their own languages, it is because language, in modern times, creates if not the nation, then at least the nationality. The development of great scientific and moral literatures, along with the cast of mind created by identical methods of education on a vigorous and undreamt-of scale, begin to shape a national mentality, even beyond the state's boundaries. There was nothing extraordinary about the various affinities of the Swiss during the war, the Swiss French favouring France and her allies, and the Swiss Germans sympathetic to the two central empires. The far more notable thing was that the coextension of language and nationality came to a head in the nation's claim – which, still unvoiced, had always been latent – over those who speak its language. The debates at the Peace Conference [of Paris, 1919] brought this to light: linguistic criteria served as arguments; the number of words in the vocabulary; geographical onomastics proving this or that by way of origin, became the objects of debate. Should a given population have been de-Slavicized, de-Germanized, or had a particular land been previously populated by a particular people whose linguistic composition had altered; these became sufficient reasons to claim a frontier or a province whose inhabitants have neither the least recollection nor the least sense of a particular nationality. The Germans, by the way, did not understand why the Flemish, despite speaking another Germanic language, were not enchanted with becoming subjects of the Reich, and the majority amongst them still do not understand that the Alsatians had never wanted to be their subjects. The Pan-Slavs proceeded in the same manner. Likewise, states intended to impose the dominant language of the nation on populations with a different language. This is what the Russians wanted just about everywhere, especially in Poland, and the Germans in Lorraine. We have just witnessed the scandal of Denikin[5] entering the Ukraine and closing, during his brief appearance, the 1200 Ukranian schools opened since the Revolution. That this had been more or less unanimously acknowledged as an offence indicates the advances made by the notion of a people's autonomy even since the war. The Treaty of Versailles was a way of protecting national minority schools in almost every region with a mixed population, and this is a sign of a people's right to have *its* language, and of national individuality. It is only regrettable that exceptions to this rule have been made for the benefit of Italy which, without any guarantees, absorbed several hundred thousand Yugoslavs. If the great powers had really intended to apply the same rule to themselves as to the lesser powers, it would not have been so damaging to the latter.

In the third instance, a nation believes in *its* civilization, in its customs, its industry and its fine arts. It fetishizes its own literature, its sculpture, its science, its techniques, its morals, its tradition; in a word, its character. It is almost always prey to the illusion of being the world's pre-eminent nation. It teaches its literature as if it were the only literature, science as if it alone had contributed to it, its techniques as if it had invented them, and its morals as if they were the best and the most beautiful. In this there is a natural complacency, partly caused by ignorance and political sophism, but in many cases by the exigencies of education. Not even the smallest nations avoid this. Each nation is like the villages from our antiquity and our folklore: convinced of their superiority over the neighbouring village, their folk fight with the 'madmen' opposite. Their public ridicules the foreign public, as in [Molière's] *Monsieur de Pouceaugnac*, where the Parisians hold the Limousins up to ridicule. They are heirs to the prejudices of ancient clans, ancient tribes, parishes and provinces, because they have become the corresponding social unities, and are individualities that have a collective character.

It would take a very long time to describe all the phenomena that express this nationalization of thought and the arts. It is not expected of us that we summarize well-known themes in the histories of literature, art, industry, morals and law. These are themes upon which the nineteenth century and the beginning of this one have perhaps insisted too much, to the detriment of humanism and in reaction against the masonic humanitarianism and cosmopolitanism of either the preceding centuries, or the progressive classes of various nations. The theories of literary history, such as Taine's *milieu*, were applied in England and France; theories such as Hegel's *Volksgeist* have been applied to the history of German civilization: all this has passed into the domain of criticism. What is happening in the domain of the arts and sciences itself is perhaps less marked, but far more serious. On the one hand, there is a conscious effort to remain within tradition, which already bears down with all its weight. Millions of imitations, citations, centos and allusions have constrained literatures within often insipid national forms. Rhythms, canons and customs have determined dances and gestures: academic authorities and the well-named 'conservatories'[6] have held invention in check. In the Middle Ages and during the Renaissance, with the unanimity of the church and the universities, despite difficult communications and the absence of printing, photography, patents and certificates, the evolution of the arts, the sciences and ideas had a unity and a logic other than that imprinted on progress by the ups and downs and clashes of thought, modes of aesthetic expression, isolations, prejudices and national hatreds; as, for example, the French cabal against Wagner, and the latter's stupid revenge. Even industrial techniques have been the object of national tradition, appropriation and opposition. The Portuguese, Spanish and Dutch held back from conceding the Indies, as the Phoenecians kept the Cassiterides[7] a secret; in the seventeenth and even the eighteenth centuries, for example in the invention of porcelain, industrial secrets were guarded as if they were military secrets; and in the twentieth century, in discovering others' secrets and guarding their own, the Germans displayed a comportment worthy of glassworkers in the Republic of Venice. The idea that a nation is the proprietor of its intellectual goods and can with impunity pillage those of others has so strong a hold that it is only very recently, with the Bern Convention, to which not every state has even adhered, that literary, artistic, technical and industrial property, after having been very gradually recognized by domestic law, passed into the sphere of private international law.

Even forms of law, of economic life, even the unrestricted exploitation of land or subjugated populations were able to be conceived as the basis of national rights. We are so convinced of the fact that what we call civilization is a national thing, that we have made it into the basis of territorial rights. It is almost comical to see the ill-understood, poorly studied phenomena of folklore invoked before the Peace Conference as proof that a given nation must expand in this or that direction because there we find once again a particular style of housing or a particular bizarre usage.

On the other hand, there has been a constant effort, especially in the Eastern European nations, to return to popular sources, to folklore, to the origins – true or false – of the nation. It is not only language that there have been attempts to reconstitute and bring back to life, but also ancient traditions – which attempts have, sometimes, been successful. The movement began in Scotland, and we are familiar with the astonishing story of the false Ossian, this allegedly rediscovered Gaelic literature. Then came the German Romantics and their philosophers, for whom Grimm's tales and the rediscovery of the *Edda* were the decisive moments. They thought they had discovered Germanic civilization itself. Poetry and music, especially of the Wagnerian variety, took great pains to live on these origins, to bring them to life; but the great names of the Germanic epic ended sadly by being given to the trenches that had to be the guardians of the routed army. The Finnish and the Slavs followed this example. And Serbs, Croats and Czechs have formed literatures of this genre for themselves. Russian music is intentionally folkloric: the principles of the renowned 'Five'[8] are well known. Ethnographic museums, the return to national arts, the successive fashions that seized people: all this is the same phenomenon, of seeking to reconstruct the nation around tradition.

It is at once comic and tragic to see the direction given, in Eastern Europe, to the notion of a dominant civilization. [...]

Within the diplomatic, folkloric, imperialistic, German or Slavic jargon used by the Pan-Germanists, the Pan-Slavs or others, the 'dominant civilization' within a heterogeneous society is understood to mean that the civilization of the dominant people has characteristically been imposed, and is often the only one the country has. In the name of this principle, the Habsburgs have, for a long time, reigned over the Slavs and the Hungarians, since the Germans in Cisleithania and the Hungarians in Transylvania, under their royal authority, have tyrannized the Slavs and the Latins. In the Serbian affair, it was the maintenance of these false rights at all costs that was one of the causes of, and the major opportunity for, the Great War. All the same, the result of this has been to make the application of these principles more difficult, if not absurd. For a people to have halted another people's entire material and intellectual development is no longer, thanks to God and [Wilson's] Fourteen Points, a licence to reign over this other people. Even if it is true that in Eastern Galicia the only 'cultural' element is Polish, and that the Ruthenes or the Ukranians are nothing but poor peasants, it no longer follows that the right belongs to this self-styled elite and not to the masses. It is no longer true that the people and their lands must belong to the Polish bourgeoisie, the landowners and jurists – to the christianized Polish Jews, in this case – to dispose of as they will. Nor is it any longer true that Bessarabia, appropriated by the Russians, must remain Russian, nor that the *Balticum* becomes German because of a predominance of Teutonic barons and partially germanized Jews.

A people's hardships in enduring a civilization not its own, its day-to-day resistance, its often heroic efforts to create for itself a morality, a tradition, and an education system: these are noteworthy, commendable and relatively widespread. A people wants to have its own businessmen, its jurists, bankers, rulers, its own newspapers and its art. It is the sign of the need for true independence and total national freedom to which so many populations, until now deprived of these goods, aspire. It is unthinkable that this situation is going to change. Many strata of populations that were subjugated until now are currently in the process of becoming wealthy, in contrast to the conquering white races who have been exhausted by war. They are going to attempt their emancipation, their liberation, and the creation of their own civilizations. The example of Japan, which knew how to retain its past and how to acquire all the advantages of modern civilization, will be infectious and spread throughout the whole of Asia. The struggle between nationalisms and imperialisms is not over. As yet, neither the popularization nor individuation of civilizations is any nearer an end. Many national characters remain to be reformed through blood, conflict, effort and time. The work of individuating the old nations goes on. Germany makes desperate appeals to Austria, while the latter strives equally desperately to be a single country. They mark themselves out, they set themselves apart; in a word, they create a collective character.

We are deliberately using the word 'character' in its psychological sense here. Character is the integrated whole of one individual's various faculties, some being more or less sensory, others being more or less intelligent or voluntary; some more or less crude or acute, strong or weak, some personal, others stripped of all personality. Now, the remarkable thing is that the development of nations, especially the formation of great nations, has resulted not in the destruction of collective characteristics, but in their accentuation. The last century saw the rise of a new kind of literature. The study of a people's character is added to what, after Theophrastus, Mandeville and La Bruyère, has become the classical study of individual character. Hence the innumerable psychologies of the French, or the English, or any other people. In Montesquieu, in Voltaire and in Kant we will find the origin of these studies where, fortunately, so many documents have been set down in advance for sociology, which has yet to enlarge upon this point. This is, however, simply the literary manifestation of the phenomenon of the conscious construction of national character. Until recent periods, the character of a society was the unconscious work of generations and of the internal and external circumstances in which they found themselves.

[. . .]

Some [nations] stick with their old folklore, others have become enamoured of an ever more refined and, of course, extra-national, civilization; even Rome was Latin in the Middle Ages, later humanist, anglomaniac, gallomaniac, later still becoming Spanish, Italianate. It is only in the Greek cities, and in Judea (which we distinguish from the rest of Israel), at the time of the development of the synagogue and the Community of the Poor, that the idea of the comprehensive education of the people as a whole came about. Thucydides speaks to us about Mycalessus, a small Boeotian city in which, at the time of the Peloponnesian Wars, the Thracians massacred the children they found all gathered together in the school. The idea of compulsory education only thrived among the Jews and the Greek cities that became Latin municipalities. It survived, eclipsed, in the Church (in the catechism), and then in the Reformation. Then, however, as with the Jews, it was entirely religious. It was in Switzerland and Germany, in the Protestant countries, that the idea formed of an education that was, at the same time, both religious and national. At this same moment, the Encyclopedists and the French Revolution, the English radicals and, above all, presbyterian Scotland, the Quakers, and the new Republic of the United States returned to the notion that a citizen of the nation must be instructed and educated by it. On the day when public and compulsory education was established, when the state, the nation, legislated effectively and universally on this question, on this day the nation's collective character, until then unconscious, became the object of a progressive effort.

Briefly, a complete nation is a sufficiently integrated society, with a central power, democratic to a certain extent, having in every case the notion of national sovereignty, and whose frontiers are those of a race, a civilization, a language, a moral code – in a word, a national character. Certain of these elements may be missing: democracy is partly lacking in Germany and Hungary, and is totally lacking in Russia; Belgium and Switzerland both lack linguistic unity; Great Britain lacks integration (Scottish Home Rule). In mature nations, however, all this coincides. Such coincidences are rare, therefore all the more remarkable and, if I may be permitted to judge, the more beautiful. For it is possible to judge societies, even without political prejudice, like one judges animals or plants.

INTERNATIONAL PHENOMENA

Nations are no more alone in the world than are all kinds of societies. Whether or not they have sorted out their relations with other societies is one of the dominant factors in their lives, and must be analysed. Of course it is possible to conceive of closed and self-sufficient societies. The populations of distant Pacific islands managed to create this illusion for the first European sailors who landed there, for novelists like Stevenson and for fanciful ethnologists such as B. H. Thomson. On the other hand, vast societies that extend across the continents, enjoying climates and soils as diverse as the United States or Russia, will one day, at a pinch, be able to exhibit an extraordinary degree of autonomy and economic independence, and effortlessly withdraw their interests from everything that is not themselves – which is what the United States is really doing at this precise moment. Historically, however, and today in fact less than ever, no society has been formed without others. Their interdependence is even increased by that phenomenon of their relational life that is war. The problem of this relational life is therefore posed in the foreground.

[. . .]

Over and above nations, international phenomena are – as national phenomena were in the past – increasingly numerous and important. That is to say that it is quite obvious that, if they have existed for all time, as we have seen as regards the notion of civilization, they have, in the last several thousand years, gained an increasing strength and frequency. Expanded businesses, a larger scale and volume of trade, more rapid borrowings of ideas and fashions, great waves of religious and moral movements, the increasingly conscious imitation of economic and juridical institutions and regimes; finally and above all, the increasing and more thorough knowledge of literatures and languages consequent upon all this, have led large and small nations, and today even the world's most underdeveloped societies, to a state of increasing permeability and mutual dependence. So that, if the formation of social groups larger than our great nations remains entirely within the realm of the idea and the ideal, by contrast, the importance and consciousness of relations between nations and societies of every order have increased to an unforeseen degree, even since the war. And in consequence, an extremely high number of the conditions are in place for a practical solution to a practical problem to become, if not immediately possible, at least conceivable.

[. . .]

It must be remembered that societies, like all natural things, only really change if their environment changes, and in themselves, have only forces of relative alteration.

Unlike historians who, on this point, have always described the reality better, sociologists have been only too ready to attribute an internal evolutionary power to social groups, and only too ready to consider the social phenomena of different societies in isolation. It is time that the notion of those contingencies, deviations and interruptions familiar to history be brought forcibly to the attention of the social sciences, a notion contradicted only by the metaphysical ideas of uniform progress, general laws and autonomous generation. On the contrary, a genuinely positive sociology must take the most serious account of the fact that it is precisely these relations between societies that properly explain the phenomena of the inner life of societies. It is in fact an abstraction to believe that a nation's internal politics are not largely conditioned by the external, and vice versa. However, the remarkable thing is that whereas societies live amongst other societies – in short, that is, to the extent that their environment is not physical or geographical, it is of the same nature and the same order as they are – other organisms, including human individuals, live in environments that are totally heterogeneous to them: either inferior to them, like the physical environment, or superior to them, like the social environment. A society that is already an environment for the individuals that compose it, lives amongst other societies that are equally environments. Therefore we would be expressing ourselves correctly if we were to say that the totality of international, or better, intersocial relations of the relational life between societies, is an environment of environments. Thus we would clearly see the immense complexity and importance of this fact, and also the difficulty that there is in describing it in everyday language.

Finally, this human environment that is a society, and this totality of environments that is humanity, are not, now that the totality of the oecumen is known, like the physical environment, beyond the reach of all human agency. Hence arises the absurd notion, but the well-grounded illusion, that man can arbitrarily change societies, when the will arises. The idea has been popular; it is one of the great and forceful ideas of history; it inspired great legislators; it is what drove the great tyrants: Alexander, Caesar, Napoleon, Robespierre and Lenin, even though the latter was a marxist.

Meanwhile, we will see later, with regard to individualism, that human environments, in contrast to others, because in fact they constitute not only biological, but also psychological environments, are influenced by individuals more than any other natural environment. They are influenced by each other, alter each other and destroy each other at a rate unknown in any other biological phenomenon. So that, to be complete, we can see that a history of societies must be a history in the ordinary sense of the word, with the whole procession of diverse facts such as Cleopatra's nose or Napoleon's cancer.

CIVILIZATION

The history of civilization from the point of view we hold is that of the circulation amongst societies of various goods and knowledge of each one. As we have said in our study of the notion of civilization, when indeed we remarked that societies do not define themselves by their civilization, and as we recalled with regard to the formation of nations, societies are in some sense plunged into a pool of civilizations: they live by borrowing, and they define themselves by the refusal to borrow rather than by the possibility of borrowing. On this matter, look at the remarkable argumentation of a king of Ch'iu, one of the realms of China, to his councillors and his great feudatories who refused to take on the Huns' (Manchus') custom of riding on horseback rather than on chariots, and how he had the greatest difficulty explaining to them the differences between their rites and customs, arts and styles. Courtesy, gestures, even kissing, all sorts of things that are currently in transit and are imitated, are precisely those things that have been known, offered and rejected by societies.

This, however, is not the place to study the negations of borrowing, which are a matter for descriptive, historical, or rather psychological sociology, much more typical of given societies and more explanatory than the borrowings themselves. It is enough for us to have indicated that groups are more marked by institutions than by trends on this point, which simply proves that borrowing is the normal phenomenon, since non-borrowing is precisely what makes one society stand out in relation to another.

The facts of borrowing, all physiological, fall neatly into the order of sociology and the so-called classical social sciences: economics, technology, aesthetics, linguistics and legal studies, to enumerate only the major ones.

[...]

We will limit ourselves to indicating a few facts more typical than others, and particularly, for each of the major categories of social facts, to registering both the degree of permeability presented by modern nations, and the degree of uniformity that has resulted from this for the civilizations of today and tomorrow. Everything that is social and is not the very constitution of society may be borrowed from a nation, from one society to another. We shall content ourselves with establishing this, since historical development has peculiarly enhanced this human character of institutions, technical and aesthetic arts, in such a way indeed, that we are now able to speak of global human civilization.

[. . .]

Even nations with vehemently closed mentalities are in reality more open to each other than ever, due to one of those about-turns to which progress is accustomed. We live in a time when the unity of the human mind – so noticeable, as we have said, in the absolute homogeneity of its primitive creations – is going to become noticeable through the nations' very progress in the paths of science, industry, art and communal life.

Everything conspires towards ever intensifying numerous and far-reaching material, intellectual and moral relations between nations. We will conclude this, the first part of our work on international phenomena, by indicating that now the oecumen forms a world; that there is no longer a single people that is not in direct or indirect relation with others and that, in spite of all the clashes and setbacks, progress – or, if you would rather not use this optimistic term – the chain of events, leads us in the direction of an increasing multiplication of borrowings, exchanges, identifications, down to even the details of mental and material life. It is a poet's, even a bourgeois poet's prejudice to mock, as Musset does, the 'cabbage patch' that is the civilized world. First, we lack cabbages at the moment. Next, nothing proves that the division of labour within and between nations that will be the rule of tomorrow's economies, laws and arts, will not result in a diversity amongst nations and countries more propitious than these forbidden and closed economies whose mentalities bristle at one another, where each society forces itself to do without the others, and all are obliged, underneath it all, to do the same thing. For the nations, solidarity will become what it has been for men inside nations; it will exempt them from having their lives devoted to multiple tasks, none of which they may excel in, and will allow them to develop their individuality to the full.

Translated by Iain Hamilton Grant

* From M. Mauss, 'Nation, nationalité, internationalisme', in *Oeuvres*,

vol. 3, *Cohésion sociale et division de la sociologie*, Paris, Editions de la Minuit, 1969, pp. 593–605, 607–10, 625.

EDITOR'S NOTES

1 Henry Thomas Buckle (1821–62), author of *History of Civilisation in England* (1857–61).
2 Before the first world war.
3 Franz Boas (1858–1942), American ethnologist, best known for his book *The Mind of Primitive Man* (1913).
4 The river Leitha divided the Austrian (Cisleithania) and Hungarian (Transleithania) parts of the Empire.
5 Anton Ivanovič Denikin (1872–1947), White Russian general, attempting to overthrow Bolshevik rule, 1918–19.
6 Colleges of music, fine arts, etc.
7 The Isle of Scilly.
8 'Group of Five' Russian composers: Balakirev, Rimski-Korsakov, Moussorgsky, Cui and Borodin.

6

NATIONAL STATES AND NATIONAL MINORITIES*

C. A. Macartney

C. A. Macartney (1895–1978) worked for the League of Nations before becoming an academic. An expert on international relations and central Europe, he was author of many works on Hungary and the Austro-Hungarian empire. Macartney was one of the small group of scholarly commentators on the contemporary scene (including E. H. Carr) drawn together in the interwar years by A. J. Toynbee at the Royal Institute for International Affairs. This remarkably documented study, published by the RIIA in 1934, demonstrated the incompatibility and conflictual consequences of the territorial claims of nationalists that resulted from the treaty of Versailles.

THE NATIONAL MOVEMENT DURING THE WAR

The present political structure of Europe is the result of the violent resolution, into what are in theory uninational states of the modern type, of the great super-national empires which (in whole up to a century ago and for the greater part up to 1914) had divided between them the belt of mixed population.

Although the peculiar conditions in that area had for many centuries prevented the formation of such states, the states of 1914, multi-national in fact but generally uninational in intention, had failed to supply a satisfactory alternative. Some of them treated their national minorities benevolently enough, but that had ceased to satisfy. Well treated or no, the submerged nationalities had come, with hardly an exception, to entertain as their true and ultimate ambition the ideal of complete independence. The danger to the existing empires was greatly increased by the fact that most of the national states bordering on them had as yet realized their national ambitions only partially and had now come to hold it a grievance that any of their own kinsmen should live as minorities under the sovereignty of another state – believing sincerely and passionately in their right to unite them with themselves at the first opportunity.

The desires of the subject nationalities for freedom enjoyed considerable sympathy among Liberal opinion in western Europe, which saw in them a struggle of democracy against tyranny. Such opinion did not, perhaps, fully realize the difficulties inherent in the question. It was notable, for example, that the aspirations of the Poles and the Magyars received far more widespread support than those of the Ruthenes or the Slovaks; and yet the former were no more, although no less, respectable than the latter. But this general, if vague, popular sympathy for the oppressed nationalities was widespread, and in certain cases influenced governments decisively.

On the other hand, neither the Powers in general, nor diplomacy as such, had reached the point of recognizing the inalienable right of any people to self-determination. Opportunist rulers like the Napoleons might exploit the principle of nationality to their own advantage. Individual statesmen, a Palmerston or a Gladstone, might on humanitarian and religious grounds give help and encouragement in special instances where a population revolted against intolerable tyranny. In cases of Christian peoples in revolt against the Turk, such sympathy was fairly widespread, and something like a doctrine of the right of intervention on grounds of humanity seemed to be held in many quarters. It was, however, far from general, and in any case was based on strictly humanitarian considerations. Where the treatment of a subject nationality was not so bad as to endanger peace, no Power was prepared to infringe the sovereignty of the ruling nation by intervention, and the action of states which used the national question as a pretext for interference in their own interests was condemned by the world. It was obvious that a Europe whose international relations were governed by the Concert of the Powers, three of which contained important and discontented national minorities, would hardly admit the general validity of a principle so dangerous to its own structure.

If, then, we are to explain the enormously important part played by self-determination in the Peace Settlements, we must bear in mind the very peculiar circumstances prevailing at the time, where, of the four super-national empires, three had been defeated and were at the mercy of their enemies; the fourth was in the hands of men who took an entirely novel view of political relationships; and the law was laid down by an American democrat, and applied by the representatives of the national states of western Europe.

The national question was not only the immediate occasion of the World War (and it is worth remarking that the motive which lay behind the Serajevo murders was not indignation at ill treatment of the Bosnian minorities but rather the conviction that the only proper government for Serbs was government by Serbs). Serajevo was only a single disastrous manifestation of a feeling which had dominated the political situation in central Europe for half a century. Austro-Hungarian policy, domestic and foreign, had long since come to be governed by the national question; and as Germany was closely allied to Austria, her situation, too, was indirectly but no less certainly ruled by the same question.

Thus the grouping of forces in Europe in 1914 had been determined very largely by national issues, and the event soon proved that the national factor was even more important than had been anticipated. For the original structure had been elaborated on a system dictated chiefly by considerations of the balance of power. Italy and Roumania were, in 1914, bound to the Central Powers by treaty obligations which actually ran contrary to their national aspirations. The war once engaged, however, both these countries believed that they could better realize their ambitions by joining the Entente Powers; and Italy did so in the name of 'her most sacred aspirations', while Roumania, in her declaration of war, expressly invoked the principle of nationality. Thus it came about that once the lists were fully joined in Europe, one side was found to consist almost entirely of states with unsatisfied national ambitions, the other of states containing dissatisfied minorities.

There was one exception on the side of the Central Powers in the shape of Bulgaria, to whom, owing to the accident that her ambitions conflicted with those of Serbia, already fighting on the side of the Allies, the Central Powers were able to offer the better terms. On the Allied side, Russia formed a most notable exception, but an isolated one. France, Italy, Serbia, Roumania, and even Greece stood to gain more than they would lose by the application of the principle of self-determination.

Neither side could, however, invoke it without danger as a general principle, nor did either attempt to do so during the early period of the War.

[...]

Both sides concluded treaties by which they bought the help of new allies, and in each case the price was a concession to national ambition and thus envisaged a partial adaptation of political to ethnographic frontiers. Yet the purchasers did not scruple to violate ethnographical claims where the seller demanded it. The Treaty of London, by which the Allies brought Italy into the War, promised her the Brenner frontier (which involved presenting her with 250,000 Germans) and ample Yugoslav, Greek, and Albanian territory. The treaty with Roumania envisaged assigning to her hundreds of thousands of non-Roumanians. As for the secret treaties between the Allies regarding Turkey, Russia was to have received Constantinople, eastern Thrace, the Asiatic Bosporus, Gallipoli, and some of the Islands, while the Allies promised themselves, and one another, large concessions in Anatolia. On the other side, Bulgaria exacted from the Central Powers, promises of territorial aggrandizement in the Balkans which went far beyond what she could have justly claimed on ethnographical grounds.

Both sides, again, exploited the principle of nationality in individual cases, where they thought that they could weaken their adversaries by doing so. It speaks volumes at once for the thoroughness and for the political blindness of the Germans that they acted in this respect far more energetically than the Allies during the early part of the War, at least in Europe.[1] In Ireland they lent what help they could to the movement which culminated in the outbreak of Easter 1916, and in Belgium they encouraged a Flemish movement which in 1917 demanded the separation of Flanders from the Walloon countries and the assumption by the German Emperor of a protectorate over it. It was the Germans, too, and not the Allies who gave a friendly reception to the 'Congress of Nationalities' which met at Lausanne in June 1916 and was, indeed, largely composed of representatives of the subject nationalities of Russia. Russia was naturally the country upon which Germany could concentrate her chief attention. Occupying Lithuania in 1915, the Baltic provinces in the following year, she did much to detach them from Russia, although the régime which she set up in the Baltic provinces was almost purely German, and in Lithuania, for practical reasons, she favoured the Polish element. But here and indeed in Finland also (where the Russian Government had taken repressive measures in December 1914) she helped the final dissolution by her propaganda and her administration.

Poland was a more difficult case, since neither side dared promise too much to the Poles living under the enemy flag, for fear of whetting inordinately the appetite of its own Polish subjects, while each felt bound to make some offer, lest it be outbid.

[...]

The Central Powers were at the disadvantage of being unable to agree between themselves. The Austrians were prepared to create a genuinely autonomous state composing the whole Polish territory, but the Germans wished to reserve the blessings of liberty for Russian Poland alone. It was not until November 1916 that the Central Powers made up their minds to hold out the prospect of the restoration of an independent Poland; and, meanwhile, they administered the country through military governments, under which it was anything but independent.

In comparison with all this busy activity, the Entente appeared almost to neglect the national question, although it would have seemed their obvious point of attack against Austria. But a fear that if Austria-Hungary were dismembered, Germany would in the event be strengthened; social considerations for the Dual Monarchy; the difficulty of satisfying both Bulgarians and Yugoslavs; and, finally, prevailing ignorance of Central European politics, stayed their hand, and although Czech and Croat emissaries early began to beg for their support, they received only very lukewarm encouragement. The first definite change came at the end of 1916, when President Wilson asked the Allies to state their war aims.

[...]

During something over two years of the War, the belligerents of neither side had adopted the principle of self-determination as a general part of their policy. On the other hand, by their intrigues with the minorities in the enemy camp, each had fed the ambitions of the submerged nationalities, while the enfeeblement of authority, impoverishment, and the growth of revolutionary feeling had brought the day nearer when those nationalities would be able to take their destinies into their own hands. Now two events occurred, each of which was destined to throw the card of nationality into the hand of the Allies.

The first was the entry of the United States, led by President Wilson, into the War.

[...]

Wilson, although the ideas of justice and reparation for past wrongs played their part in his philosophy, sought, above all, peace, and he believed that the subjugation of one nation by another always constituted a threat to peace.

Thus it may be said that on broad lines Wilson believed that justice demanded the general satisfaction all round of the principle of nationality.

[. . .]

The results of the Russian Revolution, [the second event] of the principles proclaimed by its authors, and of the reception accorded to them by Germany, were very far-reaching. On the one hand, the revolutionary sentiment throughout Europe was greatly strengthened; on the other, it was turned very directly against the Central Powers. The submerged nationalities now believed that they had a chance of achieving their full ambitions, but they saw that they could so only if Germany, Austria-Hungary, and Turkey were defeated. From the beginning of 1918 onward the Western Powers, freed from the necessity of further considering Russia's feelings, came out ever more boldly on the side of self-determination.

[. . .]

THE ESTABLISHMENT AND BASES OF THE NEW FRONTIERS

Thus the fortunes of four years of war had brought about a situation of which none of the combatants had, most likely, dreamed in 1914. Throughout almost the whole belt of mixed population, the great super-national empires had crumbled away, and were to be replaced by a new order, based on the principle of the national state.

In the case of the states which had detached themselves from the Russian body politic this process had already occurred, or was in process of occurring, when the Peace Conference met. The Conference as such had nothing to do with regulating the relations between Russia and these states. Each Power had only to decide for itself whether or not it would recognize the new formations. In most cases recognition was granted as soon as there seemed any likelihood that they would prove stable.[2] The duty of the Powers was confined to concluding peace treaties with Germany, Austria, Hungary, Bulgaria, and Turkey respectively; and even here, they were not working on a clean slate. The recognition of Poland and Czechoslovakia, the agreement – if it can be so called

– reached between the various branches of the southern Slavs, and the formation in these three states of governments which had already to some extent established themselves when the Conference met, marked out the broad lines of the settlement which was to be made. It would not have been possible to put the clock back and re-establish the old Austria or the old Hungary. Thus it was not difficult to say which were the national groups which were destined to become states. The only genuine ambition to form a state which might have been respected, and was not, was that of the Ruthenes, i.e. those Ukrainians who had previously been Austrian or Hungarian subjects. Another important decision to be taken concerned German Austria where, on the contrary, the people primarily concerned wished to be merged in what they regarded as their true national state, Germany, while the Conference wished them to pretend to a separate 'Austrian' nationality.

In most other cases where a small 'independent' state was proclaimed, but failed to survive, the ambition to become independent had not been genuine. Such formations as the Mirdite Republic on the borders of Albania, or the Republic of Baranya in southern Hungary, were only called into being by a neighbouring state with a view to subsequent annexation. It was not, as a rule, difficult to see through such ingenuous pretensions.

If, however, the main lines were laid down in advance, the determination of the frontiers was a very much more complex affair. In defending the settlement ultimately made, in so far as the German frontiers were concerned, the Allied and Associated Powers claimed definitely and emphatically that they had acted in accordance with the principles of self-determination enunciated by Wilson.

'Every territorial settlement of the Treaty of Peace' (i.e. with Germany), they wrote, 'has been determined upon after most careful and laboured consideration of all the religious, racial and linguistic factors in each particular country. The legitimate hopes of peoples long under alien rule have been heard; and the decisions in each case have been founded upon the principle explicitly enunciated in this same address: that "All well-defined national aspirations shall be accorded the utmost satisfaction that can be accorded them without introducing new or perpetuating old elements of discord and antagonism that would be likely in time to break the peace of Europe and consequently of the world".[3]

There were, however, certain modifications and reservations. The German Government having complained that the principle of self-determination had not been followed, but that the basis of the territorial settlement was 'indifferently, now the consideration of an unchangeable historical right, now the principle of ethnographical facts, now the consideration of economic interests', the Allies replied ingeniously that far from acting unjustly towards Germany, they were exactly following out Wilson's principle that – 'Each part of the final settlement must be based upon the essential justice of that particular case and upon such adjustments as are most likely to bring a peace that will be permanent.' The departure, in certain cases, from the ethnographical principle was 'the inevitable fact that an appreciable portion of the territory of the German Empire consisted of districts which had in the past been wrongfully appropriated by Prussia or Germany'. Finally, yet a third demand of Wilson's had been for 'the destruction of every arbitrary power everywhere that can separately, secretly, and of its single choice disturb the peace of the world or, if it cannot be presently destroyed, at the least its reduction to virtual impotence' – a principle which, if interpreted, would justify almost any strategic frontier.

In the case of Finland, the Allied and Associated Powers had to bear practically no responsibility, either for its existence or for the determination of its frontiers. The Finnish Diet had proclaimed the independence of Finland within its historic frontiers, and it appears that the cleavage which was manifest in the vote was rather social than national. Finland's independence had been recognized by Russia, according to Lenin, so that 'the bourgeoisie could not say that the Great Russians were chauvinistic'. Moreover, 'one cannot refuse to recognize what is; one is forced to recognize it'. The Allies intervened only in the single case of the Aaland Islands, where a dispute between Finland and Sweden was brought before the Permanent Court by Great Britain, and the League Council finally confirmed Finland in her sovereignty over the Islands.[4]

Estonia and Latvia separated similarly from Russia in conformity with the Bolshevik doctrine of self-determination. The action of the Allies was again almost confined to recognition, and to enforcing the retirement of the German troops of occupation;

although the frontiers between Lithuania and Latvia, and between Latvia and Estonia, were actually settled in each case by British arbitrators. The frontiers with Russia were settled by agreement with that Power, and roughly along ethnographical lines. In both of these states, however, the revolution was carried through almost solely by the majority nations, and against the wishes and, in part, the resistance of various minorities.

The independence of Lithuania was, again, the work of the Lithuanian nation, but her frontiers with both Poland and Germany were laid down by the Powers – in each case bowing to force. The Supreme Council first laid down a boundary with Poland which followed the ethnographical lines as closely as it thought possible, but after Poland, by a *coup de main*, had seized the disputed territory, the centre of which was Vilna, it recognized her possession. With regard to the German–Lithuanian frontier, the Conference forced Germany to renounce her sovereignty over a strip on the right bank of the Niemen, including the port of Memel, and to accept the settlement to be made by them, 'particularly in so far as concerns the nationality of the inhabitants'. The motive of this decision was mainly economic, as Lithuania would have found it difficult to exist without this port, but it was also argued that although the town was in part German, the majority of the population of the district was 'Lithuanian in origin and in speech'[5] – a statement contested by Germany in her reply. The Powers administered the port and district themselves for some time, and most unsuccessfully. In 1923, however, Lithuania seized Memel by a *coup de main* and the Powers eventually assigned the district to Lithuanian sovereignty, but as an autonomous area with a statute guaranteed by the Principal Allied and Associated Powers.

The problems connected with Poland were more complicated. All the Allies had, from the earliest days of the War, made promises to Poland, but without explaining very exactly what they understood under the name. The Russian Provisional Government had been the first to recognize the complete independence of Poland, i.e. of the old 'Kingdom of Poland' in Russia. Afterwards violent fighting between Poles and Russians broke out, Poland receiving considerable help from France. Her eastern frontier, with Russia, was then fixed by treaty with that nation, on the basis of the military *status quo* – a frontier which was very unfavourable to Russia, as it left large districts inhabited by White Russians within the Polish frontiers. The Lithuanian–Polish frontier was also settled, in effect, by force, and here, again, favourably to Poland.

With regard to Poland's other frontiers, something more of an attempt was made to apply Wilson's principles. The Allies had laid down, and Germany had accepted, the principle that the restored Poland should include 'the districts inhabited by an indisputably Polish population'. A 'free and secure access to the sea' had also been stipulated, but it had never been stated whether this implied a territorial access. At the Conference, the Allies, rather unexpectedly, revived the historical argument, stating that

> there is imposed upon the Allies a special obligation to use the victory which they have won in order to re-establish the Polish nation in the independence of which it was unjustly deprived more than one hundred years ago. . . . To undo this wrong is one of the first duties of the Allies.[6]

They maintained, however, that in certain cases they had 'deliberately waived the claim of historic right because they wished to avoid even the appearance of injustice' in favour of the national principle. In fact, the Supreme Council modified to a not inconsiderable extent the original proposals made by the Polish Commission.

The settlement was as follows:

All territory south of the old frontier of East Prussia was considered as 'indisputably Polish'. In the southern and south-western districts of East Prussia, which are inhabited largely by so-called 'Masurians' akin to the Poles by race and language, but, unlike true Poles, Protestant by religion, plebiscites were taken. These went overwhelmingly in favour of Germany, who was allowed to retain the areas in question, with insignificant modifications.

Westward of this, Danzig and the area immediately surrounding it (which are, and had long been, purely German) were separated from Germany on account of their overwhelming economic importance to Poland; but in obedience to the national principle, were not assigned to Poland, but constituted a Free State, standing in a special relationship to Poland and administered by a League Commission – an attempt to safeguard the interests of all parties concerned which accorded with history and deserved a better fate than it has enjoyed.

Farther west an attempt was made to achieve an ethnographical frontier. This historic frontier between Pomerania and West Prussia was left intact; southward of it, while the provinces of West Prussia and Posen (Posnania) (annexed to Germany under the partition of Poland) were assigned to Poland, the frontier was modified, in Germany's favour, to secure a better ethnographical line. Large German minorities remained, however, within Poland. The Kashubs, it must be noted, were reckoned as Poles, and the assumption was also accepted that they would desire union with the Polish state.

The Silesian boundary was left unchanged, except for small modifications in Poland's favour, made on the ethnographical principle, until its extreme south-eastern corner – the highly industrialized and all-important Upper Silesia – was reached. It had at first been proposed to assign this area *in toto* to Poland, but in reply to Germany's protests a plebiscite was held, and it was partitioned, to the dissatisfaction of both parties. The ethnographical line was perhaps as just a one as could be found, approximately equal numbers of minorities being left on either side of it; but the economic unity of this area was completely destroyed.

The southern frontier followed, on the whole, the historical and ethnographical lines, which approximately coincided, until eastern Galicia was reached. This is a large and important district inhabited mainly by Ukrainians, or Ruthenes, who are racially and linguistically identical with the Ukrainians of Russia, but attached by historical tradition to Austria, and for the most part members of the Uniate Church. They are bitterly hostile to the Poles, under whose oppression they suffered grievously in past centuries. Alone among the Slavonic nationalities of Austria-Hungary, they stood by Austria to the last, in the hope of thus retaining some protection against the Poles, but like the rest they established their own autonomous government, which was duly recognized in November 1918 by the Lammasch Cabinet. They were immediately involved in fighting with the Poles, which was greatly complicated by the fact that the Russian Ukrainians were at the same time engaged in hostilities with the Bolshevists, and had proclaimed a union between the Russian Ukraine and East Galicia. The Powers found it very difficult to know what to do about this territory, but on March 1st, 1919, President Wilson, in their name, definitely promised the west Ukrainians to find an equitable solution of the difficulty between them and the Poles. In June 1919 the Supreme Council authorized Poland to occupy the territory and to establish a civil government after having fixed with the Allied and Associated Powers an agreement whose clauses shall guarantee as far as possible the autonomy of this territory, and the political, religious and personal liberties of the inhabitants. This agreement shall be based on the right of free disposition, which, in the last resort, the inhabitants of East Galicia are to exercise regarding their political allegiance. The period at which such right shall be exercised shall be fixed by the Allied and Associated Powers or by the organ to which these shall delegate their power.

In November 1919 the Supreme Council actually granted Poland a twenty-five years' mandate over East Galicia – being the only instance in which an attempt was made to apply the mandatory principle in Europe, although the application of it to Albania was seriously suggested. Neither party agreed to the mandate, but the Poles remained in occupation, and in March 1923 the Conference of Ambassadors assigned East Galicia to Poland in full sovereignty, the decision being prefaced by a clause stating 'that it is recognized by Poland that as regards the eastern part of Galicia, the ethnographical conditions necessitate a régime of autonomy'.

The story of Czecho-Slovakia is even more complicated. At the Peace Conference the Czecho-Slovak Delegation claimed the 'lands of the Bohemian Crown' (Bohemia, Moravia, and Austrian Silesia) in virtue of historic right and juridical continuity. This claim had been advanced early in the War by President Masaryk, and seems to have occasioned some surprise. It had been expected that the Czechs would adhere more closely to the principle of national self-determination,[7] since in Bohemia and Moravia the Czechs constituted only about two-thirds of the population, and in Silesia they were actually in a minority. As soon as the Czechs declared their independence the Germans constituted themselves in various bodies which claimed the right to attach themselves to German Austria. Czech troops occupied the disputed territories, and both sides and Austria appealed to the Allies, the Germans pleading the right of self-determination, the Czechs 'the position of the Czecho-Slovak State as a state recognized by the Allies during the war and the Allies' promises touching the historic frontiers of the Czech lands'.[8] These 'promises' are not very definite,[9] but the French decided to allow Czecho-Slovakia to occupy the historic frontiers of Bohemia, Moravia, and Silesia until the Peace

Conference. The British acquiesced, but the United States extracted from the Czechs a promise that they would submit unreservedly to the decisions of the Conference.

The Conference then admitted the Czech claim in its entirety, except that it modified the frontier in Silesia in favour of the Poles, mainly on economic grounds. The Czechs were even granted some territory outside the historic frontiers, at the expense of Germany (on ethnographical grounds) and of Austria (to ensure their communications). In justifying their decision, the Allies advanced a unique argument. 'They have thought', they wrote, 'that the populations of German speech inhabiting the borders of these provinces should remain associated with them in the development of the national unity with which history has bound them up (*les a rendu solidaires*).' The violations of this historic principle in favour of Czecho-Slovakia were actually advocated as ensuring 'the best pledge of that national unity'.

The Allies overrode historic and economic considerations in favour of ethnographical and strategic ones as decisively in Slovakia as they had done the opposite in Bohemia and Moravia. It was not even quite agreed what were the wishes of the inhabitants, but a number of them – probably the majority – favoured joining the Czechs, on some basis short of complete unification. Representatives of Slovak parties passed a declaration to this effect on October 30th, 1918. Afterwards the Czech and Hungarian troops fought for the possession of Slovakia. The former were supported by the Allies, who eventually forced Hungary to accept a line which left all the Slovak parts of north Hungary in the hands of the new state. Subsequently considerable blocks of territory, some of which were purely Magyar in population, were included in Czecho-Slovakia on strategic and economic grounds.

On the other hand, the Conference rejected, as too artificial, a scheme (which had apparently originated in a French brain)[10] for joining up Czecho-Slovakia with Yugoslavia by a 'corridor' between Austria and Hungary. The justification for this plan would have been purely military.[11] It also refused to allow special treatment for the Czechs of Lower Austria, or the Lusatian Serbs. By another unique concession, however, it allocated to Czecho-Slovakia the district known as Sub-Carpathian Russia, in the extreme north-eastern corner of the Carpathians, and inhabited mainly by Ruthenes. The Ruthene leaders had themselves voted for union on a basis of autonomy with Czecho-Slovakia, if they could get nothing better; and the Peace Conference, while placing them under Czecho-Slovak sovereignty, stipulated that they should receive 'the widest measure of self-government compatible with the unity of the Czecho-Slovak Republic'.

Roumania, whose representatives enjoyed far less personal popularity in Paris than did the Czechs, was treated with less indulgence, although she, too, could hardly complain of ungenerous treatment. Originally formed out of the two 'historic' Danubian principalities of Moldavia and Wallachia, which were unquestionably predominantly Roumanian, she had received the northern Dobruja in 1878 purely as compensation because Russia had insisted on taking to herself Bessarabia. The northern Dobruja was a land of very mixed population, which fifty years of occupation had made, on the whole, mostly Roumanian. Then, in 1913, Roumania forced Bulgaria to cede her the southern Dobruja, the population of which was almost entirely Bulgarian, Turkish, and Tatar. Her secret treaties with the Allies during the War had opened to her the prospect of a very large extension of territory at the expense of Austria and Hungary. These became null and void when she concluded a separate peace in 1918, under which she receded to Bulgaria almost the whole of Dobruja. On the other hand, Bessarabia had declared itself autonomous on the outbreak of the Russian Revolution and had formed a National Council, in which the Roumanians were in a majority. The Council proclaimed its complete independence on January 24th, 1918; and on March 27th the Roumanian majority voted for union, with local autonomy, with Roumania.[12] When the Central Powers collapsed, the Council voted for complete union with Roumania, and the Roumanian authorities subsequently extended the scope of this declaration to those districts which, being under the military occupation of the Central Powers, had not participated in the previous voting. The Peace Conference sanctioned the military occupation of Bessarabia by Roumania, and on March 9th, 1920, the British Empire, France, and Italy recognized the political union. On October 28th, 1920, this recognition was sealed by a treaty which, however, has not yet (1933) become legally binding, as one of the signatories (Japan) has not ratified it.

The Bukovina came to Roumania in somewhat similar fashion. The retiring Austrian governor had placed the administration in the hands of the Ruthene majority, but the local Roumanians proclaimed union with Roumania and called in troops from Old

Roumania, who occupied the country. The Supreme Council, after considering a redrafting of the frontier which would have excluded some compact Ruthenian districts, allowed Roumania to retain the province within its historic frontiers. In the Dobruja, the frontier of 1913 was restored, thus leaving a large Bulgarian minority within the Roumanian frontier. In the Banat, which was claimed by both Roumania and Serbia, although the population was largely German with Magyars and Jews in the towns, a rough ethnographical line was drawn dividing the country between Serbia and Roumania, with each claimant receiving some important towns, and the minorities being balanced out against each other. In Transylvania, the Roumanian majority voted for union with Roumania, the Saxons adhering to this decision, which the Magyars, on the other hand, accepted only under *force majeure*. During the early part of 1919 Roumania was at war with Hungary, and her troops occupied much of eastern Hungary, advancing in August west and north of Budapest. They were with difficulty induced to withdraw. The final frontier was advanced far westward of the optimum ethnographical line to give Roumania possession of certain towns, and of the communications between them.

Reference to some of the main decisions affecting Austria has already been made. The German-Austrian Deputies of the Reichsrat had on October 21st, 1918, passed a resolution that 'the German people in Austria is resolved to determine for itself its future form of State, to form an independent German-Austrian State' (which was to comprise 'all districts inhabited by Germans'), 'and to regulate its relations to the other nations by a free agreement'. The first Provisional Government, of November 12th, 1918, proclaimed this state a part of the German Republic. The Powers vetoed this, forcing Austria to drop even the prefix 'German' from her title; and a provision was inserted in the Austrian and the German treaties forbidding Austria to forgo her full independence except by the unanimous consent of the whole Council of the League. Further, as has been remarked, the Germans of Bohemia, Moravia, and Silesia were denied the right to join with Austria, and even some small districts of Upper and Lower Austria were detached and assigned to Czecho-Slovakia. The southern half of the Tyrol, up to the Brenner, was given to Italy, on strategic grounds. In the south-east, the predominantly Yugoslav districts were detached and attributed to Yugoslavia, on ethnographical grounds, the benefit of the doubt, so far as the Styrian districts were concerned, being given to the Yugoslavs. In Carinthia, however, a plebiscite was held in one zone where the wishes of the population seemed doubtful, and the district was left with Austria in accordance with the result of the vote (which showed, incidentally, that many Slovenes must have voted for Austrian citizenship). Only in the east did Austria receive an accession of territory at the expense of Hungary, being given some German-speaking districts of west Hungary. A plebiscite was, however, allowed for the chief town of this district, Oedenburg (Sopron), and this resulted in favour of Hungary, which accordingly retained the town and its immediate surroundings.

The nucleus of Yugoslavia is formed out of the kingdom of Serbia, composed first of those districts (mainly inhabited by Serbs) which successfully revolted against the Turks at the beginning of the nineteenth century. It received several increases of territory, based partly on ethnographic considerations. In 1913, as a result of successful wars, Serbia acquired the Sanjak of Novi Bazar (inhabited mainly by Serbs) and northern and central Macedonia, in which the population was exceedingly mixed, the purely Serb element being very small, while the majority was intermediate between Serbs and Bulgars, but sympathized more strongly with the Bulgars, and there was a large sprinkling of Albanians, Turks, pure Bulgars, Vlachs, and other nationalities. Some of the purely Albanian territories in the west were, however, separated off to form a principality of Albania. During the War Serbia was occupied by the Austrian and Bulgarian troops, and Bulgaria would have annexed not only all Macedonia but much of Serbia proper. After her defeat, however, Serbia recovered all that she had lost in Macedonia, and was granted rectifications of her eastern frontier on purely strategic grounds, the inhabitants of the district in question being pure Bulgars. As against Albania, the line fully sanctioned was that of 1913, which separated some 400,000 Albanians from their fellow-countrymen in Albania, a frontier which was neither ethnographically nor economically justified.

At the end of the War, all the historic units of the Austro-Hungarian Empire which were indisputably Yugoslav in the majority (Bosnia and Herzegovina, Dalmatia, and Croatia-Slavonia), with the kingdom of Montenegro, proclaimed their union with Serbia. There remained a number of Austrian Crownlands and a part of southern Hungary which were mainly Yugoslav. These were claimed for the new Serb–Croat–Slovene State on ethnographical grounds, a newly-constituted Slovene National Assembly taking over the government of all the Southern Slav provinces of Austria, while the Croatian Diet, speaking for Croatia, Slavonia, and Dalmatia, including Fiume, expressly claimed 'the whole area belonging ethnographically to this [i.e. the Yugo-Slav] race without regard to the territorial and state boundaries within which the Slovenian, Croatian and Serb people live at present'.

For these frontiers, therefore, the ethnographical test was adopted, except in the case of Montenegro, which contained many Albanians in its southern territory, acquired by conquest. The optimum ethnographical line was eventually modified, to Yugoslavia's disadvantage, as against Italy. The line with Austria was fairly regulated by a plebiscite, as described above. In Hungary no plebiscite was allowed, and a line drawn greatly to the Yugoslavs' advantage, Yugoslavia being allowed to annex no less than 250,000 Magyars in order to enable her to retain the town of Subotica, with its Bunjevac (Catholic Serb) population. The settlement of the Roumanian frontier is described in connexion with that country.

Little more need be said of Hungary, Bulgaria, or Albania. Hungary was left only a torso. In practically no case was she given the benefit of the doubt when her frontiers were being drawn, and only in the case of Sopron (Oedenburg) was a plebiscite allowed. Bulgaria was allowed to keep a portion of what she had gained in the Rhodopes at the expense of Turkey in 1912, but she lost western Thrace, and her losses in Macedonia and the Dobruja were sealed. Albania received in the north and east her inadequate frontiers of 1913, but in the south Northern Epirus, about which there had been a dispute which was still unsettled in 1914, was finally awarded to her. All of these three states were losers by this settlement, in which large numbers of their nationals were left outside their frontiers. All of them, however, also contained considerable percentages of national minorities.

Greece had a very chequered career. Even before the War her frontiers had contained many Albanians and some other minorities. In the Balkan Wars she acquired Crete and various islands in the Aegean, being predominantly Greek, although with Turkish minorities, and, by conquest, a part of Macedonia in which the population was exceedingly mixed. After the World War she was at first assigned the greater part of Thrace and the basin and hinterland of Smyrna, in Ionia, but after she had fought an unsuccessful war against Turkey, the districts in Ionia and eastern Thrace were taken from her. She was, however, assigned western Thrace, with a large Bulgarian and Turkish population, on grounds not very easy to ascertain.

Turkey was at one time destined for a drastic parcellation, but by virtue of her military resistance recovered eastern Thrace in Europe, and a frontier in the south which went beyond what had been predominantly Turkish territory. In the east she retained much of Kurdistan, and in the north-east, where her frontiers were settled by agreement with the Soviets, a large district which had been chiefly Armenian in population. 'Irāq became a mandated territory, and subsequently (1932) independent, the Kurds of its northern frontier being divided between 'Irāq and Turkey.

Finally, the Peace Conference made certain other territorial adjustments affecting the more western states. Italy received the Italian Trentino, but also the Brenner frontier, which was designed to give her strategical security, but placed 250,000 German-Austrians under her rule. Farther east, she obtained, on grounds most simply described as *Machtpolitik*, a large Slovene hinterland behind Trieste, while getting Fiume and Zara and some small islands on ethnographical grounds, and another island farther south on strategic grounds. France re-annexed Alsace and Lorraine on historic grounds, as redressal of 'the wrong done by Germany in 1871 both to the rights of France and to the wishes of the population of Alsace-Lorraine, which were separated from their country in spite of the solemn protest of their representatives at the Assembly of Bordeaux'.[13] Perhaps unwisely, she did not carry through a plebiscite, which would have undoubtedly gone in her favour. She was also ceded the Saar coal-mines in reparation, the Saar territory being placed under League administration for fifteen years, after which a plebiscite was to be held. Belgium was given Eupen, Malmedy, and Moresnet on strategic and economic grounds, and with no plebiscite, although the inhabitants (five-sixths of whom were Germans) were allowed to make signed protests. Denmark was assigned part of northern Schleswig on ethnographical grounds, after a plebiscite had been held in the more doubtful areas. The line which resulted was substantially the optimum ethnographical line.[14]

C. A. MACARTNEY

THE NEW NATIONAL STATES

All of these states – and this is a vital factor in the situation as it developed subsequently – constituted themselves as national states.

[...]

Modifications and exceptions apart, all the new states are more or less consciously the national states of the single nation which forms the majority of their population. Most of them take pains to express this fact in their Constitutions. Thus the Estonian Constitution opens with the words:

> The Estonian people, in the firm conviction and with the unshakeable will to create a State founded on justice, right and liberty. . . .

That the Estonian nation, in the personal sense of the word, is meant, is proved by the statement that the territory of the new state is to comprise 'the districts of Voru, Petseri and the other limitrophe districts inhabited by the Estonian people'.

The Polish Constitution begins:

> In the name of Almighty God,
>
> We, the Polish nation, thanking Providence for having restored us liberty after a century and a half of servitude. . . .

The Czechoslovak:

> We, the Czecho-Slovak nation, wishing to consolidate the complete unity of the nation. . . .

The personal interpretation of the central phrase is, again, undoubted, and was, indeed, officially confirmed by a decision of the Czechoslovak Supreme Court of Justice, of March 23rd, 1929, which lays down that:

> The Czechoslovak language is the official State language of the Republic, i.e. of the Czechoslovak State constructed by the Czechoslovak people, and consequently, of a national State.

Whence it is deduced that: 'Czechoslovaks, where they are in a minority (i.e. locally) enjoy quite different rights in relation to the local authorities than those enjoyed by members of a German minority in relation to the State authorities.'[15]

Roumania is the most uncompromising of all, for her Constitution actually begins with the words:

The Kingdom of Roumania is a national, unitary and indivisible State.

Even Austria would appear to have altered her previous conception of the relations between state and nation, for her present Constitution contains the provision that:

The German language is the official language of the Republic, without prejudice to the rights accorded by the Federal Republic to linguistic minorities –

a stipulation which seems to place the minority languages on quite a different footing from the old nominal equality guaranteed under the law of 1867, and to mark a changeover from the supernational conception of the state to which, with all her shortcomings, Austria still adhered up to 1918, to a national philosophy. As Hungary, Bulgaria, and Turkey were already constructed on these lines, the result of the Peace Settlement was that every state in the belt of mixed population, with the few modifications mentioned above, now looked upon itself as a national state.

But the facts were against them. Not one of these states was, in fact, uni-national, just as there was not, on the other hand, one nation all of whose members lived in a single state. Given the inextricable tangle of nationalities existing in this part of Europe, no state could have been formed without leaving minorities within its frontiers. But besides this, although the Peace Settlement had aimed, nominally, at satisfying the claims of national self-determination wherever possible, actually many departures had been made from this principle; and while in some cases, such as that of Bohemia, the historical and economic considerations had made it reasonable to suppose that a departure from the strict ethnographical line would be in the best interests of the minorities themselves; in others, as those of the Bulgars assigned to Yugoslavia and Roumania, the Magyars of the Schütt Island, the Germans of Italy, or the Albanians of Yugoslavia, the minorities concerned had been simply sacrificed to the interests of their new masters. Taken all in all, the number of persons left as, or made into, minorities by the Peace Treaties was probably not less than some 25–30 millions, constituting the substantial proportion of some 20–25 per cent of the populations of the states to which they were assigned.[16] They were of all types and classes, ranging from small, humble, and politically inactive groups, to which a change of masters meant little, up to great, highly-civilized communities, who had formerly been masters in the countries where they were now to become servants, who protested violently against their fate, and whose complaints found an answer in the hearts of great European Powers. Together, they constituted a problem with which the Peace Conference could not escape dealing.

* From C. A. Macartney, *National States and National Minorities*, Oxford, Oxford University Press, 1934, pp. 179–86, 189, 191–211.

NOTES

1 The intrigues of both sides in Asia form a story too complex to be more than mentioned here.

2 President Wilson was curiously hesitant in this respect. Great Britain and France were, in most cases, more prompt in granting recognition.

3 *Reply of the Allied and Associated Powers to the Observations of the German Delegation on the Conditions of Peace* (Cmd. 258, Misc. No. 4 of 1919), Introduction, Basis of the Peace Negotiations, p. 5.

4 Finland also attempted to raise the question of eastern Karelia before the Court, but that body declared itself not competent to deal with it, and eastern Karelia consequently remained with the Soviet Republic.

5 *Reply of the Allied and Associated Powers* . . . Parts II and III, Boundaries of Germany and Political Clauses for Europe, Section X – Memel.

6 Ibid., Section VII – Poland.

7 T. Masaryk, *The Making of a State* (1927), p. 28.

8 J. Opočensky, *The Collapse of the Austro-Hungarian Monarchy and the Rise of the Czechoslovak State* (1928), p. 191.

9 J. Papoušek, *The Czechoslovak Nation's Struggle for Independence* (1928), p. 73, quotes a letter from M. Pichon, then French Foreign Minister, to Benceš, promising that the French Government would do its utmost to secure the fulfilment of the desires of the Czecho-Slovak people for independence within its historic frontiers. It is difficult to see what this meant, for if the Czech nation might perhaps claim historic frontiers, the Czecho-Slovak people certainly could not do so.

10 Temperley, *A History of the Peace Conference of Paris* (1920–4), vol. iv, p. 273.

11 The district in question contained, besides Germans and Magyars, a certain number of Croats, refugees from the days of the Turkish advance; but the great majority of the population was German.

12 Besides the Roumanians, the Polish Deputy voted for the Union; but the German, Russian, Ukrainian, and Bulgaro-Gagauz groups did not recognize the competence of the Council to take this decision.

13 Treaty of Versailles, Section V, Preamble.

14 Schleswig was taken from Denmark by Prussia in 1864, but Prussia undertook in 1866 to cede the northern parts to Denmark if a free vote of the population expressed the wish to be united with Denmark. The plebiscite was never held, and the local population and the Danish Government asked the Peace Conference for a vote.

15 E. Ammende (ed.), *Die Nationalitäten in den Staaten Europas* (Vienna, 1931), p. 208.

16 The figures are necessarily rough, for complete accuracy is impossible, both in view of the difficulty of obtaining reliable statistics, and of the large number of genuinely doubtful and border-line cases.

7

THE IDEA OF NATION*

Federico Chabod

Federico Chabod (1901–60) was an academic with a deep moral commitment, who fought as a partisan in his native Aosta valley during the nazi occupation of Italy. A historian of early modern Europe and the political thought of Machiavelli, he was led by the experiences of the second world war to study the origins of the highly contemporary themes of the historical evolution of the concepts of the nation and of Europe: the course from which the following text is drawn was delivered at the university of Milan in 1943–4, immediately following the collapse of the fascist regime and the German occupation. These classic lectures, in which Chabod underlines the contrast between the Italian and German idea of the nation, provide a lucid example of how nazism obliged historians to rethink nationalism in the light of the contradictions of its consequences, both liberating and aggressive.

The sense of national and historical 'individuality' is less deep in Rousseau than in Herder, but the political thrust, the collective will to action is much stronger and more lively. The appeal to a *volonté générale* is something new which, indeed, was completely lacking in earlier authors. From the observation of a fact – the nation – created above all by the past, which is to be found in earlier authors, there is a shift towards the 'will' to 'create' a new fact, that is, a state founded on popular sovereignty, and hence – the transition is inevitable – a 'national State'.

This is an innovation of extraordinary importance. An act of will, previously missing, is substituted for, or rather joined to the simple recognition of the nation. Nostalgia for those long-lost happier times, of a 'past' where men were free and strong, is converted into the desire for a happy age of the 'future'; complaints

124

about the decadence that the centuries have brought about in ancient customs, about the corruption and humiliation of ancestral liberties, are transformed into the intention to realize, in the near future, a state of affairs in which mankind is truly happy and free. The nation, which previously was only 'felt', will now be 'desired'.[1]

This passage from 'judgement' to 'will', in general, marks the transition from the reformist mentality of the eighteenth century to the revolutionary mentality of 1789 and the nineteenth century. And Rousseau was correctly felt as a revolutionary stimulus, because of the clear and decisively political message in his writings which was not present in others, even in Herder.[2] It is precisely this novelty that profoundly and substantially differentiates the nineteenth-century idea of 'nation' from that of the eighteenth.

What happens here is what happens in a more complex field with regard to the Risorgimento.

In the last twenty years many of the so-called 'Risorgimentalists' have tried to move the origins of the Risorgimento as far back as the beginning of the 1700s.

[...]

But it is important to emphasize unequivocally that, after the French period, there is a new element, something profoundly new, which gives impetus to the real Risorgimento, to the 'political' Risorgimento of Italy; or, to be yet more precise, which is responsible for the creation of an Italy which is *political*, and not just geographical, linguistic and cultural. The spirit is profoundly changed: the eighteenth-century reformism of a Verri, a Filangieri, a Genovesi, becomes the revolutionary 'will' of a Mazzini; the demand for reforms in this or that sector, in the administration or the economic life of the country, moves on to become the demand for the *political liberty and independence* of the nation, and then its *political unity*. It is a profoundly different moral climate.

There is a completely different general climate in Europe, whose fundamental characteristics are merely reflected in Italy in a particular way. The climate is different, not only in relation to one or another nation in particular, but in its general 'tone'. What has been written about the opposition between Romanticism and Enlightenment, between appeals to 'reason' and exaltation of imagination, sentiment and passion, characterizes well the substantial differences between these two worlds.

Compare eighteenth-century politics, the art of government of the major representatives of the century, of Frederick II of Prussia, of Kaunitz, Maria Theresa's minister, to that of the great politicians of the nineteenth century, a Cavour or even a Bismarck; compare how the people participate in the political events in the two periods: and you will have the exact measurement of the abyss which separates the two eras.

[. . .]

A purely rational political calculation, wholly detached from the 'passions': the 'citizen', says Frederick the Great, king of Prussia, 'must not realize that the king is waging war'.

Just compare that to nineteenth-century politics, when even the least 'sentimental' statesmen, even the most sceptical and internally driven by a pure desire for power, like Bismarck, nevertheless felt the need to win the support of so-called public opinion and organized press campaigns to arouse it, and searched in every way possible to 'heat up' national passions in order to use them as a weapon of diplomacy. Look, for example, at the press campaign cunningly fomented by Bismarck in the summer of 1879 to give the impression that public opinion was deeply concerned and alarmed by Russia's behaviour, and thus gain Emperor William I's approval of the Austro-German alliance.[3] A hundred years earlier, a Kaunitz would never have dreamed of needing such support for his policies.

The nineteenth century, in short, experienced what the eighteenth century ignored: *national passions*. Politics had appeared as an art in the eighteenth century, all calculation, careful weighting, balance, precautions, wholly rational and without passion. With the nineteenth century it became notably more tumultuous, torrid and passionate; it acquired an impetuosity, I would almost say the fire of great passions. Politics became a driving and proselytizing passion, as religious passions had once been, three centuries earlier in the age of the cruel, implacable struggles between Huguenots and supporters of the League, between Lutherans and Catholics, in the years of the 'Night of San Bartholomew'.

Politics took on a religious pathos; and ever more so with the passage of time, into the twentieth century – which explains the *furore* of the terrible wars of our times.

How can we explain this pathos except by the fact that nations transfer, as it were, from Herder's purely cultural plane to a political plane. As we have already said, the nation ceases to be only *sentiment* in order to become *will*; it ceases to look back towards the past, behind us, and is projected towards the future before us;

it ceases to be a pure historical memory but is transformed into a way of life for the future. In the same manner, liberty changes from a myth of ancient times to become a light for the future, a light only to be reached by abandoning the shadows.

The *nation* becomes the *patria* and the *patria* becomes the new goddess of the modern world: a new divinity and hence *sacred*. This is the great novelty that emerges from the period of the French Revolution and the Napoleonic Empire.

The first to announce it is Rouget de Lisle in the penultimate strophe of the *Marseillaise*:

> Sacred love of the patria,
> Guide and support our avenging arm.

Fifteen years later, Ugo Foscolo repeats it in the conclusion of the *Sepolcri* ('Sepulchres'): 'Let the blood shed for the patria be blessed and wept over.'

The *patria* as sacred; blood shed for it as sanctified. From then on, in effect, one hears of martyrs for independence, freedom, the unity of the *patria*: the martyrs of the Risorgimento in general, and in particular the martyrs of the prisons of Spielberg, Belfiore, etc.

Words have changed! For eighteen centuries the term martyr had been reserved for those who shed their blood in defence of their own religious creed; a martyr was whoever fell with the name of Jesus Christ upon his lips. Now for the first time, the term is used to indicate values, affections, purely human, political sacrifices – which acquire the importance and the depth of values, affections, and religious sacrifices which themselves become religion.

The 'religion of the *patria*' is the religion of the nation. The two terms are interchangeable: in fact, in the only European supra-national State, the Austro-Hungarian Empire (the Swiss and Belgians felt themselves no less a nation than the others), the religion of the motherland was replaced by the cult of the *dynasty*, the only moral force that managed to keep together, for some time yet, that agglomerate of various peoples.

This is truly what is 'new' about the modern world, compared with the periods that preceded it: at least when compared with the ages following the spread of Christianity.

Nothing similar, in fact, had ever occurred before. Cola di Rienzo[4] speaks of a *sacred Italy*.[5]

[...]

For Cola, Italy is sacred because it is the seat of the successors to Peter, Christ's vicar on earth; it is also sacred as the seat of that Empire which (let us never forget) for medieval man was not simply a 'political power' as it would be for modern man, but also a 'sacred' power, ordered by God, established by God, with an ultimately religious, not a political purpose. Sacred, therefore, as Rome is sacred, because it is the land of martyrs and great Christian basilicas, according to writers and poets of the Middle Ages, ever since Prudentius,[6] and – as Cola di Rienzo repeated[7] – sacred because predestined by God to be the centre of the two powers, the two sides of the *Ecclesia*, the spiritual and the temporal. This was a way of feeling light years away from that of Foscolo or Mazzini.

Not even in Machiavelli, despite his political passion, despite his intense love for Italy, can we find anything similar. He vows that he loves his *patria* more than his soul; he affirms that 'where anything to do with the good of the Patria is decided, all other considerations, whether just or unjust, must fall' (*Discourses*, III, 41) and that 'no good man will ever reprove someone who seeks to defend his Patria, whatever the means he adopts' (*Florentine Histories*, V, 8). But he cannot even imagine transferring to the love of country the characteristics always attributed to love for God and the church of God. Machiavelli removes politics from religion; but, from the nineteenth century, religion is transferred over into politics, politics is made into a 'religion'; in other words, a 'religion of the *patria*' is created, which in turn, becomes the supreme aim of politics, the goal to be achieved.

This is done, we repeat, for the first time by nineteenth-century men; and it is pointless wasting much time to stress how much stronger the idea of the *patria* becomes in consequence. A sacred quality is attributed to worldly matters; the political struggle acquires a religious, and for that matter even a fanatical character that it has shown ever more destructively with the explosion of different nationalisms.

[. . .]

The *nation* thus now becomes an ideal to be realized in the near future. Already in Alfieri[8] it was easy to perceive a notably more resolute tone, more 'political' and revolutionary than in other writers of the eighteenth century: revolution against tyrannic rule and freedom – here, again, is that magic word, already spoken by Swiss, by Germans, and now by Italians, but, with a completely different soul, not looking back to the past but aspiring to the future: it is the unity of Italy, prophesied in the conclusion of Alfieri's essay, *Of the Prince and of Letters*.[9]

These two motifs of revolution and freedom, fundamental in Mazzini's sermons, are already present in Alfieri. Then comes Foscolo,[10] and his sanctification of the *patria*; and Mazzini, in the fullness of the Risorgimento and the unfolding of the principle of *nationality*, which means that transition of the nation from sentiment to will, from past memories to future hopes.

It is obvious that the idea of nation will be particularly cherished by peoples who are not yet politically unified. The 'principle of nationality' – its application in the field of politics – will be most favoured by those who, only on this basis, can hope to unify the still scattered limbs of the common *patria*. Hence, it will be primarily in Italy and Germany that the national ideal will find enthusiastic and continuous advocates; and close behind, the other divided and dispersed peoples, first and foremost the Poles.

In France, the principle of nationality had been affirmed from the early decades of the century in the works of Philippe Buchez (1796–1865). In the first half of the nineteenth century, Italian thought is completely permeated by nation and nationality, to the point that Italian cultural life of the period would be inconceivable without thinking contemporaneously of those principles that continuously burst forth in political thought, as in art, in Gioberti and Mazzini, in Balbo and Durando, as in Foscolo, Berchet, Guerrazzi, and even in Manzoni and Leopardi, although they are less 'political'. French thought of the Restoration and Orleanist period, on the other hand, is in its main lines essentially indifferent, sometimes even hostile to problems of nationality – and the proof of this is the French attitude towards the problems of Italian nationality. Only after 1870, after the loss of Alsace-Lorraine, did the principle of nationality become a live and effective element in French culture, because it alone could legitimate the protest against the German occupation of the two regions and allow for hopes of a 'return'. The famous lecture on nationality given by Ernest Renan at the Collège de France ('What is a nation?'[11]) – where we find one of the most noble formulations of nationality itself – was delivered in 1882: that is, very much later.[12]

Italy and Germany, then, are the classic examples of the idea of nationality in the first half of the last century. And in both nations the appeals to their own past and history sounded identical, because the demonstration of an age-old and glorious Italian (or German) nation in every field, but above all in culture, art and thought, legitimated the hopes that such a presence would also become real in the political world and that the nation would transform itself from a purely linguistic–cultural entity into a political fact or 'state'. To transform the *cultural* national into a *territorial* nation was the aim: but its cultural titles served as the justifying documents for the latter claim to emerge.

Hence the appeal to past history, which is a continuation of that of the eighteenth-century writers, but with a political end that was previously lacking. We find this appeal in Italian and German writers: Novalis[13] exhorts his readers 'to history', to examine 'in their instructive complexity the ages that resemble each other' and to learn to use 'the magic wand of anthology'.[14] Exactly ten years later, in his famous inaugural lecture to his course on eloquence at the University of Pavia, Ugo Foscolo insisted: 'Italians, I exhort you to turn to histories': because her titles to glory lay in the past history of the Italian nation, which was also the pledge for her future. But already earlier, in the *Sepolcri* ('Sepulchres'), the poet had translated the same thought into an image, the image of Santa Croce,[15] the temple of 'italic glories' where one must go to 'read the auguries', 'where hopes of glory may shine for courageous intellects and all Italy'.

Santa Croce, with the tombs of the great Italians, Machiavelli, Michelangelo, Galilei, was as it were the sacred place of national consciousness. We should not forget the great importance that Florence had as an ideal for educated and patriotic Italians in the Risorgimento, at least up to the years of Neoguelphism when it was decisively replaced by the idea of Rome.

But if these characteristics are common to the Italian and German movements, it is necessary to point out that, in other respects, the two movements are, instead, substantially and profoundly different. So different and with regard to such fundamental questions that the overall judgement of the historian can only be one: the national movements in Germany and Italy, notwithstanding some affinities and similarities, are completely divergent, perhaps even opposed.

[...]

We have already said that there are two ways of considering the nation: *naturalistically*, which inevitably develops into racism, and *voluntaristically*. It is evident that the opposition is not always so total and resolute: even a naturalistically based doctrine can appreciate to a certain extent voluntaristic factors (education, etc.), just as a voluntaristic doctrine is not bound to deny every influence or all influences of natural factors (geographic environment, race, etc.). But, all told, a doctrine receives its particular shape by a greater or lesser emphasis on one or the other of these two elements.

In Germany, the ethnic (that is, naturalistic) connotation is observable from the very beginning. It is enough to think of Herder's way of considering the nation as a 'natural' fact, of the 'permanent' physical characteristics that he assigns to the various nations, on the basis of 'blood' (the generation) and 'soil', to which that specific blood remains attached.[16]

And then, at the beginning of the nineteenth century, Friedrich Schlegel, in his *Philosophical Lectures* of 1804–6, argues for the importance of the ethnic factor: 'the older and purer the stock, the more deeply rooted are the customs, and the stronger the attachment to these customs, the greater the Nation will be'.[17]

Logically, we find in Schlegel, as in Möser and Herder, hostility towards any mix with foreign blood, a closure, so to say, of one's own world against any influence from outside. Naturally, only Germanic stock begins to appear as 'old and pure'. As early as the beginning of the sixteenth century, the historian Aventinus, in his *Annales ducum Boiariae*, had extolled the affinities between the Greeks and the Germans;[18] this presumed affinity was praised even more loudly in German culture at the end of the eighteenth century, all based on the idea that, as the Greeks had once been the purest reflection of humanity, so the Germans would now take over as the true representative people of humanity.

Friedrich Schiller states it, with great conviction. In a preparatory fragment of a lyric later entitled *German grandeur* (probably of 1801) he exclaims:

> even if the world has decreed differently, it is inevitable that whichever people expresses the spirit, even if it is dominated initially, will end up dominating. The other peoples will have turned into dead flowers, whereas this people will be the lasting golden fruit. The English are greedy for treasure, the French for lustre,

while fate has reserved the highest destiny for the Germans,

131

to live in contact with the spirit of the world... Every people has its day in history; the day of the Germans will be the harvest of all the ages.[19]

These naturalistic elements we have just mentioned were to be developed in German thought through the nineteenth century and were to tend increasingly to attribute the nation to external factors, above all race and territory (the German school of geography of Ratzel contributed extensively to the importance attributed to territory).[20]

Language, for Herder, in his *Abhandlung über den Ursprung der Sprache* ('Treatise on the origin of language'), had appeared as a spiritual creation, 'a treasure of human thoughts, in which everyone created something in his own manner', to the point that there could never be only one tongue in the mouths of two men (an exquisitely modern concept). Increasingly, the same language tended to be seen as an expression of 'race', and thus to become more rigid in a naturalistic sense. And as writers spoke of 'pure' stock, of a pure race, so they spoke of a 'pure', an 'uncontaminated' language. Fichte had already written of it, naturally claiming that the Germans were the only ones who could boast such a pure language, capable of conserving the clarity of images and the freshness and perennial fluidity of consciousness.

[...]

Italian thought, instead, bases its idea of nation on decidedly 'voluntaristic' grounds. The exquisite formula of the nation as a 'plebiscite of every day' was expressed by Renan: but the substance is already to be found in Mazzini, as in Pasquale Stanislao Mancini.[21]

Mazzini, as is well known, was not systematic in his writings. We have to reconstruct his thoughts on various and even the most important problems, scattered across his numerous writings. But the essence of his thoughts on nationality remains the same; and it is as obvious in his writings of 1834 and 1835, and possibly more so, as it is in the writings of his last years. In 1835:

A nationality includes a common thought, a common law, a common end: these are its essential elements ... Where men do not recognise a common principle, accepting it in all its consequences, where there is no identity of intent for all, there is no Nation, only a fortuitous crowd and multitude, which breaks up at the first crisis.[22]

132

In 1859:

> The Patria is a Mission, a *Common Duty*. The Patria is your
> collective life, the life that links all the generations that have
> risen, acted and passed on your land in a tradition of like
> tendencies and affections [...] The Patria is above all else
> the *consciousness* of the Patria. However, the territory on
> which you walk, the boundaries which nature has placed
> between your lands and those of others and the tongue that
> is spoken there are no more than the visible *form* of the
> Patria: but if the *spirit* of the Patria does not throb in that
> sanctuary of your life that is called Conscience, the form
> remains like a corpse, without the movement and breath of
> creation, and you are a nameless crowd, not a Nation; a
> populace, not a people. The word *Patria* written by a foreign-
> er's hand on your flag is meaningless, like the word *liberty*
> that some of your fathers wrote on the doors of prisons. The
> Patria is *faith* in the Patria. When each one of you will have
> that faith and will be ready to seal it with your own blood,
> only then will you have a Patria, not before.[23]

In 1871:

> The Nation is not a territory to be made stronger by enlarge-
> ning its size, it is not an agglomeration of men speaking the
> same idiom ... but an organic whole through unity of ends
> and faculties [...] Language, territory, race are no more
> than signs of Nationality, insecure when not all entwined,
> and in any event demanding confirmation in historical tra-
> dition, in the long development of a collective life designated
> by the same characteristics.[24]

The contrast between the two conceptions, Italian and German,
becomes open and apparent in 1870–1, on the outbreak of the
Franco-German war and the German decision to annex Alsace-
Lorraine. The Germans (including famous scholars like Mommsen
and Strauss) maintained that Alsace was German through language,
race and historical traditions. Many Italian journalists of the
Destra[25] (Bonghi writing in *Perseveranza* and *Nuova Antologia*,
and Giacomo Dina, editor of the *Opinione*) responded that the
question could not be solved just on this basis, against the 'vote
of the people and consciousness of nations'. And bitter discussions

followed which brought into full daylight the substantial diversity of the two viewpoints.

Full consciousness, or the will of a people to achieve what it desires: this was the determining factor of nationality for the Italians. Of no importance, the Germans retorted, promptly creating the theory of 'unconscious nationality'.[26]

The only exception in Italy is Crispi and his group of friends who collaborated with *La Riforma*. The paper took part in the polemics between the Italian journals of the Destra and German papers on the question of Alsace-Lorraine, formulating the doctrine that the character of nationality is by nature *prior* and *superior* to any singular or collective will, that the principle of nationality has precedence as a natural right existing in every Italian, that the citizen's will can be interrogated about the form of the state, but for no other reason; whereas it would be unjust and absurd to have part of the nation decide if it wished to be Italian, German or French.[27]

In later years, Crispi would reaffirm the idea of the 'Riforma', namely, that the concept of nation had precedence, independent of the will of men; that it was preconstituted, unchangeable in absolute time, external and indestructible;[28] he would create the formula *natio quia nata* ('a nation because born as such'),[29] a definition of the nation that locates its basis in the naturalistic, ethnic–geographical element as an unquestionable and unsurmountable fact.

But Crispi's voice was, at that time, completely isolated, and the Italian doctrine of nationality remains as explained: a doctrine that rests completely on spiritual factors, on the soul, will, faith, which sees in external material factors – race, territory, the same language – simple countermarks or evidence of nationality, which thus exists only due to something deeper and internal; a doctrine that is founded, in Bonghi's words, on 'an interrogation of the present consciousness of peoples'.

Translated by Kathy Wolff

* From F. Chabod, *L'Idea di Nazione*, Bari/Rome, Laterza, 1961, pp. 44–5, 47–62, 65–7.

NOTES

1 Cf. L. Salvatorelli, *Il pensiero politico italiano dal 1700 al 1870*, Milan, 1959, p. 44.
2 For this absence of a 'political sentiment' in Herder, cf. C. Antoni, *La lotta contro la ragione*, Florence, 1942.
3 Cf. B. von Bülow, *Memorie*, Italian trans., IV, Milan, 1931, p. 510.
4 Cola di Rienze (1313/14–1354), tribune and would-be reformer of the Papacy [Editor's note].
5 In the circular to convoke the Roman 'synod', dated 7 June 1347, in the decisions of the 'synod' itself, in the circular of 19 September 1347 (*Briefwechsel des Cola di Rienzo*, ed. Burdach-Piur, III, lett. 8 and 27; IV, n. 32).
6 Aurelius Prudentius Clemens (348–c.410), Christian poet [Editor's note].
7 Cola's circular of 7 June, sent to the commune of Perugia to invite it to take part in the Roman synod, stated: 'and of the other holy apostles, whose bodies lie in that city [Rome], and of the infinite other martyrs and virgins, *in whose blood that holy city was founded*; nor should it cause surprise, because this *sacred city which was built for the consolation of souls*, and which must be the refuge of all the faithful . . .' (*Briefwechsel*, III, lett. 8)
8 Vittorio Alfieri (1749–1803), playwright of heroic tragedies [Editor's note].
9 Salvatorelli, *Il pensiero*, p. 89.
10 Ugo Foscolo (1778–1827), romantic poet and writer [Editor's note].
11 See above, chapter 3 [Editor's note].
12 Cf. F. Ruffini, 'Nel primo centenario della nascita di Pasquale Stanislao Mancini', in *Nuova Antologia*, 16 March 1917, pp. 6 and 9 of the offprint.
13 Friedrich von Hardenberg, called Novalis (1772–1801), romantic poet [Editor's note].
14 Ruffini, 'Nel primo centenario . . .' p. 17.
15 The great church at Florence, with the fame of Westminster Abbey [Editor's note].
16 Antoni, *La lotta*, p. 160.
17 F. Meinecke, *Weltbürgertum und Nationalstaat*, Munich, 1908 (It. trans. 1930, I, p. 81).
18 'Indeed our speech, especially that of the Saxons . . . is the closest to and has the main exchanges with the language of the Greeks. There are infinite words that mean the same to us and the Greeks' (*Werke*, II, p. 54).
19 Meinecke, *Weltbürgertum* pp. 54–5.
20 Ruffini, 'Nel primo centenario . . .', p. 8.
21 P. S. Mancini (1817–88), legal theorist and statesman [Editor's note].
22 'Nazionalità. Alcune idée sopra una costituzione nazionale' in *Scritti editi ed inediti*, Rome, Ed. nazionale, 12 (1883), p. 84
23 'Ai giovani d'Italia', in *Scritti editi ed inediti*, 12 (1882), pp. 65–6.

24 'Nazionalismo e nazionalità', in *Scritti editi ed inediti*, ..., 17 (1891), pp. 165–6.
25 The Destra was the moderate conservative government party following the unification of Italy [Editor's note].
26 Ruffini, 'Nel primo centenario...', p. 6.
27 'Il principio di nazionalità' (*La Riforma*, 20 December 1970). *La Riforma* returned to the question of Alsace-Lorraine on 8 October 1872 in relation to patriots of the two regions: on this occasion too it insisted on the 'unrenounceable rights' of the nation, which always exist 'as long as the natural confines that separate nation from nation continue, and in their absence, so long as a race, a history, a common language exists'; it insisted equally on national unity 'which *exists in its own right*, independent of any vote or any plebiscite'.
28 'The existence and independence of nations cannot be subjected to the decision of plebiscites. Nations live of natural law, which is eternal and unchangeable. Such a law cannot be modified in any way by the passage of years or the will of the populace', Crispi to Raiberti (Paris) 14 November 1891 (in *Carteggi politici inediti di Francesco Crispi 1860–1900*, Rome, 1912, p. 641; cf. pp. 458–9).
29 'In any case, as I have often said, our nation exists *quia nata*: and it had no need of plebiscites to come into being' (letter to Primo Levi), *ibid.* p. 466; cf. p. 471: '*Natio quia nata*, remember it'.

8

REFLECTIONS ON NATIONALISM*

John Breuilly

Nationalism in recent years has attracted the attention of many social scientists. Among them, the social anthropologists Ernest Gellner and Benedict Anderson, both with experience of field work in extra-European contexts, have offered important and very different approaches to the conditions that explain why individuals become nationalist. **John Breuilly**, author of a wide-ranging work on *Nationalism and the State*, outlines and offers his critical reflections on their views and his own contribution about the role of power and the state in this important debate.

Nationalism is the most important political ideology of the modern era. It is also the one on which there is the least agreement. There is a gulf between ideological commitment and theoretical reflection. No one would consider the nationalist writers Mazzini, or Heinrich von Treitschke, or Palacky important theorists of nationalism in the way one would consider Karl Marx on socialism, or John Stuart Mill on liberalism, or Edmund Burke on conservatism. There is a gulf between those who regard nationalism as the product, in however exaggerated or distorted a form, of an underlying national reality, and those who regard it as myth, the cause rather than the product of nationality. There is a tension between those who see the nation as a political association and those who regard it as a cultural community. There are further differences concerning the type of political association or cultural community which is envisaged as the aim of nationalism.

There are two major reasons for this failure to agree even on fairly basic questions. First, the sheer universality and apparent power of nationalism has created a vast range of cases and vested interests which make it difficult to agree upon basic approaches to the subject. Second, nationalism is peculiar in that it combines a descriptive with a prescriptive claim, There *is* a nation and it *should be* free. Some students of nationalism focus on the descriptive claim: *are* there such entities as nations, and, if so, how do we account for them? Others focus on the prescriptive claim: *why* do nationalists make such a claim and *why* do others support it? The net result is a literature that grows larger every year but does not progressively advance knowledge of nationalism as it grows.

Instead one confronts an immense variety of historical and theoretical writings on nationalism the findings of which are impossible to compare, let alone integrate. In order to appreciate fully the two books under review it is necessary briefly to indicate what have been the major types of approach to nationalism.[1]

To begin with, there are particular histories of particular nationalisms. These tend to become absorbed into their subject. The very restriction to a 'national' framework implies agreement with the nationalist argument that there is a nation, though it is difficult to subject this implication to criticism. As any good history is responsive to the nuances of the subject of inquiry it is also difficult to compare and contrast the findings of various histories.

More general histories go a little further. There are histories which simply see nationalism as an aspect of modernity and describe its development in the context of a broad history of the making of modern times.[2] The problem with such histories is that it is never clear what it is about modernity which promotes nationalism. What is needed is a more explicit and selective view of the modernity/nationalism relationship.

Preferable as a general historical approach is one which regards nationalism as a political expression of the emergence of nations and relates the varieties of nationalism to the varieties of nations.[3] But that begs the question of the nation/nationalism relationship which must be at the heart of any inquiry into nationalism. A more sharply focused historical approach sees in nationalism the rise of a political doctrine to power.[4] This usually begins by outlining the character and novelty of the doctrine and moves on to describe how this doctrine becomes a political force. There is a tendency to see the development of nationalism in terms of the working through of a logic of ideas, achieving power by means of ideological conversion or manipulation. This approach has a fairly crude understanding of how ideologies develop and influence

138

people. Even when some broader context than that of ideas is sketched out it tends to take the form of an account of the 'rise' of the intellectuals who then hold sway over the gullible masses.

A more abstract and theoretical approach involves going 'beneath' the surface of nationalism to discover the underlying reality which is responsible for nationalism. Nationalism may be related to modern forms of class conflict, to the psychological losses of identity brought about by the erosion of tradition, to the needs of modernization, or to the development of new patterns of communication and culture. There are problems peculiar to each of these approaches.[5] A common problem is that they tend to work better for some cases than for others (thereby calling into question their status as general theory) and are difficult to frame in such a way that particular cases can be analyzed and the evidence built up in a way which could be used to test an approach.

What is needed is a fruitful combination of historical analysis and theory. My own attempt at this has involved defining nationalism rather narrowly as nationalist politics and developing methods of classification and analysis which allow a wide range of cases to be grouped, analyzed and compared.[6] From this theoretically informed collection of case study material I went on to make general claims about nationalism. With this background in mind we can turn to the two books under review.

Both authors are (rightly in my view) agreed that nationalism is modern. There are 'in-group' sentiments in every society as well as the projection of feelings of hostility and superiority upon 'out-groups'. Clearly nationalism can be regarded as one form of expression of such sentiments. But it is a very special form. The claim that there exists a group with a specific cultural identity and that, as a consequence, this group should possess a territorial state of its own, is modern and peculiar, as is the belief shared by many people that this is a valid, even a 'natural' claim. Gellner makes the point vividly:

> A man must have a nationality as he must have a nose and two ears; a deficiency in any of these particulars is not inconceivable and does from time to time occur, but only as a result of some disaster, and it is itself a disaster of a kind. All this seems obvious, though, alas, it is not true. But that it should have come to *seem* so very true is indeed an aspect, or perhaps the very core, of the problem of nationalism.

139

Having a nation is not an inherent attribute of humanity, but it has come to appear as such.

In fact, nations, like states, are a contingency, and not a universal necessity. Neither nations nor states exist at all times and in all circumstances. Moreover, nations and states are not the *same* contingency. Nationalism holds that they were destined for each other; that either without the other is incomplete, and constitutes a tragedy. But before they could become intended for each other, each of them had to emerge, and their emergence was independent and contingent. [p. 6.]

The second point of agreement is that any adequate generalizing approach must seek out those aspects of modernity which relate particularly to nationalism. Nationalism will, therefore, be understood neither as an expression of some enduring reality such as the nation nor as an arbitrary ideological construction, but rather as one response to certain crucial aspects of modernity. The major issue, therefore, becomes what one selects as the central features of modernity to relate to nationalism. This will not necessarily lead to a 'single factor' theory which could never be sustained with something as various and complex as nationalism. Rather it will serve as the departure point for a 'contextual' explanation of nationalism, that is an explanation which does not seek the 'cause' of nationalism, but instead seeks to show which situations favour the development of nationalism.

For Gellner the key to modernity is 'industrialism'. Industrialism, whether organized through the free market or centrally controlled, brings with it rapid and continuous change and a much higher level of social mobility than had existed in earlier societies. Industrialism involves a complex division of labour and this requires a rather different, specialized and universal educational system which provides people with the basic tools for employment such as a standard language and literacy. To sustain such an educational system one needs a centralized state and the effect of such a system is the production of a 'standard culture'. Gellner also argues that the 'modern spirit' is not one which recognizes that different sorts of knowledge are confined to different spheres. Rather the world is regarded as a 'single logical space' where everything is capable of analysis and further analysis, and in which such 'analyzability' promises perpetual innovation.

With these ideas, contrasted to the situation in agrarian societies, Gellner has constructed a powerful model which can be related in various and very persuasive ways to nationalism. Nationalism does not just develop in response to something rather vague and negative called the 'breakdown of tradition' but also in relation to new patterns of social movement, state activity, and cultural and intellectual innovations. The development of a standard culture clearly promotes and makes plausible notions of national identity. Increased social mobility favours a shift of social identity from position in the social structure to cultural characteristics. The powerful central state controlling major concerns such as the educational system extends political awareness and intensifies the desire to control 'our' state. Whereas earlier social structures encouraged particularism – for example, the horizontally divided peasant communities and the vertically divided elites (merchants, nobles, guildsmen) above them characteristic of what Gellner calls 'agrarian empires' – the social structure of industrialism encourages more extensive, culturally based identities. Nationalism as a response to these developments is appropriate in three ways. First, it gives a specific, ideological expression to the emergence of a standard culture. Second, it can become a weapon on the part of certain groups threatened by the growth of industrialism and a new standard culture. Third, nationalism can operate as a force helping in the process of industrialism and in the construction of a standard culture. Let us look at these claims more closely.

The first two are fairly specific and see nationalism as a response to other developments. They thus avoid the two great problems of functionalist explanation: vagueness and teleology. Nationalism is related to elites seeking control of the state and justifying that to fellow members of their standard culture or to elites seeking separation from the state and appealing for support from members of 'their' culture group who are threatened by the emergence of a standard culture which is far more accessible to members of other culture groups. The third idea is a much more difficult one: nationalism is regarded as functional for industrialism (vagueness) and its function serves to explain its existence (teleology). Gellner shifts emphasis at this point and argues that nationalism can be a response to the industrialism of others. Industrialism is now less a process of social change underpinning nationalism and more a perceived need which motivates nationalists.

One can also criticize the assumptions about industrialism itself.

It is doubtful whether social mobility becomes much more rapid with industrialism. Geographical mobility certainly increases but whether the rural labourer who moves to a mining town has an increased chance of moving up the social scale is another matter. Second, although I accept the point that ethnic and religious tensions often take on a new importance and form in the urban–industrial environment, such tensions are often not expressed in nationalist forms, and strong nationalist movements can be found in the absence of such tensions. This points, I think, to the importance of a political dimension to convert ethnic tension into nationalist politics. Third, Gellner's point that a mass education system is a universal product of industrial societies is well-made. But does the answer lie in the 'generic training' such education offers? There is again the problem of functionalist explanation: education may eventually function in this way but does that explain its development? Unless one specifies either a deliberate intention on the part of key groups to produce this result or some feed-back mechanism which will 'select' generic training patterns of education against other patterns, this cannot count as an explanation. At the same time one can think of other explanations: humanitarianism, the growing distinction between home and work which excluded children from the labour force and made them a special problem requiring special treatment, the need to train citizens or conscripts for the mass politics and mass armies of the modern age.

Gellner also argues that nationalism has a particular force in the early stages of industrialization when conflict and tensions are particularly acute. I doubt that. The period of industrialization in Europe and the USA between 1815 and 1914 was the period of the longest and greatest peace in modern times and such wars as did occur had little to do with any virulent or popular nationalism. Nationalism was not of central importance in politics until after mid-century and even then it had little appeal to the group most closely associated with industrialization, the urban working class, which gravitated rather to class-based ideologies. Nationalism as a powerful and popular politics seems to me to be more closely associated with the mature industrial societies of twentieth-century Europe and the non-industrial societies beyond Europe.

One can also question the industrialism/nationalism link by pointing to the development of nationalism even before the development of industrialism. The French Revolution directly promoted various sorts of nationalism but at that time industrialism even as a model to pursue did not exist. Gellner discusses the existence of nation states prior to the process of industrialism as something contingent which is important for the subsequent development of nationalism but need not be brought into the general framework of interpretation. But if one thinks, as I do, that nationalism is linked to new state forms and patterns of political conflict, a different view can be developed. This might involve distinguishing between national sentiment, nationalist doctrine, nationalist politics, and ethnic tension as well as the processes which promote each of these. Thus I think one could argue that national sentiment as a widespread attitude within a large society can only develop in relation to the growth of a 'standard culture' on the lines Gellner indicates. Ethnic tensions are liable to be deepened when groups with different cultural characteristics meet in the fluid and uncertain world of the industrial town. But these sentiments are not to be equated with nationalism which may be able to become significant in the absence of widespread national sentiment or ethnic tensions or industrialism.

A final criticism concerns Gellner's treatment of nationalist ideology. In positive terms it seems to me that Gellner is making two important points. First, he points to an essentially modern form of knowledge which sees no part of the world as beyond the reach of certain standard procedures of analysis. Second, he points to the development of new standard and widespread cultures which are underpinned by the education system and controlled by the state in one way or another. The first development has the effect of destroying the 'mystique' of various groups – priests, guildsmen, kings, etc. – and means everything can be investigated by the same methods of reason. A proliferation of secular ideologies which claim to base themselves upon knowledge of the world is one result. Clearly this can be related to nationalism. The second point can lead to the idea that nationalist ideology partly reflects and partly promotes the development of a standard culture and a situation in which culture rather than social structure underpins social identity. But nationalism cannot be reduced to these intellectual and social trends. One must recognize that there is a more specific intellectual tradition which is itself a response against modern science and the claim to be able to understand the whole world by means of universal reason. The development of historicism, the idea that what is human cannot be understood by the methods of reason employed in the natural sciences, but only through empathy with the unique history of each society (nation), underpins nationalist ideology and conflicts with the more universalist and rationalist concepts which are at the heart of socialism and liberalism. This historicist current of thinking can in turn be linked to changes in the social consciousness of key political elites such as bureaucrats and members of new professions. It is difficult to derive this current of thought and the types of political ideology and action which it stimulates from industrialism.

Let me sum up my major criticisms of Gellner. There is a strong argument for saying that increased social movement (geographical rather than up or down), a growth of standardized languages and mass educational systems, and the increased power of a territorial state are features of modernity. It is also plausible to argue that such developments will promote those views of the world which see it in terms of a number of culture groups occupying particular territories and either possessing or needing their own state. However, it is not clear to me that these developments are to be closely associated with 'industrialism'. It seems to me that capitalism (a term Gellner deliberately plays down) can have many of these effects without necessarily giving rise to industrial society. Equally the general crises produced by the breakdown of a centralized state such as the ancien regime of France into revolution and war can very rapidly create such conditions. On the other hand it is possible for industrialism not to possess some of these characteristics.

Second, I would argue that these developments promote extensive national sentiment, a potential popular base for nationalism under certain conditions, and can shape and intensify ethnic tensions and conflicts. But nationalism can develop as a significant politics at an elite level in the absence of such developments. Gellner's retreat from industrialism as the major generator of nationalism to industrialism as something nationalists want or nationalism promotes is an indication of the failure of this central argument. A more differentiated model is needed both in terms of what is to be explained (nationalist politics, widespread national consciousness, ethnic tensions and conflicts, etc.) and what can help explain it (an interventionist state, the growth of a standardized popular culture, increased social mobility, the breakdown of privileged spheres of knowledge). Finally one needs to pay close attention to what turns the preconditions of nationalism into a specific political movement. In his chapter 'What is a Nation?' Gellner composes a brilliant fictional tale about the development of nationalism in Ruritania. But in this story the last episode, the emergence of a nationalist political movement, is seen as something almost automatic, unproblematic, and requiring little attention. But that is a crucial stage in the development of nationalism and it has its own dynamics which are to do with the nature of elites in that society and the type of state they confront. Furthermore the processes sketched out in this fiction form only one model for the development of nationalism. Other models, without the patterns of industrialism Gellner describes here, can give rise to powerful nationalist movements as well.

One problem Gellner faces is how to move from the idea of the 'cultural community' as a set of relationships to the idea of the 'cultural community' as consciousness. There seems to be an unbridgeable gulf between the structural changes and imperatives associated with industrialism and the actual construction of a sense of nationality, especially a sense so strong that it can demand and receive the ultimate sacrifice of human life. That is the fundamental question with which Anderson begins. He starts with the assertion that the nation is an imagined community. No one can experience membership of the nation in a way that one can experience membership of a face-to-face group. But any community beyond that level (perhaps, one might argue, even at that level) can only be experienced through imagination. The question, therefore, is less whether nationalism is true or false but how the community it imagines is different from other ways of imagining a community.

> Communities are to be distinguished, not by their falsity/ genuineness, but by the style in which they are imagined. [p. 15.]

Anderson argues that the style of the nationalist imagining is of the community as limited (there are other nations, or at least people who do not belong to one's own nation), sovereign, and as a community for which sacrifices can be made. This is a dramatic and compelling point of departure. One could add to the imagined elements of the nation – I would add the idea of the nation as a comprehensive and self-sufficient group. One should also distinguish between the imagination of what the nation is and what it should be. Finally, despite what Anderson argues about the irrelevance of the truth/falsity distinction, one would want to reserve the right to dispute the truth of the claims of those nationalists who imagine themselves bound by ties of blood and race to others. The extent to which what nationalists imagine about a community is untrue will have profound implication for that nationalism. Nevertheless, this starting point immediately directs us to the issue of what shapes the form and content of the imagination of community.

Anderson then deals with some of the things which could erode other imaginings and promote the nationalist imagining. The breakdown of religious communities and of dynastic empires undermine certain ways in which people can imagine themselves relating to one another. The development of vernacular languages, of a 'print culture', and of capitalism (seen as interconnected developments by Anderson) provide a basis for a national imagining.

So far one could relate these arguments to those of Gellner. Capitalism looms larger than industrialism, but apart from that the stress is upon changes in structures and forms of communication. But Anderson then lays great stress upon the ways in which people will reflect upon this new situation. A brilliant section analyzes the significance of a literature (popular novels, the daily newspaper) aimed at an audience both anonymous and assumed to be at one culturally with the writer. The writer will assume the audience as a cultural community 'out there' which he addresses. The reader will be aware of himself as one of a community of readers. In this way a culture comes to be constructed through representation. Representation is, indeed, a crucial modern concept with its assumption of an extensive reality which can only be understood and operated through the focusing method of representation – be it the scientific representation of the experiment, the cultural representation of the exemplary art form, or the political representation of public opinion and elective institutions.

Anderson goes on to show how these cultural representations of community are developed within certain political–linguistic frameworks. The passages on the 'pilgrimages' of the indigenous administrators of European empire moving within a framework bounded by the colonial frontier and where upward movement involves a spiralling progress between colonial periphery and colonial centre – are brilliant and illuminating. They do much to explain why the liberation movements which did develop in eighteenth-century America largely worked within the territorial framework set down by the colonial system. I would be inclined to make the political aspect the crucial one: the colonial state became the focus of the national movement and its structure and boundaries shaped the structure and boundaries of the national movement. Anderson does not consider how national political movements can be constructed with very little in the way of such 'pilgrimages' and where the major thrust of the movement comes from stable sub-territorial groupings which form 'national' coalitions in order to wrest control of the colonial state from the colonial power. Here the more specifically cultural arguments are weaker than is the case for eighteenth century America or, to judge from Anderson's account, for twentieth century South-East Asia. But the picture is very different in many parts of Africa and in India where, perhaps, local political–cultural ties play a more important part. I would not deny the importance of the cultural dimension (e.g., the form and location of colonial educational policy) for the understanding of particular nationalist movements, but the near universality with which colonial nationalist movements are confined within the framework of the colonial state, whatever the particular cultural aspects of nationalism, suggests to me that it is the political aspect which is crucial.

This relates to the way in which Anderson's argument falters when he moves from eighteenth century America to nineteenth century Europe, and outlines the development of cultural, especially linguistic nationalism. Suddenly, the interplay between political structure and cultural representation disappears, and the burden of argument is placed upon cultural factors. Much of this is presented in a fairly standard form which is surprising after the freshness of the argument up to this point. Anderson exaggerates the significance of cultural nationalism in nineteenth century Europe. He does not tackle the thorny problem of the lack of congruency between 'cultural' and 'political' nationalism (e.g., the 'unification' of Germany seen as a political event, can be contrasted with the division of Germany seen as a cultural event). He introduces a new, functionalist point about the 'need' bourgeoisies have for imagined solidarities and jumps from that to nationalism. But it is by no means clear to me that the bourgeoisie did need solidarities of that sort, that if they did they had to be provided by cultural nationalism, and that this was in fact the function performed by cultural nationalism.

There are similar weaknesses in this chapter on official nationalism, that is nationalism promoted by existing governments to help sustain them in power. The problem here is that Anderson brackets some genuine cases of such a movement (Russia, Siam) where an authentic nationalist idea is first developed from above by a government with cases that should be understood in quite different ways. Magyar nationalism cannot simply be understood as an aristocratic power response to nationalist threats from subordinate groups. Indeed the chronological sequence is the other way around – it was the development of aristocratic Magyar nationalism which helped promote nationalist movements amongst subordinate groups. This had a major influence upon the subsequent career of a more reactionary form of Magyar nationalism after 1867. Again, one must see nationalism in Japan as beginning in response to international pressures and being associated with real alterations in the political structure in the Meiji period, even if this nationalism did take on a governmental and reactionary character later on. At least these movements do take on at some stage the character of an official nationalism. That cannot be said of what Anderson calls a policy of official English nationalism in India. There were undoubtedly assumptions of cultural superiority and a policy of Anglicizing a small group of educated Indians who were seen as playing a role in the governing of India. But this policy was never conceived of along nationalist lines. A closer analogy would be with the Habsburg policy of adopting German as an official language of government which had nothing to do with ideas of German nationalism but rather with choosing the most suitable vehicle for the exercise of rational government. Indeed, the problem, as Anderson makes clear, is that the transfer of certain English (sometimes western would be a more appropriate term) qualities to Indians was not envisaged as being synonymous with the transfer of 'Englishness', and this led to cruel disillusionment amongst some Indians. The point is that the British government was never really trying to convince all, or any part, of the subject population that it shared a common national identity with those in power. Insofar as nationalism was promoted in India it was in the form of Muslim nationalism (sometimes seen by British officials as a genuine nationality as opposed to the 'artificial' nature of educated Hindu Indians), though even here the role of instrumental power considerations must not be exaggerated. So these are very different types of nationalism which are all bracketed together under the heading of official nationalism. Partly this is because Anderson does not sufficiently take into account the very different political purposes served by ideas of cultural identity in the various cases.

Where Anderson falters is where the political framework is largely neglected. The cultural nationalism of mid-nineteenth century Europe and the adoption of cultural nationalist ideas by some governments is not related to the political context in which such movements developed, nor to any penetrating evaluation of the real appeal and significance of such movements. When Anderson moves to twentieth century European empire (again, therefore, where the political–cultural separation of ruler and ruled becomes as clear, albeit in different forms, as in eighteenth century America) the power returns to his account. The political dimension returns. The argument, for example, as to why racism is found amongst the colonial rulers (one of their ways of imagining what sort of people they rule and exploit) but not amongst the colonial ruled (they learn enough about their rulers not to need to resort to such puerile imaginings) is brilliant, precisely because the connection between power and culture is once more restored to the centre of the analysis.

Generally Anderson can cope with a problem Gellner finds difficult: the indubitable emergence and significance of nationalism in societies that have not remotely begun upon the process of industrialism. Thus Anderson outlines the development of a Cambodian elite which came to imagine that there was a Cambodian nation and were able to act, with terrible consequences, upon that imagining. Industrialism and the notion of a standard culture (as opposed to some sort of cultural agreement within a key elite) give way to patterns of political–cultural communication and action, often on the part of small groups. Capitalism rather than industrialism becomes the dynamic economic change of modern times which sustains empire, the commerce of print culture and makes possible the nationalist imagination. In short, by focusing on the specific cultural processes at work Anderson can give a more subtle and specific account of the development of nationalist ideology than Gellner. In particular, when this is closely related to the political framework within which nationalism develops, above all the structure of the state which nationalism both opposes and claims as its own, the analysis has great power. But this can only explain why certain, often small groups, might be disposed to imagine that they belong to a nation and to act politically on the basis of this assumption. But why are those groups important?

Why does anyone either above (in power) or below (in the society claimed to be national) take these arguments seriously? Here Anderson's approach reveals its limits. Gellner at least tries to pinpoint some basic changes in social structure which might underpin, even generate, the type of cultural processes Anderson considers. Work on the links between the modern state form and nationalism might provide some suggestions on how to relate Anderson's arguments more closely to the politics of nationalism.

Both approaches have, therefore, their costs as well as their benefits. But both also, I would argue, suffer from common and avoidable problems. They both assume that the self-evident success of nationalism means that nationalism is very strongly rooted in the thought and behaviour of people. Clearly it would be absurd to go to the other extreme but one can be sceptical of some formulations to which this assumption can lead. Anderson stresses that the imagined community of nationalism can call forth the ultimate sacrifice of one's life. But I would want to look at this much more sceptically. Can one even describe the massive casualties of the 1914–18 war as direct testimony to the power of nationalism? What of the technology of war, the controls and disciplines of a society and its organizations, the very mediated and differentiated forms in which views of the nation were held within different social groups? How often has a national message been made relevant by its linking to pre-defined and particular interests or significant by virtue of the response of those in power for reasons which have little to do with the power of the nationalist argument or movement? On closer analysis Anderson's 'imagined community' may turn out to be the affair of very small and, in themselves, rather unimportant groups of people; and it may be that, contra Gellner, powerful support can be given to a nationalist case and movement where nothing remotely approaching industrialism or a standard culture can be discerned.

Part of the reason for this is to do with another weakness of both books. They both rather indiscriminately consider diverse matters such as national consciousness, nationalist doctrine, and nationalist politics. But these are very different matters and what might account for the development of one will not account for the development of another. There are numerous cases of societies with highly developed national cultures but little overt nationalist doctrine or politics (nineteenth century England), with poorly developed national cultures and highly developed nationalist politics (many twentieth century colonial territories), with elaborate cultural nationalist arguments and weak nationalist politics (Wales), or poorly developed nationalist doctrines but powerful nationalist politics (Ulster Unionism). One must take a narrower approach which tries to construct a framework for the understanding of one or other of these matters, before trying to understand them all at once.

It is also clear that both sets of arguments work better for some sorts of nationalism than for others. To test the arguments properly one would need to develop methods of classification and analysis which would enable one to take a wide range of nationalist cases and test the arguments in some detail against the evidence of these cases. The method of general argument with brief references to some examples does not suffice because the choice of examples may be unbalanced and because a more detailed consideration of those examples may undermine the original point that was being made.

This is why my own approach has been to focus on nationalist politics (it is, after all, the political success of nationalism which largely causes us to devote so much time to trying to understand it) and to see its significance not so much in the intellectual–cultural appeal of nationalism, but rather in the relevance of political nationalism (including its ideology) to the task of seizing and exercising power in the modern state system. From that narrow position it was possible to build up a comparative analysis of cases which a broader view of the subject would make difficult, if not impossible, but without which any argument remains little more than (possibly stimulating and illuminating) speculation.

I will conclude by relating my approach to those taken by Anderson and Gellner. Each of us assumes that nationalism is modern and that the task for any general theory of nationalism is to identify the key aspects of modernity to which one can relate nationalism. None of us imagines that any 'single-factor' explanation will work. But one must begin somewhere and that departure point will shape the whole theory. Broadly one can begin with changes in social structure, changes in social consciousness, or changes in political structure or consciousness. The focus on political consciousness is exemplified in the work of those intellectual historians, usually rather conservative, who see nationalism as arising out of pernicious modern political ideas. It is a very narrow departure point and can be left aside.

JOHN BREUILLY

Gellner's departure point is at the level of social structure. It is the broadest point of departure. He selects a particular notion of what happens to social structure in the modern period and relates that to nationalism. For a speculative argument about the impact of industrialization upon general social consciousness, and in particular the role of culture in the construction of social identity, this has great force. It provides one with a broad background against which more specific changes may be understood. But its broadness is its main handicap for an understanding of nationalism. If the subject was the development of real, broadly diffused, national cultures, one could accept much of the argument. But the subject is nationalism, and that is a very different subject.

Anderson's departure point is at the level of social consciousness. Broader underlying changes are only sketched in and it is rather specific aspects of those changes (commerce, print-culture), seen in terms of how they can shape patterns of communication and cultural understandings, that occupy pride of place. By being more specific the arguments bear more directly than those of Gellner upon the emergence of nationalism. But they tell us more about how nationalist consciousness develops at an elite level than about how either popular support or effective political activity can develop. The arguments have more force where, as with eighteenth century America and twentieth century colonial cases, these cultural processes are related to political considerations. But even then Anderson does not consider how far similar political developments can take place in the absence of these cultural processes. Just as Gellner conflates the conditions for the development of a broad-based national culture with those for the emergence of effective nationalist politics, Anderson conflates the conditions for the development of a cultural sense of nationality (mainly at an elite level) with those for the emergence of an effective nationalist politics.

Generally I would argue that the departure point for an understanding of nationalism (meaning nationalist political movements of some significance) should be a specifically political one: the development of the modern 'public' state which has made politics a distinct and specialized form of action which has to forge connections with other forms of action and to justify itself in terms of some sort of general interest. However, a great danger of such an approach is that it will treat political arguments as simple instruments of power. I tended to treat 'culture' as an increasingly

152

separate and specialized sphere of life which was then exploited as such in nationalist ideology. My main concern was to specify the forms of exploitation (mobilizing popular support, co-ordinating the interests of different elites, legitimating objectives to those with power 'outside' the nation). I still think this is preferable to an approach which sees the source of nationalist arguments in some underlying structure or type of consciousness which has a real national dimension. If I had to choose between what A. D. Smith has called the 'primordial' and the 'instrumental' approaches to nationalism, I would choose the instrumental.[7] But Gellner and Anderson, in very different ways, show that a choice of this sort is not necessary. Gellner helps one understand that culture should not be seen as just one possible source of social and political identity, but as something which stands in a different relationship to modern social structures compared to earlier societies. As a consequence political arguments building upon notions of cultural identity will develop in a strong and distinct way in the modern world. Anderson helps one understand more specifically why certain structures and patterns of communication can give a national form to the cultural imaginings of community. I would still wish to move from the political context in which nationalism develops to the cultural and social contexts which give a particular relevance and function to the nationalist argument. But these two books should transform the ways in which we understand how changes in social structure and consciousness can be related to the rise of nationalism.

* J. Breuilly, 'Reflections on Nationalism', *Philosophy of the Social Sciences*, 15 (1985), pp. 65–73. Reprinted by permission of Sage Publications Inc. A review of *Nations and Nationalism*, by Ernest Gellner, Oxford, Basil Blackwell, 1983, p. 150, and *Imagined Communities: Reflections on the Origin and Spread of Nationalism*, by Benedict Anderson, London, Verso Editions and NLB, 1983, p. 160.

NOTES

1 For a detailed consideration of different approaches to the subject see A. D. Smith, *Theories of Nationalism*, London, 1971; and for bibliographical guidance, A. D. Smith, 'Nationalism: Trend Report and Bibliography', *Current Sociology*, 21 (1973), no. 3, pp. 7–180.
2 See, for example, Boyd C. Shafer, *Faces of Nationalism: New Realities and Old Myths*, New York, 1972.

3 As in Hugh Seton-Watson, *Nations and States: An Inquiry into the Origins of Nations and the Politics of Nationalism*, London, 1977.

4 This is the broad approach of older, classic studies by Hans Kohn, *The Idea of Nationalism*, New York, 1967; and Carlton Hayes, *The Historical Evolution of Nationalism*, New York, 1931. It is more sharply and narrowly formulated in Elie Kedourie, *Nationalism*, London, 1960, and the introduction to a collection of nationalist statements edited by him under the title *Nationalism in Africa and Asia*, London, 1971. Another exponent of the approach is J. L. Talmon: see his recent study *The Myth of the Nation and the Vision of Revolution: The Origins of Ideological Polarisation in the Twentieth Century*, London, 1981.

5 See A. D. Smith, *Theories of Nationalism*; and the introduction to my book *Nationalism and the State*, Manchester and New York, 1982, pp. 1–41.

6 *Nationalism and the State*, op. cit..

7 A. D. Smith, 'Ethnic Identity and Nationalism', *History Today*, 33, October, 1983, pp. 47–50 (at p. 49).

9

LANGUAGE AND NATIONALISM*

Joshua Fishman

Joshua Fishman, who taught at the Yeshiva University in New York, has long been a leading figure in socio-linguistics. From his interest in the formalization and standardization of languages in the new states of the former European empires, he was led to reflect increasingly on the particular role and significance of language in the process of construction of nationalism, which he illustrates with a wealth of historical examples.

THE VERNACULAR AS THE MEDIUM OF NATIONALISM

As in many other respects nationalism's *utilization* of the vernacular is not so much a clear break or departure relative to earlier periods as much as is the intensity with which it pursued this utilization and, in particular, its rationalization thereof.

The functional dependence of new protoelites on the vernaculars was a reflection of the need of these elites to communicate with, organize, and activate recently urbanized but still predominantly illiterate populations. Less obvious is the fact that these populations often had neither a single vernacular (but, rather, a socially, regionally, and experientially differentiated *continuum of vernaculars*), nor a vernacular that could readily be put to the modern ideologizing and organizing purposes that new protoelites had in mind. Even less obvious is the fact that many would-be elites themselves did not know the vernacular that had to be utilized if their goals were to be attained. The sociocultural alienation of the aristocratic and bourgeois leadership of the pre-

155

nationalist period had produced an imposing array of discontinuities between the masses and those normally expected (and expecting) to be their leaders. The early and mid-17th century Irish chronicler Conell McGeoghagan laments that 'because they cannot enjoy that respect and gaine by their said profession as heretofore they and their ancestors receaved, they set naught by said knowledge ... and choose rather to put their children to learne English than their native language'. Two hundred years later we encounter the same lament not only in nationalist writing of awakened protoelites of Western European minorities (e.g., 'We have no Royal, princely nor aristocratic families among us to influence our customs. The few rich ones who live in the country [Wales] are strangers to the people as regards language, and foreigners in respect to religion') but in similar writings throughout Central, Eastern and Southern Europe as well. By the end of that century the linguistic reethnification of new protoelites was far advanced throughout formerly 'nonhistoric' Europe.[1]

[...]

The protoelitist conversion comes prior to mass nationalist mobilization. The former also has more than a tinge of *mea culpa* to it.

The reethnification of protoelites is no less an authentification experience for the fact that it served personal and class interests.

> Had the mineral wealth of the principality been discovered by the natives, and could it have been properly put to use before they were subdued to English rule, they might have preserved their language and been the foremost among British subjects in wealth, manufacture and arts. (H. L. Spring, *Lady Cambria*, 1867; cited by D. G. Jones 1950, pp. 113–14).

How much more appropriate then that this wealth be returned to the nationality to which it rightfully belonged by self-proclaimed guardians who not only appreciated this wealth but the language as well. The control of the one legitimized the control of the other. Indigenization of the language, at the very least, was 'a great stirring up [that] portended no one knew exactly what; meanwhile it was a useful lever for doing many desirable things' (a paraphrase of the views of the Irish nationalist leader Moran), including, of course, 'excluding from their jobs the old bourgeoisie and substituting for them new men', men who identified with the people, who were increasingly of the people, and, therefore, genuinely deserving of their stewardship. For all of these reasons nationalist protoelites have been much more than 'theoretically' interested in the vernacular, as well as in language learning *per se*. For prospective protoelites the vernacular was (and is) very much an instrument of power – for themselves and for the people.

[. . .]

Even those nations following the state-nation pattern toward nationality formation are often dependent upon vernacular literacy, if not upon vernacular education, in order to secure the modern political–operational stability and participation without which ultimate socio-cultural integration cannot come to pass. Thus, nationalist theoreticians need not be suspected of either conscious or unconscious self-aggrandizement when they stressed the need to recognize, utilize, standardize, and modernize the vernaculars. Some saw it simply as a military necessity ('How were recruits to be instructed if they did not understand the language of their leaders? How were orders to be rapidly transmitted to these immense moving bodies of men? Above all, how was moral cohesion between them to be attained?'). Others saw it as an invaluable tool for the spread of nationalist ideologies in the light of which nationalism itself was merely a first stage. Most recognized that it not only had 'identitive integrating power', but that such power was *useful*, all the more so because its broad boundaries were vague and manipulable.

The instrumental dependence of unificatory nationalism on the vernacular is, therefore, not greatly different from that of other modern mass movements, whatever their political or economic coloration. Thus, it is particularly in connection with the authenticity emphases of nationalism that its more unique interrelationship with the vernacular becomes manifest. Modern mass nationalism goes beyond the objective, instrumental identification of community with language (i.e., with communication) to the identification of authenticity with a *particular* language which is experientially unique and, therefore, functional in a way that other languages cannot match, namely, in safeguarding the sentimental and behavioural links between the speech community of today and its (real or imaginary) counterparts yesterday and in antiquity. *This* function of language tends to be overlooked by other mass modernization movements and *its* utility tends to be ignored by them. Nationalism stresses this function, a deeply subjective function, as a *summun bonum*, and demonstrates decisively that 'the rational and the romantic are not wholly alternative or antagonistic but are at least in some measure, complementary ... The romantic form is essential to the solution of the problem of identity, for *its* content can only be categorical' (Binder 1964, p. 136).

LANGUAGE AS [PART OF] THE MESSAGE OF NATIONALISM

[...]

Language as the Link with the Glorious Past

One of the major motivational emphases of modern nationalism has been that the ethnic past must not be lost for within it could be found both the link to greatness as well as the substance of greatness itself. It was on both of these accounts that 'the mother tongue became almost sacred, the mysterious vehicle of all the national endeavors' (Jaszi 1929, p. 262), particularly for those whose current greatness was far from obvious. For the 'peoples without history,' history and language were two sides of the same coin. The vernacular was not merely the highroad *to* history, it was *itself* 'the voice of years that are gone; they roll before me with all their deeds' (from Macpherson 1760, cited by Hayes 1937, p. 16). It was felt that 'in its mother tongue every people honors itself; in the treasury of its speech is contained the charter of its cultural history' (Ludwig Jahn, cited by Rocker 1937, p. 295). As a result 'a language [and] a history' were viewed as twins since together they constituted 'the two first needs of a people.... There is not a new nation in Europe which has not been preceded by from fifty to eighty years of philology and archeological studies' (Etienne Fournol, *Les Nations Romantiques*, Paris, 1931, p. 206; cited by Sulzbach 1943, p. 24). Little wonder then that linguists were, on occasion, 'compared to surgeons who restore to its natural function a limb which had been almost paralyzed but not severed from the national body' (Kahn 1950, p. 157).

Lest it seem that only the 'upstart' nationalities of Central, Eastern, and Southern Europe viewed their vernaculars as direct bonds with historical glory (and, therefore, with either the reality or the potentiality for current glory), it should be pointed out that the historic nations too were not averse to such views. Michelet, in mid-nineteenth century, held that 'in this [French] is continued the grand human movement [so clearly marked out by the languages] from India to Greece and to Rome, and from Rome to us' ([1846] 1946, p. 240), while the first stirrings of Pan-Indian nationalism produced claims that 'Sanscrit was the most enduring monument of the past greatness of the country and was destined to act as one of the most powerful agents in India's future regeneration' (McCully 1940, p. 255). As for Arab thinkers in the latter part of the nineteenth century, 'the "great days of their past" were not just, as in the West, the flowering of a vaguely related culture – the way that Greece and Rome were vaguely related to Britain and France – but were directly related to the men of this period linguistically, religiously, and, as the Arabs loved to emphasize, by ties of kinship' (Polk 1970, p. xiii). The heirs of past greatness deserve to be great again. The heirs of triumphant unity in the past must themselves be united in the present and future. The heirs of past independence cannot but be independent again. The purported continuity of the language was the authenticating device for finding, claiming, and utilizing one's inheritance.

Language as the Link with Authenticity

Directly, via the language per se
History consists of names and dates and places but the essence of a nationality is something which is merely implied or adumbrated by such details. This essence exists over and above dynasties and centuries and boundaries; this essence is that which constitutes the *heart* of the nationality and which leads to its greatness; the essence of a nationality is its spirit, its individuality, its soul. This soul is not only reflected and protected by the mother tongue but, in a sense, *the mother tongue is itself an aspect of the soul*, a part of the soul, if not the soul made manifest.[2] The major figure in placing language squarely at the emotional and intellectual centre of modern nationalism's concern for authenticity was doubtlessly Johann Gottfried Herder (1744–1803). Although he was himself influenced by others (particularly by the works of Vico, e.g., *The New Science*, 1725) in developing his views, as well as associated with others in propagating them (e.g., Fichte), the phrases, concepts and emphases that have cropped up again and again during the past two centuries, throughout the world, wherever vernaculars are defended or admired, tend to be his. His writing was seminal in developing the complementary views that the mother tongue

expressed a nationality's soul or spirit, that since it was a collective achievement par excellence, language was also the surest way for individuals to safeguard (or recover) the authenticity they had inherited from their ancestors as well as to hand it on to generations yet unborn, and, finally, that worldwide diversity in language and in culture was a good and beautiful thing in and of itself, whereas imitation led to corruption and stagnation.[3] The Slavs openly recognized him as the fountainhead of Slavic nationalist thought. Consciously or unconsciously his words have been repeated by those who claimed that 'without Finnish we are not Finns' (Wuorinen 1931, p. 62) or that 'the role of Arabic in the life history of the Arabs . . . is [to be] the register of their creativeness, a symbol of their unity, and an expression of their mental and artistic aptitudes' (Nuseibeh 1956, p. 69) or that 'Our language, the expression of our people, which can never be given up . . . is the spiritual foundation of our existence' (Catalonian Cultural Committee 1924, p. 13).[4]

The contrastive position of 'Germany' vis-à-vis its insultingly proud Romance neighbours to the west and its hopelessly crude Slavic neighbours to the east may have contributed to the Herderian view that languages were huge natural divides. Perhaps personal preoccupation with the literary, standard language was also contributory to the view that the boundaries between languages were more fundamental, lasting, clearer, and implicational than political boundaries, religious boundaries, or other behavioural systems. Politically, religiously, and behaviourally Germany was even more fractionated than the Slavic east! Only language implied an ideal genotypic unity that could counteract the phenotypic horrors of the day. From the very first a distinction of the langue-parole type permitted Herder and other language nationalists both to have their cake and to eat it too: to champion an ideal norm and to create it at the same time.

Both the exact nature of the nationality-and-language link, and the strength of this link, have been argued by seemingly dispassionate social commentators and social scientists on the one hand and by proudly passionate nationalist writers and activists on the other. The views of these two types of participant observers are typically and predictably different. In the first case we find doubt if not derision. The 'requiredness' of the link, i.e., the view that it is unquestionable and given-in-nature, is obviously questioned by those who consider that social conventions have social rather than supernatural or species-wide bases. Thus, Pfaff states that 'considerations of language, history or geography are valuable, to justify what one already believes, but they do not necessarily lead to that belief' (1970, p. 159). Sapir is more charitable. He admits that 'a particular language tends to become the fitting expression of a self-conscious nationality' but adds that 'such a group will construct for itself ... a race to which is to be attributed the mystic power of creating a language and a culture as twin expressions of its psychic peculiarities' (1942 [1930], p. 660), i.e., the link is ultimately man-made but ascribed to supernatural forces in order to hallow it.

[...]

Between the foregoing views (essentially that nationalisms tend to find or inflate the symbols that they require in language as in other respects) and those of most involved nationalists there is a huge chasm. Between the two major positions only few adopt the view that language has *become* symbolic and as such *should* be preserved, cultivated, protected, and advanced. Such moderate views were more common in premodern settings (e.g., 'Methinks the nations should make their language triumphant also, and the rather because there are Laws against it. For why should a free people retain any marks of slavery?' Robert Huntingon, Provost of Trinity College [Dublin], 1686), but are still sometimes encountered (e.g. 'Are we not able to rise above our sectional interest and local patriotism and adopt as our national language the mother tongue of Dr. José Rizal, our greatest hero and martyr, who ardently wished that some day we should speak one language' [Rojo 1937, p. 60]).

[...]

What is striking about such views is, on the one hand, their awareness of language as a prime and fitting group symbol, and, on the other hand, of the need for organized human intercessation on its behalf.

The view that language and nationality are inextricably and naturally linked also begins in a low key. When St. Stephen's crown was offered to Ferdinand of Austria (1527), in order to strengthen Hungary's resistance against the Turks, the new ruler pledged 'We intend to conserve your nation and language, not lose them' (cited by Dominian 1917, p. 154). Spenser, in his *View of Ireland*, indicates the naturalness of the link by a single phrase: 'So that the speech being Irish the heart must needs be Irish' (cited

161

by Flannery 1896, title page), as does a Welsh writer of the same period ('Our tongue cannot be learned by a stranger; its fire burns only in a native breast,' cited by Southall 1893, p. 212).

With the coming of modern nationalism the entire relationship is not only more urgent but more demanding as well. What was hitherto often enough viewed as a natural link is now also a cause, a goal, and obligation. 'Without its own language,' Herder wrote, 'a Volk is an absurdity (*Unding*), a contradiction in terms' (vol. 1, p. 147; cited by Barnard 1965, p. 57). As a result 'language is not separate from man, rather, man has the duty to honour language as a national idol.... Language, unlike man, contains Law' (Koppelman 1956, p. 93). From modern Germany this emphasis spreads its way throughout Europe. In Ireland Davies writes (in English) precisely what Herder might have written:

> To impose another language on ... a people is to send their history adrift ... to tear their identity from all places ... To lose your native tongue, and learn that of an alien, is the worst badge of conquest – it is the chain on the soul. To have lost entirely the national language is death; the fetter has worn through ... Nothing can make us believe that it is natural ... for the Irish to speak the speech of the alien, the invader, the Sasanoch tyrant, and to abandon the language of our kings and Heroes ... No! oh, no! the 'brighter day shall surely come' and the green flag shall wave on our towers and the sweet old language be heard once more in college, mart and senate. (Davies 1945 [1845], p. 73)

How natural then that the slogan of the times became 'Ireland, not free only but Gaelic as well; not Gaelic only but free as well!' (Beckett 1966, p. 417).

Language equals nationality and nationality equals language; the slogan finally reverberates far beyond its initially European boundaries. 'A land qualifies as part of the Arab patrimony if the daily speech of its inhabitants is the Arabic language' (Izzedin 1953, p. 1) is essentially a modern European view of the matter (indeed Chejne claims that 'It was at the insistence of Christians and Westernized Muslims that the language took on a new dimension and became a secular symbol of a national creed as embodied in the concept of 'urūbah (Arabism)', 1969, p. 172).

[...]

However, the inseparability of the God-given link between language and nationality is not the most that can be claimed. Such a claim might well be advanced for other desiderata as well. The ideological pinnacle of language nationalism is not reached until language is clearly pictured as *more* crucial than the other symbols and expressions of nationality. This pinnacle too has been scaled time and again in the annals of modern nationalism and in very characteristic contrastive contexts at that. In prenationalist days the primacy of the language–nationality link, on the rare occasions that such primacy was claimed, was in terms of its greater collective significance than the symbols with which elites alone (or primarily) were involved. 'A language is mightier far than any number of books which may have been written in it, for such productions, great though they be, at best embody what was in the hearts and minds of individual men; but language, on the other hand, is the impress and life of a nation' (cited by Southhall 1893, p. 236). When viewed from the perspective of nationalist ideology, however, language primacy is claimed precisely in comparison with other collective symbols, in comparison with other referents of mass participation, mass involvement, and mass sanctification. Language is worthier than territory. 'A people without a language of its own is only half a nation. A nation should guard its language more than its territories – 'tis a surer barrier, a more important frontier than fortress or river' (Davies 1945 [1845], p. 71). Language is worthier than the institutions of government. 'Even if a Volk's state perishes the nation remains intact, provided it maintains its distinctive linguistic traditions' (Herder 1877/1913), vol. XIV, p. 87; cited by Barnard 1965, p. 58) and, therefore, 'Although the Arabs find themselves politically divided, their language betrays a unity more basic than any single institution' (Chejne 1969, pp. 174–5). 'Language is not an art form, it is *the* art form of the Arabs' (Polk 1970, p. xvii). Indeed, language is even worthier than religion, for 'There is no doubt that the unity of language is more durable for survival and permanence in this world than the unity of religion' (Rendessi 1958, p. 125).

[. . .]

The same conclusion has been reached by the theorists of other modern nationalisms as well. Political fortunes wax and wane. Religions are often shared with other peoples and, at any rate, have a too firmly established elite of their own, tradition of their own, and task orientation of their own to be easily captured and manipulated by newly aspiring protoelites. Religion is often viewed as an embarrassment by modern man. In language, on the other hand, one has a secular symbol (if such is desired) that can simultaneously draw upon and lean upon all of the sanctity that religion has given to texts, to writing systems, and to word imagery per se (see below), at the same time that it is manipulated by and that it serves a basically new elite and a new set of problems, goals, and methods. Modern societies have an endless need to define themselves as eternally unique and language is one of the few remaining mass symbols that answers this need without automatically implying one or another short-lived and non-distinctive institutional base. Institutions may come or go, but none of them get to the heart of that which is eternally unique. Institutions must routinize in order to maximize and therein lies their failure, emotionally, and ultimately, practically as well. Language, on the other hand, is viewed as contra routine. It is for its readers a universe which is simultaneously constantly expanding and, yet, very much their own. 'And the immense sea of Castilian extends as if it met no shores or limits. Its sun never sets' (Capdevila 1940, p. 164).

Indirectly, via widespread oral and written imagery

Nationalism glorifies the vernacular not only directly but indirectly as well, by honouring and experiencing as symbols of collective greatness and authenticity the most pervasive products of verbal versatility. 'The sagas of the Norsemen, the vedas of the Hindus, the Pentateuch ... of the Hebrews, the Homeric poems, the Virgilian hexameters, all the famed deeds of the brave men before Agamemnon ... have served to inspire linguistic groups with corporate consciousness and to render them true nationalities' (Hayes 1937, p. 17). The mother tongue was the vehicle whereby history reached the lower mass and whereby folklore reached the upper class. Poetry, songs, proverbs, mottos, and tales – these all involve basically language behaviors and language products and both history and authenticity are manifestly made and safeguarded by their recitation. Over and over again one finds that both the context and the form of vernacular oral and written literature are pointed to, by elites and laymen alike, as inspiring, unifying, and activating nationalist stimuli. It was even so in the case of Latin literature, 'Rome is the heroine inspiring Romans to heroic deeds to fulfill her destiny' (Barrow 1949, p. 117). In the case of nationalist literature, however, the target population was no longer elitist but, rather, the largest audience attainable.

The interaction between the mother tongue and experiences of beauty, devotion, altruism, and righteousness – in short, the tie between the mother tongue and collective 'peak' experiences – does not depend on abstract ideologies concerning the 'ethnic soul' or the 'national spirit.' Such experiences are more directly and formatively provided via the oral and written literatures in the vernacular that both anticipate and accompany mass nationalism. Herder's view that national character was an impossibility in the absence of a folk-song tradition has since been echoed by others, both laymen and literati, in the East as in the West. 'Literature has always consolidated the nation-forming power of language ... For men of feeling, destiny will ever be hailed in the word that stirs. The harvest reaped by Cavour was of Dante's sowing' (Dominian 1917, pp. 318–19). Whereas Macpherson merely claimed that his forged fragments had been collected 'among a people so strongly attached to the memory of their ancestors' 'as to have preserved' 'in a great measure uncorrupted to this day' the poetry of their ancestors, nationalist spokesmen also recognized a crucial causal nexus in the opposite direction, i.e., the literature (oral or written) preserves the nationality, rather than vice versa. Thus '[Grimms' fairy tales] have enabled us to understand that we, the German people, bear the power and the conditions in ourselves to take up and carry on the civilization of old times, that we are a folk with a high historical mission' (Franke 1918, p. 176) and 'In his [Runeberg's] poems we recognized ourselves and felt that we were one people, that we had a fatherland and were Finns' (cited by Wuorinen 1931, p. 79). Similarly, the *Marseillaise* is sung 'so solemnly, so ceremoniously' that it and the language of which it is a part must be viewed as 'outpourings of an eternal French soul' (Hayes 1930, p. 235). The Kalevala (self-styled as 'Songs of ancient wit and wisdom / Legends they that once were taken / from the pastures of the Northland / from the meads of Kalevala') is hailed as a 'Homeric poem which the people had brought forth in times immemorial ... handed down from generation to generation in the course of centuries ... A mighty monument to the genius of the Finnish people ... no foreign influences had ever marred it' (Wuorinen 1931, p. 75). Similarly, 'the guzlar's ballad is the symbol of national solidarity. His tunes live within the hearts and upon the lips of every Serbian. The pjesme may, therefore, be fittingly considered the measure and index of the nationality whose fibre it has stirred' (Dominian 1917, p. 322). We find the link between language, language product and nation expressed even more directly in Arndt's patriotic hymn:

> What is the German fatherland?
> So name me thus my land!
> Wherever rings the German tongue
> And God in Heaven sings,
> So shall it be, so shall it be,
> It shall be all Germany.

[. . .]

Such examples can be multiplied endlessly. One point that these examples serve has already been made, namely, that vernacular literature (oral and written) provides the masses with the emotionalized link between language and nationalism that exists for elites at the level of ideological and intellectual program. The beauty of the vernacular, the greatness of the nationality, the purity of the common cause are grasped by many for the first time – and thus associated with their personal emotional and intellectual 'rebirth' – via the popular literature of nationalism. The Finnish writer Estlander (early nineteenth century) realized this link when he wrote 'No fatherland can exist without folk poetry. Poetry is nothing more than the crystal in which nationality can mirror itself; it is the spring which brings to the surface the truly original in the folk-soul' (Wuorinen 1931, p. 69).

[. . .]

However, a second and related point still remains to be mentioned: that the link between vernacular literature and nationalism provides yet another avenue for the influence of nationalist sentiments and principles upon language planning. The lexical, phonological, and grammatical forms which become popularized and emotionalized via the moving literature that is prompted by or contributory to the mass awakening of nationality sentiments and nationalist activity have a subsequent directional grip upon language planning which it may well be impossible to displace. Just as Lönnrot's reconstruction of the Kalevala 'revealed the startling resources of the Finnish language and came to play a decisive part in the development of modern Finnish both as a spoken tongue and as a literary vehicle' (Wuorinen 1931, p. 75) so other inspirational literatures in periods of developing nationalism have influenced the subsequent development of languages all over the globe.

* From J. Fishman, *Language and Nationalism*, Rowley, Mass., Newbury House, 1973, pp. 41–52, 122, 127–8.

NOTES

1 Learning (or relearning) the vernacular was an integral part of the reethnicization of Czech, Slovak, Polish, Ukranian, Jewish, Rumanian, Estonian, and other later nineteenth-century and early twentieth-century protoelites drawn from middle-class (or better) sociocultural backgrounds. Thus, Arwiddson, a mid-nineteenth century leader of the pro-Finnish Swede-Finns held that 'the Finns could never become a truly united nation while the upper classes were separated from the lower by a linguistic gulf. The gulf could be bridged and the people united only by reversing the process which had made the upper classes increasingly Swedish. In a word, they would have to adopt Finnish as their mother tongue' (Wuorinen 1931, p. 53). A similar linguistic reethnization was frequently necessary in late nineteenth-century India.

2 Wilhelm von Humboldt expressed this view most succinctly, as follows: 'Their speech is their spirit and their spirit is their speech. One cannot express too strongly the identity of the two' (cited by Rocker 1937, p. 228)... Its original presentations are indicative of the nationalist contexts in which the conviction arose that language must be taken 'not merely as a set of words and rules of syntax, not merely as a kind of emotional reciprocity, but also as a certain conceptualization of the world' (Minogue 1967, p. 120). Thus, Schleiermacher held that 'only one language is firmly implanted in an individual. Only to one does he belong entirely no matter how many he learns subsequently... [for] every language is a particular mode of thought and what is cogitated in one language can never be repeated in the same way in another... Language, thus, just like the Church or state, is an expression of a peculiar [i.e., of a distinct way of] life' (cited by Kedourie 1961, p. 63). That such views quickly lent themselves to sweeping invidious comparisons is obvious from Hamann's observations that 'Every people reveals its mode of thought through the nature, form, rules and mores of its speech... The legalism of the Jewish people, which rendered it so blind at the time of the divine visitation, is fully revealed in its language' (Johann Georg Hamann, *Schriften*, vol. II, [Berlin: 1821]; cited by Baron 1947, p. 132).

The continued emotional hold of this view, in the absence of confirmatory evidence, notwithstanding repeated efforts to provide such via controlled experiments, is evident from the fact that most cultural anthropologists today would doubtlessly agree with Vossler's intuitive claim that 'there rests in the lap of each language a kind of predestination, a gentle urge to this or that way of thinking' (1932, p. 137).

3 Although Herder's devotion to linguistic and cultural authenticity and

167

diversity was certainly sincere, it was equally certainly anti-French, at least in origin (Barnard 1969, Clark 1955, Wells 1959). It is interesting, therefore, to find a very similar view being expressed at approximately the same time by the French philosopher Limoge, who in a letter of 1790 to Bishop Gregoire of the National Assembly, observed that 'the spiritual wealth of the nation was stored in its language and could only be tapped by those understanding it; the true spirit and character of a nation could only be expressed in the national tongue' (paraphrased by Shafer 1955, p. 122). Certainly Herder was not alone in his recognition of the link between language and national authenticity. His contribution to this view and its subsequent espousal and intensification by generations of German philosophers and scholars must not be over-looked. Herder, Wilhelm von Humboldt, the Schlegel brothers, the Grimm brothers, Bopp, Schleicher, Dier, and many others '... established the attitude of the German mind to the language of its own people and to other languages. The whole of modern philology is essentially and almost exclusively a German product' (Vossler 1932, p. 130).

4 The unimportance of the distinction between languages and dialects, from the point of view of this argument, is revealed by the following claim on behalf of preserving Swiss-German: 'Our dialect is more than a language of exchange and social relations: it is the expression of a fully-developed way of thinking. It has grown beyond other dialects because in Switzerland this dialect has continued to exist as the language of sociability of all classes ... ; for us it is a marker of social unity and the symbol of our democratic thought' (Sommer 1945, p. 100). Thus, the same arguments utilized to distinguish between recognized varieties ('languages') were easily transferred to distinguish between less privi-leged ones, the status of the latter as languages (rather than as dialects) coming to be a reflection of *the societal success of the argument pre-sented* rather than of the distance between any variety of reference and any other. Modern sociolinguistic theory takes full cognizance of the fact that the distinction between 'language' and 'dialect' is essentially linguistically arbitrary and societally reversible by treating both within one and the same theoretical framework (Fishman 1971).

REFERENCES

Barnard, F. M. (1965), *Herder's Social and Political Thought: From Enlightenment to Nationalism*, Oxford.

—— (1969), *J. G. Herder on Social and Political Culture*, London.

Baron, S. W. (1947), *Modern Nationalism and Religion*, New York.

Barrow, R. H. (1949), *The Romans*, Baltimore.

Beckett, J. C. (1966), *The Making of Modern Ireland*, London.

Binder, L. (1964), 'Ideological foundations of Egyptian-Arab nationalism', in D. Apter (ed.), *Ideology and Discontent*, New York.

Capdevila, A. (1940), *Babel y el castellano*, Buenos Aires.

Catalonian Cultural Committee (1924), *Appeal on Behalf of Catalonia*, Geneva.

Chejne, A. G. (1969), *The Arabic Language. Its Role in History*, Minneapolis.

Clark, T. T. Jr. (1955), *Herder, his Life and Thought*, Berkeley.

Dadrian, V. N. (1965), 'Major patterns of social and cultural change of the Armenians', *Year Book of the American Philosophical Society*.

Davies, T. (1945), *Essays and Poems with a Centenary Memoir*, Dublin.

Delaise, F. (1927), *Political Myths and Economic Realities*, New York.

Dominian, L. (1917), *The Frontiers of Language and Nationality in Europe*, New York.

Etzioni, A. (1965), *Political Unification*, New York.

Flannghaile [Flannery], T. O. (1896), *For the Tongue of the Gael*, London.

Fishman, J. A. (1971), *Bilingualism in the Barrio*, Bloomington.

Franke, C. (1918), *Die Brüder Grimm, Ihr Leben und Wirken*, Dresden-Leipzig.

Herder, J. G. (1877–1913), *Sämtliche Werke*, Berlin.

Hayes, C. J. H. (1930), *France, a Nation of Patriots*, New York.

—— (1937), *Essays on Nationalism*, New York.

Izzedin, N. (1953), *The Arab World*, Chicago.

Jaszi, O. (1929), *The Dissolution of the Habsburg Monarchy*, Chicago.

Jones, D. W. (1950), 'National movements in Wales in the 19th century', in A. W. Wade Evans (ed.), *The Historical Basis of Welsh Nationalism*, Cardiff.

Kahn, R. A. (1950), *The Multinational Empire: Nationalism and National Reform in the Habsburg Monarchy, 1848–1918*, New York.

Kedourie, E. (1961), *Nationalism*, New York.

Koppelman, H. L. (1956), *Nation, Sprache und Nationalismus*, Leiden.

McCartney, D. (1967), 'Hyde, D. P. Moran and Irish Ireland', in F. X. Martin (ed.), *Leaders and Men of the Easter Rising: Dublin 1916*, London.

McCulley, B. T. (1940), *English Education and the Origins of Indian Nationalism*, New York.

Meillet, A. (1928), *Les Langues dans l'Europe nouvelle*, Paris.

Michelet, J. (1946), *The People*, London.

Minogue, K. R. (1967), *Nationalism*, New York.

Nuseibeh, H. Z. (1956), *The Ideas of Arab Nationalism*, Ithaca, NY.

O'Cuiv, B. (1969), 'The Gaelic cultural movements and the new nationalism', in K. B. Nowlan (ed.), *The Making of 1916*, Dublin.

Pfaff, R. H. (1970), 'The function of Arab nationalism', *Comparative Politics*, 2.

Polk, W. R. (1970), 'Introduction', in J. Stetkevych, *The Modern Arabic Literary Language*, Chicago.

Rendessi, M. (1958), 'Pages peu connues de Djamal al-din al-Afghani', *Orient*, 6.

Rocker, R. (1937), *Nationalism and Culture*, London.

Rojo, T. A. (1937), *The Language Problem in the Philippines*, New York/Manila.

Sapir, E. (1942), 'Language and national antagonism', in A. Locke and B. J. Stern (ed.), *When People Meet*, New York.

Shafer, B. C. (1955), *Nationalism: Myth and Reality*, New York.

Sommer, H. (1945), *Von Sprachwandel und Sprachpflege*, Bern.

Southall, J. E. (1893), *Wales and her Language*, London.

Sulzbach, W. (1943), *National Consciousness*, Washington, DC.

Vossler, K. (1932), *The Spirit of Language in Civilization*, London.

Wells, G. A. (1959), *Herder and After. A Study of the Development of Sociology*, The Hague.

Wuorinen, J. H. (1931), *Nationalism in Modern Finland*, New York.

10

URBAN SPACE AND MONUMENTS IN THE 'NATIONALIZATION OF THE MASSES'

The Italian case*

Bruno Tobia

Bruno Tobia, who teaches at Rome University, is a leading exponent of recent research on the importance of the symbolic construction of the nation. Tobia illustrates how the sense of new nation statehood in Italy was reflected in the desire to create a national artistic style which would leave its imprint on the 'universal' city of Rome, and in the use of exhibitions and monuments as symbols in the process of nation-building.

Urban space and the use of monuments in the process of nationalization of the masses in Italy in the second half of the nineteenth century (from political unification onwards) were explicitly nourished by the desire to 'administer urban values' and to 'form' a city[1] as a place of self-recognition and 'didactic' demonstration of the feeling of belonging to the newly created political community. Camillo Boito was an important architect and a cultured, refined, sensitive and extremely modern restorer who for decades was also director of the Brera Academy in Milan and one of the 'dictators' of official Italy in the public competitions for monuments and works of art. In 1880, he explicitly posed the problem of the creation of a 'national style', following the example, he maintained, of the other European nations:

> nations are already searching for a style: the Germans return to their ogival style, the English to their Tudor, the Russians

171

hold on to their Byzantine, the French are undecided between their Gothic and their Renaissance style. For Italy, the marvellous richness of its past constitutes its greatest obstacle. But sooner or later, an Italian architectural style will have to emerge, especially now that Italy has become a nation, and has its capital. And it will have to be a style, as in the fourteenth century, varied, supple and adapted to the needs, climates and spirit of the different provinces; it will have to be worthy of a refined civilisation, of the advanced science of this, our nineteenth century – or indeed of the twentieth, for what we are discussing, just for pleasure, is our future to come.[2]

Boito's search for a national style was not very successful (he was in favour of the fourteenth-century Lombard style, except for Rome, where he advocated sixteenth-century classicism). But he tried to solve the problem in terms of 'buildings and architects, not architecture'; he sought to achieve 'a contemporary but national style; to maintain just enough of the spirit of the past as to give a national stamp of Italianism, but to renew and modernise everything that does not correspond to today's conditions and desires'. It was the same problem confronted by the first Italian Artists' Congress of 1872, which had complained of the paradox in Italy where, before political unity, a stylistic unity had existed (neoclassicism), which, after unification, had broken up into regional schools.[3]

Boito's reflections fitted easily into the typical context of the *political pedagogy of form*, as (and insofar as) it was exercised by the ruling classes in Italy after unification. Liberal Italy, in fact, like every political system considered in terms of what ensures its continuance and makes of it a 'regime', produced urban forms and monumental objects as an expression of a specific political pedagogy. This political pedagogy of form sought to couple two different aspects: the proud search for a founding myth of the national reality, fixed in the past, anchored to the past, nurtured by the past, and the equally proud affirmation of the new modernity, which, with the acquisition of political unity, was seen – and, above all, was anticipated – as bursting through the breach of Porta Pia.[4]

The close dialectic between *tradition* and *modernity* is the first characteristic to be noted in examining the process of nationalization of the masses which took place in Italy in the second half of the nineteenth century through the new urban structures and use of monuments. It is as if the liberal leaders were involved in an attempt to render two sentiments equally possible, two impressions of the spirit equally present and alive. These two 'souls' were expressed – we would almost like to say personified – in two great intellectuals who were not Italian but lovers of Italy. One aspect is embodied in Ferdinand Gregorovius' anguish, as he observed the seizure of Rome by the Piedmontese troops, this unexpected assault of modernity, which he judged as irreparably catastrophic for the eternal city, wholly concentrated in its august past. The other sentiment was expressed by Theodor Mommsen, when he asked the minister Quintino Sella on what principle, on the basis of what new universal idea the Italian people could remain in Rome, now that the pontiff had been chased away; to which the reply was: on the basis of science. The liberals gambled everything on the dialectic between these two terms, hinted in this exchange: how could modernity mediate with the past and grow from the past without being conditioned by it?

In fact, the revival of Italian historiography in the first half of the nineteenth century, so rich in political patriotic references, had ideologically fed on this same dialectical tension between respect of the past and desire for modernity in its search for an ideal principle underlying Italian history, as a means of contributing to the preparation of the future. The philosopher and politician Vincenzo Gioberti had followed the same logic on a political–cultural level when he had singled out the moral and civil primacy of Italians, writing of a mythical Pelasgic past of Italy, as an omen of its political reawakening. Giuseppe Mazzini had felt the same need to combine the past and modernity, when he affirmed Italy's 'European mission', epitomized in the Third Rome, that of the Risorgimento which would substitute the Rome of the Popes, the Rome that once, long ago, had conquered that of the Caesars. Finally (or, more exactly, during the Napoleonic origins of the Risorgimento), the poet Ugo Foscolo's exhortation to study history had been read, not accidentally, as a preparation for political action for the same reason (to extract auspices for the future from the past). Foscolo himself, in his poem *Dei Sepolcri* (1807) had given a short but splendid example of history as memory, in his hymn to the church of Santa Croce in Florence – as if the temple containing the tombs of Machiavelli, Galileo and Michelangelo

Buonarroti was a sort of Italian Westminster, well aware that 'The urns of the great and strong incite us to grander endeavours...'.

Another poet, the poetic voice of unified Italy, Giosuè Carducci, in a later period, would go back again to Santa Croce. He made of it the symbolic monumental setting of national consciousness, in which, on every occasion, 'our ancient *patria*' came to life; in which the 'free legions sacred until death' swore allegiance to rise against the foreigner, where the 'martyrs' and the 'fraternal quivering shadows' invoked God in the war against Austria. He described the church as the fantastic meeting point of three 'grand and stupendous' forms, radiating the colours of the national flag, ready to liberate Sicily, Venice and Rome.[5]

Carducci praised Santa Croce a final time, when the Risorgimento was over, as a 'place of glory', the 'solemn and solitary Temple of our fathers', worthy seat of Foscolo's ashes, Foscolo who before all others 'opened to his people / From the depth of his heart and the superiority of his mind / The swell and light of the new life', only to ask himself, without hope and with disappointment in his heart, what had been the true result of the Risorgimento. In the light of subsequent events, it seemed inadequate, full of unfulfilled promises, to the point of his doubting, when faced with so disappointing an outcome, the very destinies of the *patria* and the value of monuments: 'Patria of great and strong men, / What is your destiny? If the reply / To their ancestors remains today's ill-living / People, why Engrave in marble / The bones of the dead?'

But Carducci was in opposition, and whatever his authority, in 1871, his was an isolated voice. Besides, is it not usually the case that a certain *deprecatio temporum* (disparagement of the age) is indispensable as a counterpoint to other voices that are raised enthusiastically? The acquisition of Rome for Carducci was a total betrayal of the hopes of the Risorgimento because of the moderate and indecisive way in which it occurred ('A sluggish mind subdues but poorly / Poorly it ascends the Campidoglio and Rome!').

But for others it appeared not only as the glorious crowning of the liberation of Italy, but a terrain carefully prepared by history *visibly* to represent the announcement of new times. An excellent example is the journalist-writer Edmondo De Amicis, correspondent for the *Opinione* in the wake of the victorious troops. To dispel any doubts about the transfer of the capital to the city of the popes, he described Rome emphatically as 'one of the most beautiful and confortable cities of Italy', with the makings of a 'European capital'. With barely any effort, just demolishing a few houses, an 'immense and stupendous' plan for the city could be prepared.[6] Leaving aside such naivety, there were others who had immediately posed the problem of how to give the capital a representative value in political terms. Only ten days after its conquest, Rome's liberator, General Raffaele Cadorna, had already created a commission of engineers and architects to elaborate a plan for the 'enlargement and embellishment' of the city. It was the first of a series of commissions, for the production of an urban plan for the capital was a long and difficult process (it was not until 1883 that something more stable than a provisional plan was established); and this is not the place to follow its successive stages. But one major point needs to be underlined. Rome's new face was explicitly defined by the national–liberal ruling class in contrast to the age-old image that the eternal city had acquired through its restructuring by the great building popes. The model to which to turn, in the attempt to transform it, was drawn from the celebratory representation of the ancient and magnificent Catholic city. It was a cumbersome and yet splendid model, which explains the many difficulties in creating a successful comparison. But the problem was not only – one could say, not even essentially – an aesthetic one. It was supremely political and ideological.

In fact, after 1870 relations between the Italian state and the Church worsened: the Roman question now existed; the pontiff considered that his rights had been usurped, that he was a prisoner in the Vatican. Hence, the Italy that was shaping its capital, had, as a matter of principle, to turn its back on the Vatican. But Italy also had to know how to distinguish between the eternal city as the spiritual centre of Catholicism (from which it only needed to differentiate itself) and Rome as the ancient seat of the temporal power of the Pope-King (*Papa-Re*) (against which it necessarily had to set itself). This was a complex and arduous operation, virtually impossible, since under the popes, and especially under the last of the great town-planners, Sixtus V, acclamatory urban values expressive of universal Catholicism and visual values celebrating the theocratic power, were intermeshed and bound together indissolubly. Italians had to reckon with the Rome of Sixtus V, with its political, religious, and devotional layout, perfected over the following two-and-a-half centuries. It was an urban plan characterized and endowed by a strong 'panoptic' structure which linked the two cardinal points of papal power (St Peter's and the Lateran) and the basilicas[7] in a celebratory route marked by extraordinary monumental objects (the obelisks) that encircled the city centre; far from being spoiled by successive alterations the urban layout was, on the contrary, emphasized and enriched.

This is why, in Rome, the dialectic between past and modernity which we are discussing was particularly difficult, precisely because it underpinned the new representation of a national self-consciousness which was to be taught through visual form. The presence of a municipal tradition was too weak in Rome: for centuries the Capitol (Campidoglio) had been overwhelmed by the Vatican and could not provide a strong enough element of support. Everything had to be invented. The problem was complicated by the fact that, while the capture of Rome was, objectively speaking, a revolution, those responsible for it were moderate, standing well clear of extreme Garibaldian or Mazzinian solutions. This is why the development of the idea of a city that *as a whole* would show the signs of an explicit symbolic monumentality was slow and difficult. Its course was not clear and the almost casual end-result occurred as the outcome of a long but bitty campaign of public works and road building between 1875 and 1895. It is not by chance that the effective destruction of the panoptic monumental city of the popes did not take place until a political decision was made in 1882 to erect in the city centre (near Piazza Venezia) the gigantic marble monument to Victor Emanuel II, 'Father of the *Patria*' (the so-called Vittoriano). More precisely, it was *that* decision which finally determined the celebratory urban centre of the new capital which none of the previous plans had been capable of establishing. The polycentricity of papal Rome was thus destroyed and Rome returned to a monocentricity which had been forgotten over centuries, sealed by the homage to the Great King, the 'Unity of the *Patria*' and the 'Freedom of the Citizens', at the crossing between the millenary via del Corso (the *via lata* of ancient Rome) and the very modern artery that extends from the railway station, obviously called the via Nazionale.

What a difference from monumentality as an itinerary offered by the Sistine mode, obviously with its own political–religious significance! Along via XX Settembre (the old via Pia, renamed in memory of the date of the liberation of the capital), the merest trace can be found of a sort of Roman Whitehall, with the ministries of Finance and War and the ministry of Foreign Affairs in the Piazza del Quirinale, the official residence of the King. The possibility of exercising control through the incorporation of other representative buildings of the city never came about: the project for a new Parliament in via Nazionale failed and it was never constructed; the enormous ministry of Justice would later be built on the opposite side of Rome, in the new Prati district. Mazzini would be commemorated with a monument on the slopes of the distant Aventine hill; while the other national monument of significance, the equestrian statue of Garibaldi on the Gianicolo, would find an appropriate seat in the capital for celebrating the epic story of its hero, in the same spot where the historic events took place. But the huge size of the monuments was not enough to hide the poverty of a renewed urban form which was unable, through its exaggerated monocentrism, to construct a truly panoptical monumental city: a city in which the link between architecture and representation would be highlighted by an apposite design that would permit the entire urban space to be ideally traversed as if it contained a celebratory unity. Nor was this initial impression corrected by the destruction of old districts (the Ghetto and Parione) for reasons of public health and speculation, nor by the building of modern infrastructures (the Tiber riverfront area, the Polyclinic, military barracks, the military hospital, the Art Exhibition Centre). At Rome, commemoration and modernity would continue their paths, divided and separate when not in conflict, and the plan to subvert the layout of the papal city would never materialize. What became the alternative was a half-way plan, rhetorically ideological and intimately linked to the cult of the deceased king, celebrated in the monumental route that has its fulcrum in the massive structure of the Vittoriano in Piazza Venezia. The immense monument destroys the slopes of the Campidoglio, crushing and hiding its form: in this relationship of overpowering juxtaposition between old and new can be read the urbanistic–architectural metaphor of the commemorative link between past and present, far beyond the intentions proclaimed in the official rhetoric. And thus, not by chance, cloaked in rhetoric and set against this funerary background, it was here that Liberal Italy witnessed the greatest patriotic parade it would ever know in honour of the national institutions: the pilgrimage to the tomb of King Victor Emanuel II at the Pantheon of Rome in January 1884, eight years after the death of the sovereign, on the occasion of the twenty-fifth anniversary of the second War of Independence.

The occasion was of great importance, above all because of its scale. The provincial delegations of pilgrims that marched in front of the King's tomb on three different days (9th, 15th and 21st of January) totalled 68,000 persons who, taken together with those who came from the province and city of Rome, added up to 76,000 in all. Given that the organization was in the hands of a national committee, assisted by provincial committees organized on a voluntary basis, one cannot deny that the parade was an unexpected success: even more so, if one thinks of the difficulties at the time of organizing transport by trains, finding accommodation and synchronizing arrivals and departures. A second proof of success was the ability of the organizers to produce a strong feeling of *social* involvement. The central committee at Rome was composed of constitutional[8] politicians of all hues (whether or not in support of the government), of nobles and landowners, state officials and professional men. But if we look at the executive committee, the presidency and the secretariat (that is, not the honorary but the important operative bodies), we note that 'their social representativeness diminishes, their conservative character increases, the role of members connected with the army and military–patriotic tradition becomes overwhelming'.[9] Conservative politicians, officers, and veterans, active in the ex-soldiers' associations, were the key figures in the organization of the pilgrimage in the provinces as well, where the mayor (or his representative) played an equally crucial role.

The participants who took part in the act of homage can be divided into two main categories: those participating individually as private citizens (55 per cent of the total) and those representing associations. Among the latter, workers' and mutual benefit associations and municipal delegations are the most strongly represented. A pyramidal structure emerges, with officers and veterans at the top and citizens at the base, for the most part organized within the only associative structures within civil society that the Italy of the period could identify for purposes of broad political mobilization: the municipality and the trade association which had not yet become a trade union. Despite the obvious success of the parade, the overall picture is thus one of weakness: on the one hand, we have an educated bourgeoisie, the mediator of consensus, together with a business and landowning bourgeoisie, that preferred to *delegate* a wider representative function to organisms whose political role was strongly mediated by their institutional responsibilities (army and municipality); on the other hand, we are faced with a political articulation of civil society which, if it wanted to demonstrate its monarchical and constitutional convictions, was basically dependent on either an institutional structure (once again, the municipality) or an associative form characterized by a paternalistic interclassism.

All this allows for some further reflections on the characteristics of the nationalization of the Italian masses in the liberal period. We have already identified the first aspect in the insistent dialectic between past and modernity. Now we must highlight its centralizing character. The most important and passionate moment for the 'mass' revelation of patriotic values was staged in Rome and involved the figure of the sovereign, the symbol of national unity. The organizing committee had thought of arranging contemporaneously with the pilgrimage a 'decentralized' tribute at the tombs of Charles Albert in Turin, Cavour in Santena, Mazzini in Genoa, and Garibaldi in Caprera. The idea was abandoned, the gesture of recognition to the so-called 'four factors' of the Risorgimento did not occur, because in the end a different commemorative vision prevailed over this attempt at the pedagogy of Unity. Both the conservative and pro-government wings of the political line-up and the constitutional 'left' agreed on the centrality that needed to be attributed to the monarchy, as the only institution capable of representing the unity of the *patria* either by the immediate identification of country and dynasty (the government view), or as an expression of the nation–king tie, to be constructed dynamically through a popular monarchy (the view of the constitutional opposition). The pilgrimage was visually to realize such an aspiration. The fact that the provincial delegations, after placing their wreath on the tomb of the deceased king (Victor Emanuel), were to be given an audience at the Quirinal by the living king (Humbert) is highly significant: it is evidence of the will to establish and exhibit a bond of double institutional fidelity, displayed in the devotional tribute to the past, but then prolonged in the political act of reverence toward the present. The albums of signatures in tribute to Humbert collected in the provinces and brought to the king are proof of the same intent. In such a context there was no room whatsoever for any different type of demonstration of patriotic fervour: the Garibaldian organizations indignantly gave up the fight to have the right to participate in the processions in a distinctive and recognizable fashion.

179

The pilgrimage was to take place in Rome, nor could it be otherwise, for it was here that the capital and the king's tomb were to be found. But if the itinerary was obligatory, this was not the case with the highly propagandistic function that was attributed to the image of Rome. Variations on the theme were sounded. On the one hand, an exaggerated value was attributed to Rome compared to other Italian cities; on the other hand – and it is not contradictory – the indisputable right of all Italy to possess the eternal city was asserted. The initial version of the plaque to be placed on the Campidoglio to record the pilgrimage recalled classical Rome in its effort to express the special, incomparable character of the new capital of Italy. The pilgrims were invited to ascend the fateful hill in order to fulfil their patriotic vow in front of the Forum, 'so that Italians may feel their sacred duty to carry out deeds worthy of the ancient grandeur'.

For the most part, the same tone marks the messages sent by the mayors of the cities of Italy to the mayor of Rome in thanks for the hospitality given to the delegations during the pilgrimage. Rome is 'the noble city of the Caesars', once queen of the world and now 'worthy capital of Italy' (thus the mayor of Palermo); or the tie between 'noble Rome' and the Italic cities of the Republican era is evoked (words of the mayor of Siena). For his part, in his reply, the mayor of the capital, Prince Torlonia, vindicated the rights of Italy to possess Rome: the aim was explicitly unitarian and against the temporal rights of the pope. The overall result, on the occasion of the pilgrimage, was to weave a myth of Rome as a supremely rhetorical place which provided a geographical and ideological equilibrium as the sole reminder, the only driving force capable of overcoming localistic rivalries through mediation and the moment of construction of such mediation. Rome, in short, was represented as the indispensable link in the centre of the country of the hundred cities, the meeting point through which it became possible for municipalism to be projected directly towards a *national* dimension.

It is important to note that such a result could not have been taken for granted. It is true that the majority of the political actors of the Risorgimento – Cavour above all – saw the conquest of Rome and the transfer of the capital to the eternal city as the completion of national unity, as only in Rome could particularistic jealousies be silenced: in place of the myth of Florence, as the cradle of Italian culture and hence symbol of a politically divided country that strove for unity, was substituted the myth of Rome, as the only place in which that unity, once acquired, could be represented. Nevertheless, there had been strong resistance to the move. There had even been the proposal to construct an entirely new capital in Umbria, the geographic centre of the peninsula, almost like founding an Italian city of Washington. And in 1881, when the needs of Rome as capital were discussed in Parliament, there was no little resistance to voting the State aid necessary for all the infrastructures required to modernize the city and render it functional for the new role that it was now given. The new modernizing and ideologically representative public works appeared to many deputies as useless 'building ostentation', London and Paris were cited as terrible models of 'engorging cities', megalopoles that negated the true Italian tradition, with its rich provincial presence. The value of centralism, which on the political–administrative level was affirmed without hesitation, indeed with a determination that has been defined as 'jacobin', was also proposed by the most fervent supporters of the symbolic value of Rome on the grounds of its pedagogic value for a monumental and urbanistic national unity. Francesco Crispi, member of parliament and future prime minister, intervened vehemently during the parliamentary debate, calling to mind the precedent of the American legislators who had voted the funds necessary to build the new capital of the United States, despite the serious financial situation; he spoke of public competitions launched by the French Convention [1792–5] in the midst of the upheavals of the Revolution, because, he maintained, 'governments and institutions must not only concern themselves with the well-being of nations but also have the obligation to perpetuate themselves in marble and monuments'.[10] Crispi was particularly alive to issues involving political lessons of form. This former revolutionary and follower of Garibaldi had rallied to the monarchy; but he hoped for a 'left-wing', popular, and subsequently Caesaristic version of monarchy (not by chance would he become a great admirer of Bismarck). In 1878, as Minister of the Interior, Crispi had organized the funeral rites of Victor Emanuel, paying particular attention to the ceremonial aspects: the Prefect of the Court, Cesare Correnti, writing to him about the details, displayed an extraordinary touch of modernity: 'We have no precedents. So much the better. Invent them.'[11] And so Rome had lived the exceptional days of 17 January, the funeral procession, and 16 February, the day of the State funeral at the Pantheon, where the king's catafalque surrounded by statues representing the virtues of the deceased was dominated by the dome in which 140 gas-lit stars, set into the vault, burned brightly, covered by a gigantic star of white muslin, the Star of Italy.

To sum up: the excessive value attributed to the monarchy as the symbol of unity, represented as Father of the Nation in monuments throughout Italy, was supremely manifest in Rome, in the Vittoriano which became a sort of centre of an ideal diffusion of the myth of the Risorgimento on a national scale, but in the process provoked one more general dislocation of the urbanistic–commemorative layout of the capital. In this sense, in Italy – unlike Germany – a true national monument, understood as a place that stood above geographical, political and social divisions and aroused a common national feeling, can only be found in Rome, in the monument to Victor Emanuel II, the Vittoriano.[12]

[. . .]

Yet we know that the Risorgimento had not been only – nor, one must say, even fundamentally – a royal initiative. It is ultimately not surprising that no real national monument was ever dedicated to the principal and most brilliant figure of Italy's rebirth, Count Cavour, who had to be content with the 'simple' naming after him of squares and streets (albeit important ones), possibly adorned with his statue (the most notable are those in Milan and Rome). A myth, in order to grow, evidently must find its way to the heart: and culture, political wisdom, diplomatic ability, solid knowledge and capacities in the field of economics may not seem ideal virtues to enthuse spirits and enter into the imagination. Nor does a very bourgeois death in one's own bed, even if such a death is precocious and provoked by the killing strain of ten years of overwork, lend itself easily to glorification. It was probably much easier to invent the strategic and warlike virtues of King Victor Emanuel, on the basis of a certain personal scorn of danger that the deceased king undoubtedly possessed, and from that basis construct a mythical image. More difficult to understand is the subordinate treatment of Giuseppe Garibaldi.

Garibaldi incorporated all the elements for a highly effective commemorative use of the political pedagogy of form: his fame was encompassed by an air of adventure which derived from the distant Americas and from the public echoes aroused everywhere by his success. So the 'Lion of Caprera', the 'Hero of the Two

Worlds', was variously portrayed; and Italy was obliged to name squares and roads after Garibaldi too and covered itself with monuments in memory of his actions. Some were grandiose, like the one on top of the Gianicolo in Rome, surrounded by busts of his fellow-soldiers, to which a monument to his companion Anita was added in the Fascist period, so that the tree-lined avenues of the hill became a sort of Garibaldian shrine. Historians have written well of a sort of 'commemorative diarchy', correlating the cult of Victor Emanuel and that of Garibaldi,[13] as if it were in eulogistic correspondence to the process of political dialectic out of which the newly unified state was born. This is acceptable, so long as the clear subordination of one term (Garibaldi) to the other (Victor Emanuel) is clearly stressed. Indeed, it is worth adding that the insistence on the warrior-like habits and military capacities of the king (in reality, very thin) was meant to adjust the balance of the relative weight of the two figures, precisely on the terrain most immediately favourable to the hero in red. The third overall characteristic of the political pedagogy of form can thus be traced to this *commemorative 'diarchy'* in asymmetric terms: it was expressed in Italy through the formulation of a founding myth represented in monuments, epigraphs, and architectural symbols.

The problem was, thus, to 'limit' the role, meaning and function of Garibaldi, so that his figure would not obscure that of the king, even at the level of monuments and toponymy, in the creation of special 'cult' places. One example stands out. Garibaldi died on 3 June 1882 and there were instant commemorative initiatives (subscriptions for monuments, memorial stones, naming of streets). But on the very same day, a sharp exchange took place in the Chamber of Deputies between its president, Nicotera, and a member, Filopanti, who proposed the Pantheon as burial place and not Caprera, where, incidentally, Garibaldi himself had asked to be cremated. The reason for the disagreement was rendered explicit by the authoritative newspaper, the *Corriere della Sera*:

> The cremated remains, if left on the rocks of Caprera, would hardly lend themselves to *frequent* demonstrations and agitation, which we do not want. If the ashes were in Rome, they would be useful every 3rd June, anniversary of his death, every 11th May, anniversary of the battle of Marsala, every 3rd November, anniversary of the battle of Mentana, every 30th April, anniversary of San Pancrazio, etc., as a way

of annoying the government, creating confusion, letting the world know that the republican party exists.[14]

In the Risorgimental 'commemorative diarchy', a strong sense of moderation and prudence thus openly prevailed. This prudence was transformed into ostracism towards the other major protagonist of the Risorgimento, Cavour's opponent, the republican Mazzini. By the end of the nineteenth century, Genoa, his native city, was the only one of the important Italian cities to have erected a significant monument in his memory and then only in 1882 (ten years after his death!). At Rome, where he was triumvir during the republic of '48–'49, his monument, already decreed by Crispi in 1890, was only erected in 1949. Until then, the only homage to Mazzini in the capital was a modest stone bust in the Pincio public gardens, amidst those of 200 other illustrious Italians – and that only dates back to 1910. This is an extreme and clamorous case but wholly in line with the characteristic of commemorative excess towards the monarchy, personified in the figure of King Victor Emanuel, which we have already noted. It is, therefore, not surprising that the decorations of statuary to Victor Emanuel in Piazza Venezia were finally limited to allegoric statues of abstract concepts (Thought, Action, Law, War, Philosophy, Victory, Rome, etc.) and that the original idea of adding to these figures the statues of the great protagonists of the Risorgimento was abandoned, reserving exclusively for the huge equestrian statue of the king, the *realist* and *personal* features of this commemorative tribute.

This prudence operated in another sense as well, in the continual search for a *compromise* in the pedagogical–political representation, since its violation provoked the reciprocal vetoes of the political parties. In this sense, a *vocation for mediation* can always be found in the Italian tradition of the political pedagogy of form and this is the fundamental aspect in which the 'commemorative diarchy' is expressed, the monumental incarnation of that dialectic between the moderate and the democratic wings in the course of the Risorgimento. A counter-example in Milan illustrates this aspect. In this case the opposing 'parties' could not agree on a middling terrain; indeed, the reciprocal contrasts were so unresolvable that no mediation was possible and in consequence the commemorative tribute never took place. We are referring to the sometimes acute battle over two monuments that dragged on for more than forty years in the Lombard capital of Milan between those who wanted a bronze statue of Napoleon III, liberator of the city together with Victor Emanuel in 1859, and those who wanted to commemorate the acquisition of Rome by Italy with a memorial to the patriots who fell in the battle of Mentana.

It is obvious that two political programmes, two clearly antagonistic readings of the Risorgimento were at stake. All the moderates in the city identified themselves on one side: the campaign to finance the pro-Napoleon monument, launched in 1873, was supported by the cream of the Milanese and Lombard bourgeoisie, nobility and intelligentsia. The equestrian statue of the emperor was cast in 1880 and exhibited in a pavilion of the National Exhibition the following year. But the controversy had already begun. In the same year, 1873, the Milanese democrats had begun to promote another collection for another war memorial to the fallen of Mentana, the unfortunate Garibaldian attempt to liberate Rome in 1867, defeated with the help of the French troops stationed in defence of the pope. This monument was finished in 1880 and inaugurated in the presence of Garibaldi himself, who by then was already very ill. This is not the place to discuss the various stages of the controversy, which we have described elsewhere.[15] We will only note that 1886 was the crucial year for this battle. At the end of that year, during a stormy meeting of the city council, the role of Napoleon III in the Risorgimento was subjected to two opposing interpretations. On the one hand, the moderate majority was concerned to demonstrate the emperor's personal merits through his actions for Italian independence, which even went against the best interests of France; on the other hand, the democratic minority denied categorically the merits of what had happened as simply the result of mere necessity, following the same logic that had pushed Louis Napoleon to suppress the Roman Republic, to engage in the Mexican adventure, and to commit the crime of Mentana. The proposal of the council to place the statue in the new public gardens along an axis with the Arch of Peace was passed, but the agitation of its adversaries did not subside. On the contrary, by spreading the agitation throughout the country, they managed to render the council's decision inoperative. This paralysis reflected the dual political balance that governed Milan. For two majorities existed there: one resulting from local government elections to the city council, which was moderate and heavily influenced by the weight of the Catholic voters (whom the Pope had allowed to vote in local elections);[16] and the other majority, unconditioned by Catholic votes, which sent much more left-wing representatives of Milan to Parliament. The Milanese democrats were thus too weak to prevent a decision from being taken – and, in fact, had been defeated – but were certainly strong enough to prevent any decision from being put into practice. They possessed a sort of right of veto, and duly exercised it every time there was a danger that decisions might be put into practice. The question was resolved in 1927 when the fascists decided to place the emperor's statue in the public park, although not on the exact spot of the original council resolution.

We have dwelt on this episode because it shows so clearly the effects of breaking the unwritten, but not for that reason less effective, agreement between the 'winners' (the moderates) and the 'losers' (the democrats) in the Risorgimento process: on every occasion, it snapped the mechanism of the Italian tradition of pedagogy through monuments. On this occasion it was the moderates who betrayed the tacit agreement through their insistence in wanting to commemorate Napoleon III. They moved away from the traditional line of conduct, according to which what we can call official 'monumentality' had always taken on board the criticisms of the opposition, making an effort to interpret its requests, provided that in each instance a common denominator could be found. In this sense, the binomial Victor Emanuel–Garibaldi had fully expressed an inclusive inclination, in the context of monumental commemorations as well; by basing it on the monarchy as institution, and hence as we have seen, privileging the first term, it represented a monarchy which strove to express national unity. Any attempt to move away from the paradigm of the *commemorative compromise* triggered reciprocal vetoes: the tribute to Napoleon III was taken as an intolerable affront by the democrats, as an expression of the political tendency of only one party; while the war memorial to Mentana could only be accepted by the moderates as if it were payment of a toll for their own eulogistic Bonapartist intentions.

[...]

Several conclusions can now be drawn. What judgement can we make on the three basic characteristics of the political pedagogy of form to be seen in Italy in the second half of the nineteenth century? Of the attempt to combine tradition and modernity, the will to establish an ideal centre of diffusion in Rome, and the tendency to propose a mediation, a commemorative compromise between the moderate and democratic wings of the Risorgimento, which would nevertheless enhance the figure of the king? Let us start with this last aspect. The tendency towards the commemorative compromise certainly expressed a hegemonic capacity of direction of the moderates over the democrats. In fact, the attempt to propose a founding myth of the national process was a serious, intense, and uninterrupted endeavour. To the examples we have already analysed, we can add, at the least, the urban commemorative route in Milan. It begins in Piazza del Duomo with the famous ultra-modern Galleria Vittorio Emanuele – the bourgeois sitting-room of the city – and the monument dedicated to the king, ending at the restored medieval castle and its tower dedicated to Humbert I, in front of which stands the monument to Garibaldi. Such a route expresses all the characteristics of Italian nationalization of the masses through its monuments: the link between past and present, the centrality of the monarchy, the room for compromise. It was a commemorative route used opportunely on many occasions: the most important was the celebration of the fiftieth anniversary of the anti-Austrian revolt of 1848, marked by processions and speeches. But this very occasion allows us to point to the limits of the eulogistic–political capacity of the ruling class of liberal Italy. Two separate demonstrations took place on that day, in practice, using the same itinerary: the official one, liberal, monarchist, and moderate, in the morning; and the republican, radical, socialist one in the afternoon, deliberately contesting the version that the government and local council wanted to give of those days in 1848. Only ten years earlier, this would have been unthinkable; and in fact, we rightly spoke of the success of the national pilgrimage of 1884 to the king's tomb at the Pantheon. The fact is that the moment the Italian popular classes acquired an autonomous political capacity, with the constitution of the new Socialist Party (in 1892) and the renewal of the Republican Party (in 1894), the weakness of the patriotic–commemorative hegemony of Italian liberalism was revealed in all its dimensions. The commemorative compromise, therefore, the will to mediate, concealed a great fear: that the affirmation of the value of national unity could be expressed autonomously and not controlled from above, that it might go in another direction, in clear opposition to the results of the Risorgimento, wearing the guise of the most heated republicanism, perhaps then to flow progressively amongst the popular classes towards class-conscious and socially radical landing points.

The centralistic obsession of the process of the political pedagogy of form in its Italian version can also be read in this way, as another limit of the eulogistic–moderate hegemony. In the land of a hundred cities, of extreme particularisms, of age-old divisions, of the seven pre-Risorgimental states forcibly unified, a true national monument could only be located in Rome; such a monument had to have an explicitly political and non-allusive significance – as was the case with the Vittoriano. A comparison may be useful at this point: the Tower inaugurated in 1892 at S. Martino, close to Lake Garda, where one of the most bloody battles of the second war of independence took place. This, too, is a tower dedicated to Victor Emanuel: inside, there is a statue of the king and frescoes that illustrate moments of his life and military episodes of the Risorgimento. The tower is on a hill, in the open countryside, close to the ossuary of the fallen soldiers. But it was not a truly *national* monument. It was the rich bourgeoisie from the north that wanted it; they financed it, with the cities of the Po valley and the help of the government, and it retained its markedly local character. The group who promoted it were extremely patriotic, and similar to those who took analogous initiatives in other parts of Europe, for example in Germany, 'the traditional elite of the civil service, the predominant bourgeoisie of culture and property'.[17] But rather than a monument to Italian unity, it expresses pride in the contribution of the northern regions to the country's independence (and not its unification). In its aim to commemorate the royal family and the army, it is a typical example of a 'national–dynastic monument' as Thomas Nipperdey has described other German monuments.[18] It is thus an expression not of strength but of weakness, 'a situation of doubt and apprehension about an effective capacity to propose and actually establish unquestionable national values accepted in common'.[19] It is as if, once in the provinces, the value of unity fatally assumed a local and particular character. We are tempted to see a sort of metaphor of a hegemonic weakness; things which were easily realized elsewhere, for example in Germany, were unthinkable in Italy: the power of *diffusion* and *allusion* of the national monument. In other words, the 'Hermannsdenkmal', the 'Kyffhäuser', the 'Niederwalddenkmal' were inconceivable south of the Alps.[20]

And finally the last aspect: the commemorative link between

past and modernity, which needs to be related both to the actual monuments and to the use of public space. Here, too, we are faced with substantial difficulties. As a comparison, the 'Kyffhäuser' can help us. It expresses a strong temporal conception, as is necessary for spatial representations of history. Naturally, the temporal notion that is expressed in these cases is not necessarily linear. On the contrary, the greater the problem of transcodification – which is always required in the symbolic achievement of the monument – the more complex the notion of time becomes. Immersed in the eternal time of the saga, a temporal indicator is created within the complex of the 'Kyffhäuser' that also structures the hierarchy of space: from the Germanic Middle Ages (the cave where Barbarossa resides in expectation of his awakening) to the new German empire (the platform on which the equestrian statue of William I rises). Nothing similar could exist in Italy. The personalization of contemporary Italian monuments is practically absolute: there is not one important example of a monument which represents the symbolic form of 'Italy'; which means that the dialectic between past and modernity is never present in an abstract representation, but must always be reconstructed as an implicit *a posteriori*.

The same thing occurs with the use of spaces specifically created in order to suggest, this time explicitly, the dialectic between the glory of tradition and the triumph of contemporaneousness. The main theme of the National Exhibition at Turin in 1884 was the obvious one of the exaltation of technology and modern production, but it was placed alongside the utilization of the rich historical–artistic past of Italy. For this purpose a medieval castle was reconstructed 'in style' (to magnify the ancient alpine origins of the monarchy) and an exhibition on Rome was staged, from the republican and imperial period up to the more recent accomplishments. The intention was to create two interacting poles: the exaltation of the age-old cultural and artistic tradition of the country as the most solid pedestal of the current miracle of a finally unified Italy. However (and this is the point), we have to ask ourselves if the operation was successful. In this walled encyclopedia, what mattered – and the very organizers affirmed it – was the message of study and work to be transmitted. Working-class group visits were organized, following a Bonapartist pattern, and about 400,000 workers from all parts of Italy were able to admire the pavilions of this ephemeral city. Patriotic pedagogy was transformed into interclassist pedagogy. But, as we have already noted, in practice, the possibility of such a transformation was on the point of disappearing, with the foundation of the modern socialist party. For the working class on the verge of self-organization, tradition and modernity, past and present, had very different meanings: the main beneficiary of the public use of commemorative space, intent on linking the splendours of ancient Italy to those of its political Risorgimento, seemed to slip away. New actors were about to upset the game and the nationalization of the Italian masses would be left dangling at the end of the nineteenth century. The inclusion of ever larger numbers of urban and rural inhabitants in the national state would only be possible by marrying the *liberal* values of the Risorgimento to the *democratic* ones asserted by the new forces; that is, in a much wider horizon than that proposed by nationalism.

Translated by Kathy Wolff

* B. Tobia, 'Assetti urbani e monumenti nella nazionalizzazione delle masse della seconda metà dell' Ottocento: il caso italiano', International conference, *Nationalism in Europe: past and present*, Santiago de Compostela, 27–9 September 1993.

NOTES

1 G. C. Argan, *Storia dell'arte come storia della città*, Rome, 1983, pp. 236–51.
2 C. Boito, *Il nuovo e l'antico in architettura* [1880], ed. A. M. Crippa, Milan, 1988, pp. 14–15, 203.
3 F. Borsi, 'Rome capitale', in F. Borsi (ed.), *Arte a Rome. Dalla capitale alla città umbertina*, Rome, 1980, p. 13.
4 Porta Pia was where Italian troops had broken through Rome's defensive wall in 1870 [Editor's note].
5 G. Carducci, *Poesie (1850–1900)*, Bologna, 1907, pp. 98, 201, 213, 243, 364, 367.
6 E. De Amicis, *Impressioni di Rome*, Florence, 1870, pp. 63, 67.
7 The basilicas are monumental churches, with special ceremonial rights. Of the seven at Rome, the location of five constitutes an arc relative to St Peter's and S. Giovanni in Laterano [Editor's note].
8 I.e. all those accepting the monarchy [Editor's note].
9 B. Tobia, *Una patria per gli italiani. Spazi, itinerari, monumenti nell'Italia unita (1870–1900)*, Rome–Bari, 1991, p. 107.
10 Ibid., p. 26.
11 U. Alfassio Grimaldi, *Il re buono*, Milan, 1973, p. 112.
12 F. J. Bauer, *Gehalt und Gestalt in der Monumentalsymbolik. Zur Ikonologie des Nationalstaats in Deutschland und Italien 1860–1914*, Munich, 1992, p. 4.

13 M. Isnenghi, *Le guerre degli italians. Parole, immagini, ricordi (1948–1945)*, Milan, 1989, pp. 331–7.
14 V. Labita, 'Il Milite ignoto. Dalle trincee all'Altare della patria', in S. Bertelli and C. Grottanelli (eds), *Gli occhi di Alessandro. Potere sovrano e sacralità del corpo da Alessandro Magno a Ceausescu*, Florence, 1991, p. 129.
15 Tobia, *Una patria*, pp. 168–80.
16 As a consequence of the Papacy's refusal to recognize the Italian state, Catholics were forbidden to vote in parliamentary elections (1868, *non expedit*), although they were allowed to vote in local elections [Editor's note].
17 W. Hartig, *Geschichtskultur und Wissenschaft*, Munich, 1990, p. 245.
18 T. Nipperdey, 'Nationalidee und Nationaldenkmal in Deutschland im 19. Jahrshundert', in *Historische Zeitschrift*, 206, 1968, p. 533.
19 Tobia, *Una patria*, p. 181.
20 National monuments in Germany [Editor's note].

11

WHEN WAS WALES?*

G. A. Williams

Gwyn A. Williams is a radical historian of the English working classes and of the Italian marxist thinker and party leader, Antonio Gramsci. As a self-conscious Welshman in the English-dominated British state, he offers an impassioned but strongly historical account of how a minority constructs its sense of national identity within the context of a nation state and in a symbiotic relationship with the majority nation. His reflections can also serve as a salutary reminder that the British state, like the rest of Europe, needs to come to terms with the appeal or threat of the (increasing) number of social groups with national identities that co-habit in its territory, often in relations of unequal power.

The frontiers of a Welsh nation have rarely coincided with the frontiers of a Welsh people. A Welsh nation has frequently been a fraction of a Welsh people, often a small one though never of course a vulgar one. Nations have not existed from Time Immemorial as the warp and woof of human experience. Nations are not born; they are made. Nations do not grow like a tree, they are manufactured. Most of the nations of modern Europe were manufactured during the nineteenth century; people manufactured nations as they did cotton shirts. The processes were intimately linked, as peoples called non-historic invented for themselves a usable past to inform an attainable future, under the twin stimuli of democratic and industrial revolutions. In the precociously unified monarchies of Britain and France, they began to manufacture nations earlier; a British nation emerges from the eighteenth century, in the union of England and Scotland around the armature of merchant capitalism, world empire and liberal oligarchy. The ongoing and increasingly revolutionary processes of capitalism are

192

now radically restructuring and remodelling the nations they con-
jured into existence, eliminating some, transcending some, frag-
menting some. The British nation and the British state are clearly
entering a process of dissolution, into Europe or the mid-Atlantic
or a post-imperial fog. Britain has begun its long march out of
history.

How ironic it seems then, that in Referendum, General Election
and European Election during 1979, it was the Welsh who registered their country as the most passionately and totally British of
all the regions of the United Kingdom of Great Britain and about
a half of Northern Ireland. We Welsh look like being the Last of
the British. There is some logic in this. We were, after all, the
First.

When did we begin? When was Wales? Hwn yw y gododdin.
Aneirin ae cant. This is the Gododdin. Aneirin sang it. The first
lines in what is generally accepted as the first Welsh poetry to
survive. Written no later than the sixth century, one of the oldest
literary traditions in Europe and itself the heir of an even older
civilisation. Still accessible, moreover, to a modern reader of Welsh
in a way that early English is not to a speaker of modern English.
Historic immobility, even stagnation, perhaps? But that is what
one calls a tradition, you agree?

But what tradition does it celebrate? Is it a British tradition, in
the British tongue. The poem is about a battle in modern Yorkshire
between Northumbrians and the defenders of Romano-Celtic
North Britain. It was written in what is today Scotland, as were
the battle poems attributed to Taliesin. The first Welsh poetry
written in Scotland about battles north of Trent? At much the
same time, our patron saint, whom no other church recognizes,
emerged, his shrine at a hub of that complex of western sea-routes
along which Celtic civilisation and the great Irish mission church
pulsed. In the seventh century, a Welshman could serve as bishop
in Spanish Galicia; lives of the Welsh saints were written in Brittany. St. David was possibly as Irish as St. Patrick was Welsh.

What do such words as Irish, Welsh, English mean in that dark
and dramatic time when the British Diocese of the Roman Empire
shuddered apart into multiple piratical kingdoms of warring tribes?
They mean nothing. When Offa of Mercia cut his great dyke in
the 8th century as an agreed frontier, he drew a line between two
peoples, each of whom was old and between two embryonic
nations, each of whom was new.

The people to the west of that line knew where they were; they were in Rome.

Catamannus Rex: Sapientissimus, opinatissimus, Omnium Regum: so runs a memorial pillar to a seventh-century king in Anglesey. In Glamorgan they were still Roman in the eighth century, four hundred years after the legions had left. A Welsh leader Emrys, ringed by his 'bawling bards' chanting praise in intricate word-play, his rule reaching no further than his sword could reach and his stolen gold shower, could call himself Ambrosius Aurelianus and wear the purple. The last Roman monument in the western world is in Penmachno. The longest and most fecund of Welsh traditions, running an elusive thread through Mabinogion and poetry, and given a European stature by Geoffrey of Monmouth, is the British and Arthurian complex of stories, legends, mythical history and redemptive prophecy stemming from the historic Arthur, last of the Romano-Britons. As late as the tenth century, the polemical poem, *Armes Prydein*, written in opposition to Hywel Dda's pro-English policy, was directing anti-Saxon minds not to a Welsh but to a British identity. It took centuries for the peoples west of Offa's Dyke even to conceive of themselves as Welsh.

What defined the Welsh in the end were the English. In the open lowlands a strong, unifying monarchy emerged early, to become almost unique in the Europe of its day and to be strengthened still further by the injection of Norman power in the eleventh century. The relatively rapid rise of a powerful England turned the Welsh, almost from birth, penned as they were in a harshly poor upland economy staked to a bony mountain spine, into a marginal people. Talented but marginal, the talent probably a function of the marginality, light of foot, light of spirit, light of plough, they lived by their wits, the Jews of the British Isles.

The Welsh as the English called them, succumbing early to their deplorable national habit of addressing natives as foreigners, the Cymry as about half of them called themselves, emerge into history from the wreck of Roman Britain as highly self-conscious heirs of the British. There was a profound divergence between the historical experience of north and south, possibly the root cause of their divergence in language. The romanised Commonwealth of the Silures generated a kingdom of Gwent-Morganwg, heavily Roman in its style and climate, living close to Celts in the south-west and Brittany, who were excluded from the Cymry who defined

themselves in battle in north Britain. Ringed by immigrant kingdoms of Irish origin fusing, largely through the David evangelical
style of Christianity into the ramshackle confederation of Deheub-
arth, Gwent-Morganwg, for centuries an extension of the civilisation of Salisbury Plain, seems to have settled relatively easily
behind the Wye even as Gwynedd, under its north British dynasty
of Cunedda, defined itself in the struggle for north Britain before
falling apart in the eighth century as Powys emerged as the survivor kingdom of an extensive Romano-British polity on the
Severn. Hardly had these piratical little kingdoms defined themselves as British and Christian than the internal breakdown of
their inherited Roman superstructure coincided with a need to
reshape settlement and tenurial patterns in the teeth of a
voraciously land-hungry church at the very moment when the
terrible scourge of the Vikings broke on them, to drive their new
High Kings of all Wales generated by this internal crisis into the
shelter of the new English Crown focused on Wessex. In a battle
of the traditions, the old British ideology of Nennius and *Armes
Prydein* against the new Britain of Hywel Dda in which the Welsh
were a junior partner, Welsh social structure and polity were
shaped by Hywel's Laws in political dependence on the English
Crown, even as many Welsh princelings became half-Vikings
themselves within the cultural world of the Irish Sea, that mini-
Mediterranean of the north.

Hard on the heels of English and Vikings, came the Normans
who ripped half the country away into a rich and hybrid Welsh-
European civilisation, projected Welsh culture into Europe,
thrust European modes into the semi-independent west and north
and dragged the Welsh out of the Celtic-Scandinavian world into
the Latin. In response, the Welsh around the survivor kingdom of
Gwynedd struggled to build a miniature Welsh feudal state, to win
a brief success under Llywelyn ap Gruffydd, first and last Welsh
prince of Wales, who was broken by armies largely Welsh in
composition and by a Welsh aristocracy in revolt against
Llywelyn's ruthless abrogation of Welsh tradition, marshalled by
Edward I who revolutionised English society in order to destroy
Gwynedd. The colonial centuries which followed were ended by
the Rebellion of Owain Glyn Dŵr, a war of national liberation
which like all such wars was also the greatest of Welsh civil wars,
to be followed by the seminal Tudor century, when the Welsh
gentry climbed to power over the ruins of principality and aristoc-

racy alike, when the Welsh were hoisted to a temporary pinnacle of prestige, when the old British ideology of the Welsh became a new British national mythology and when Welsh society was absorbed wholesale into English. That century witnessed that characteristic Tudor contradiction, a Protestant Welsh Bible to direct and service the survival of the old language on the one hand, official discrimination against and social scorn for that language on the other. Even as the old culture stammered before the Renaissance as Protestantism rooted itself in Welsh soil, the long and rich tradition of Welsh writing in the English language was born as the Welsh language began its slow recession into a sacerdotal tongue, a sacred language, and lost contact with the fullness of modern secular living.

The century of turmoil which followed the Tudors decimated the lesser gentry of Wales, a product of its kindred social structure and critical to its separate identity and expelled it from public life, even as its landowners were clasped into the hot and clammy embrace of the broad, open, astute and ruthless oligarchy of the new Great Britain and its unprecedented mercantile empire of the eighteenth century.

The alternative society in Wales was born no less of that new mercantile Britain with its Atlantic dimension: an evangelical drive for literacy which turned a majority of the adult population technically literate in Welsh for a stretch of the eighteenth century, a Calvinistic Methodist movement independent in its origins from English Methodism, stirrings of rationalist and radical movements among the Old Dissent created by embattled Puritanism and an upsurge of interest in Welsh history and antiquities powered above all by the London-Welsh, surrogate capital of an invertebrate country. The entry of this alternative society into history was explosive. From the eighteenth century, the new industrial capitalism thrust into Wales. Over a hundred years it quintupled the population, sucked most of it into the modernising and English-speaking south-east, provided the money and the power and the will for a Welsh revival and the insidious processes which cut that revival down in its prime. Over little more than two generations, the Welsh went on their Long March out of Establishment and into the spiritual world of Dissent, even as south and east began theirs into West Britain. A further surge of growth built south Wales into an imperial metropolis of the new British world economy even as, in response, a new and semi-political Welsh nation clawed its way into half-existence, displacing and dismissing into limbo the half-formed Jacobin nation of the 1790s, to form along a language line and a religious line which was also a class line, to claim a monopoly of Welshness in the late nineteenth century even as a new industrial civilisation blossomed in the imperial democracy of south Wales and there was a massive, buoyant and innovatory immigration into that south Wales second in intensity only to immigration into the USA itself. And after a Klondyke climax to this new American Wales in the First World War, the terrible Depression of the 1920s and 1930s burned through this complex and contradictory Wales like radioactive fall-out from a distant holocaust. The Depression which plays the same social role in Welsh history, I think, as the Famine in Irish, unhinged this Welsh polity, devastated its communities, dispersed a quarter of its people and thrust a community of survivors, struggling to rebuild consensus in a precarious post-war prosperity into those crises of identity and those bankruptcies of rooted political traditions which plague our contemporary experience.

In such a people with such a history, the problem of identity has been desperate from the beginning. In recent centuries we have progressively lost our grip on our own past. Our history has been a history to induce schizophrenia and to enforce loss of memory. Professional history, history as a craft, is even more recent a phenomenon in Wales than in England. Half-memories, folklore, traditions, myths, fantasy are rampant. We are a people with plenty of traditions but no historical memory. We have no historical autonomy. We live in the interstices of other people's history.

Our survival has been a kind of miracle. What is immediately clear, from even a cursory survey of our broken-backed history, is that the tiny Welsh people, for we were always very thin on the ground, have survived by being British. Welsh identity has constantly renewed itself by anchoring itself in variant forms of Britishness. The phrase British Empire was invented in 1580 and by a Welshman, Dr John Dee, mathematician and magician, navigator and scientist of European reputation like Robert Recorde of Pembrokeshire before him, enchanter and dabbler in the occult and intellectual mentor to the exploration, colonial and piratical enterprises of the age of Drake, chief scientific adviser to that 'red headed Welsh harridan' Queen Elizabeth I. It was in British empire that a Welsh intellectual could find fulfilment in the sixteenth century. That pattern has proved recurrent.

The historic British nation was generated in Anglo-Scottish mercantile capitalism in the eighteenth century, to assume quasi-permanent ideal form and to persist until the third quarter of the twentieth century. There are nationalists among Scots and Welsh who deny the existence of this British nation. Their organic conception of nationality and nationalism requires them so to do. They are taking as an axiom what in fact they have to create. It is necessary for them to do this; in their own terms it is proper for them to do it. When they deny the historical existence of a British nation, however, what they are actually doing is asserting the power of the human will against objective historical reality. This is not to create a historic will, such as Antonio Gramsci, the Italian marxist who was the most creative marxist since Marx himself, called for, himself pre-occupied with the problem of nation-making. They are erecting human will into an anti-historic force and therefore into a myth. They are trying to shout down history to its face; they are spitting in the winds of the world.

The existence of a historic British nation, dominated by but qualitatively distinct from the English polity, is a central fact in the modern history of these islands. The history of the Scots and of the Ulster Protestants is inconceivable without it. The history of the Welsh is totally incomprehensible without it. The Welsh, the original British, have survived by finding a distinctive place for themselves within a British nation.

This is what makes the present predicament of Welsh people who wish to be Welsh so painful. The form which Welsh nationality assumed in the nineteenth century, the pseudo-nation of a 'Nonconformist people', has proved to be, historically, an instrument of middle-class modernisation. Its limited objectives attained through Liberalism, the husk fell away, leaving Labour to inherit. The residual and tougher nationalism which has today displaced it, reverted to the standard European form which the first Welsh nationalism had assumed in the 1790s. In essence, it was a form of linguistic nationalism which, in Europe, grew into a species of modern tribalism and exclusivism. The application of strict Welsh linguistic nationalism today, of course, would mean instant death to the Welsh people as a distinct people. Some individuals have followed the logic of this predicament into an historic bunker under permanent siege which would require massive invasions of civil liberty to sustain itself. On the other hand, the form of Welsh personality which historically and genuinely has existed within a

British identity seems to carry all the stigmata of the historically transient; it becomes a question of style, of accent, of historically acquired manners, of half understood hymns sung on ritual occasions, a question of trivialities. It may simply prove a station on the road to historical extinction. Central to this predicament is precisely that British nation which hegemonic British capitalism created and of which modern south Wales was not merely an element, but a central directive force.

I do not think such a history can be interpreted effectively in terms of the currently fashionable concept of internal colonialism. This, while it has now created a school of historiography in its own right, derives ultimately from one marxist interpretation of history, that first seriously applied by Andre Gunder Frank in a study of South America and the relationship between metropolis and satellite in the Third World, extending within state frontiers. It has been erected into a global analysis by Immanuel Wallerstein and has recently come under attack from Robert Brenner in a sustained controversy in both academic and marxist journals.[1] The thesis locates explanation in the extension of a market and the transfer of a surplus from satellite to metropolis with all the relations of production, social relations, ideological, intellectual and spiritual forms which follow. It is very often perceptive in terms of its analyses of the social and psychological consequences of the rapid advance of capitalism over the globe; this is precisely its strength in Wales, but in truth it derives from Adam Smith rather than Marx, it misses the centrality of a mode of production in all its social complexity. It singles out one element only, the market, from that mode of production, which embodies the transformation of human attributes and human creations into commodities in the complex class relations which derive from that process; it mishandles the central reality of uneven development and it therefore often reads consequences as causes.

The industrial development of Wales was imperial from birth. Copper around Swansea and Anglesey was a world monopoly, directed in particular at the West Indies; the rise of the massive iron, steel, coal, later tinplate industries was geared directly to the mushroom growth of British commercial empire based on Atlantic slave power during the long French wars and riveted to British industrialisation in the free labour epoch which ensued. From the 1840s Welsh industry secured another world empire in railways, incorporating the Welsh working class as a junior partner in the process, after the storms of the frontier years. The incredible world empire of south Wales coal is familiar. But this was much more than a simple matter of coal export. South Wales capital, south Wales technology, south Wales enterprise, south Wales labour not only fertilised whole tracts of the world from Pennsylvania to the Donetz basin; they were a critical factor in world economic development. The growth of Spain was completely distorted by the power of south Wales, which wrenched its natural heavy industry base from the Asturias to the Basque provinces; south Wales merchants bought up the shipping companies of French ports and of Hamburg; Italy, Argentina, Brazil worked to the rhythms of south Wales trade. In consequence a whole new industrial civilisation grew up in the south; the Welsh Outlook Press could compare the Welsh to the Japanese as an old people finding a new role; the most creative editor of the *Western Mail* was one of Cecil Rhodes's men. At the height of World War I, Stanley Jevons, professor of economics, could envisage a post-war British global hegemony centred entirely on south Wales. That this metropolis was characterised by mass poverty and exploitation and working class struggle is nothing unusual. This is par for the course for capitalism. Indeed the mushroom growth of south Wales into a major centre of the British labour movement from the 1890s, its transformation into a seminal power in that movement, followed a natural American and Atlantic pattern. The nickname American Wales in fact identifies a structural truth; the nearest and most obvious comparison is with Catalonia, another region of distinctive personality which experienced an American and Atlantic pattern of growth and slump to become a metropolis of the wider homeland of Spain.

The use of the term internal colonialism to describe this historical conjuncture precisely reverses the reality; it is the contradictions of an imperial capitalism we are dealing with, not those of one of its satellites.

In our modern history, it is possible to detect three central characteristics. The first is marginality. The original marginality, of course, was that of poverty, a cramped and pinched community of small commodity producers unable to generate capital, living in bleak and back-breaking poverty and in unremitting colonial dependence, its most vivid symptoms the great droves of skinny cattle and skinny people seasonally tramping into England to be fattened. That marginality was ended and ended decisively by the establishment of industrial capitalism. Towns, a middle class, a proletariat were created, the population was forcibly relocated; by the 1870s the marriage rate even in Merioneth was dependent on the price of coal. American Wales had emerged and the rest of Wales had to adjust; rural Wales lost over 800,000 people. The economy, however, remained marginal in one fundamental sense. The south Wales economy which enabled the country to sustain its phenomenal population increase and to retain it within its borders, was geared almost wholly to export. It worked to exactly the opposite, inverse rhythm to every other industrial region in Britain. In the first decade of the twentieth century as British industrial decline registered visibly everywhere else, south Wales reached a climax of frenetic expansion and drew in migrants at a rate second only to the USA. The Depression therefore was all the more catastrophic. What remained was a derelict society of survivors. In our own day, the continuing elaboration of capitalism has multiplied professions and white collar industries; most of us work for multi-national corporations or in the tertiary sector of bureaucracy and services; a precarious prosperity is slithering into crisis as all life is sucked away to those coasts which are becoming a coastal fringe of Europe, draining Wales' hollow heart to the point of vacuum.

A second factor has been diversity often amounting to division, itself a product of this type of capitalism, a diversity which has been able to find co-existence only within a British identity. Apart from the familiar divisions between Welsh and English speakers which, despite heroic efforts, seem to be getting worse, Wales has always been a patchwork of cultures and industry at first intensified the divergences. The massive re-stabilisation of the middle years of the century, after Chartism and Rebecca,[2] which incorporated both a working class and the new Nonconformist populism around its preacher-journalists, achieved a kind of synthesis in radicalism, which masked deep divisions and which served in historical terms as an instrument, what Gramsci would have called a gastric juice of modernisation; this synthesis fell apart with the rise of Labour out of the brash new civilisation of the south during the boom years of an imperial democracy. These variant forms of Welshness all required the power and the presence of the new Britain to be effective. This was as true of those standard hero movements of our textbooks, the builders of colleges and schools and eisteddfodau, their efforts increasingly directed as rescue enterprises to a rural Wales in permanent crisis, as of the new plutocracy of the American boom towns of the south, the new professional classes and of the new and abruptly politicised working class cadres who to combat capitalism looked for international and in practice British muscle. Two phenomena characterise the situation, I think; the emergence of Welsh rugby as a simultaneously Welsh, populist and British imperialist force and the catapulting of David Lloyd George and his Welsh populism into an imperial power.

The Depression, killer of nations, destroyed the integument which held this complexity precariously together. The massive growth of Labour, despite the fervour of a religiose ILP and the challenge of a Communist minority, was essentially a tribal defence mechanism against the slump, a warm rough blanket against the winds of the world. It could not restore that integument, by its nature it could not. It social democracy was essentially British. And today, of course, its social democracy is as bankrupt as the parliamentary democracy which was its instrument.

A third determining factor, I think, is historic melodrama. Our recent history has been sheer melodrama. After centuries of slow almost imperceptible growth, a coral-growth when the Welsh were never more than 400,000 strong and frequently much fewer, industrial capitalism tore into Wales, quintupled its population, doubled the life-span of its people, powered and then neutered a Welsh revival, planted communities and uprooted them, in a break-neck pellmell growth, endlessly revolutionising everything it touched, to climax in the middle of the slaughter of the War and then to smash up in cataclysm. We are living through the morning after a night before which lasted four generations; a psychological factor, I believe, in the present equation.

No wonder we are driven to ask when was Wales? When did we begin? We are living through what may be our end. The end of Wales and the Welsh as distinct entities.

It is apparent that Wales and the Welsh, as distinctive entities, cannot survive the capitalist mode of production in its present historic phase. A tiny Welsh nation may survive in a marginal and impotent bunker; a vivid Welsh-language culture should survive if only in aspic. But the continuous reproduction of Wales and the Welsh over generations requires the elimination and the transcendence of the capitalist mode of production. If capitalism in the British Isles lives, Wales will die. If Wales is to live, capitalism in the British Isles must die.

A vocabulary of structural dissidence is as widespread in Wales as in Britain; a movement of structural dissidence is as absent in Wales as in Britain. This was a predicament familiar to Antonio Gramsci and his generation in the 1920s as they tried to remake Italy and the west in socialism. The parallels are apt, for the Welsh, until the recent divergence, were in structure and spirit, a European people; all the valid comparisons are with European peoples of the Atlantic world. The Europe to which we belong is not the Europe of Saunders Lewis; the Europe of Saunders Lewis's *Brâd*[3] is our enemy. Our Europe is the Europe of Rosa Luxemburg and Anton Pannekoek, of Karl Korsch and Victor Serge, of Fernando Claudin and La Pasionaria; above all of that Aneurin Bevan of Italian communism, Antonio Gramsci the little hunchback who was one of the greatest creative spirits of this Europe, who was done to death in Mussolini's jails and who worked to the motto borrowed from Romain Rolland, *Pessimism of the intelligence, optimism of the will*, to make a socialist society and an Italian nation.

The human will was central to Gramsci's marxism, but it was an historic will, geared to the objective realities of history. To quote the eighteenth century, freedom is the knowledge of necessity. Such freedom is grounded in the mastery of history. No freedom is possible unless we conquer an historical autonomy, unless we can stand up among the giant cogwheels of history. History is more than a word, more than a footnote on a printed page, more than a tired smile in a shadowed study. The corpses of the dead generations do weigh like an Alp on the brains of the living. This is why we must assimilate their experience if only to get shot of them. Gramsci accurately perceived that the historic will derived from an act of choice which probably lies beyond reason.

To the question when was Wales, it is possible to return several answers. One could say, with a measure of truth within narrow limits, that Wales never was. It is equally possible to say, with equal truth within equally narrow limits, that Wales always was.

In reality, Wales is now and Wales has always been now. Wales is not an event, it is not a moment, it is not a mystical presence ubiquitous through our history like some holy ghost. Wales is none of these things. Wales does not exist and cannot exist outside the Welsh people as they exist and as they existed, on the ground, warts and all, wie es eigentlich gewesen, as it actually happened. Wales is not a thaumaturgical act, it is a process, a process of continuous and dialectical historical development, in which human

G. A. WILLIAMS

mind and human will interact with objective reality. Wales is an
artefact which the Welsh produce; the Welsh make and remake
Wales day by day and year after year. If they want to.

It is not history which does this; it is not traditions which do
this; that is Hegelian mysticism and infantilism. History does
nothing, said Karl Marx, it is men who do all this. Men make their
own history, but in the terms and within the limits imposed on
them by the history they inherit; always provided, of course, that
they master that history and make a choice. To make history, to
win historical autonomy, it is necessary to make a choice in historical awareness.

There is no historical necessity for Wales; there is no historical
necessity for a Welsh people or a Welsh nation. Wales will not
exist unless the Welsh want it. It is not compulsory to want it.
Plenty of people who are biologically Welsh choose not to be
Welsh. That act of choice is beyond reason. One thing, however,
is clear from our history. If we want Wales, we will have to make
Wales.

* G. A. Williams 'When was Wales?', BBC Wales Annual Radio Lecture,
12 November 1979, pp. 6–23 (repr. in G. A. Williams, *The Welsh in
their History*, London, Croom Helm, 1982).

NOTES

1 Gunder Frank, *Capitalism and underdevelopment in Latin America*,
London, 1967; I. Wallerstein, *The Modern World-System*, New York,
1974; R. Brenner, 'Agrarian class structure and economic development
in pre-industrial Europe', *Past and Present*, 70 (1976) [Editor's note].
2 Riots in Wales against toll-houses, 1842–3 [Editor's note].
3 Saunders Lewis, *Babbit*, New York, 1922 [Editor's note].

INDEX